ADVERTISING
COMPLIANCE LAW

Recent Titles from Quorum Books

Law and Economic Regulation in Transportation
Paul Stephen Dempsey and William E. Thoms

International Law of Take-Overs and Mergers: Asia, Australia, and Oceania
H. Leigh Ffrench

Office Space Planning and Management: A Manager's Guide to Techniques
and Standards
Donald B. Tweedy

Advertising Financial Products and Services: Proven Techniques and Principles
for Banks, Investment Firms, Insurance Companies, and Their Agencies
Alec Benn

The Political Economy of International Technology Transfer
John R. McIntyre and Daniel S. Papp, editors

Fair and Effective Employment Testing: Administrative, Psychometric, and Legal
Issues for the Human Resources Professional
Wilfredo R. Manese

Office Records Systems and Space Management
Donald B. Tweedy

Managing Real Estate Taxes
Jerry T. Ferguson and Edward C. Spede

Strategies and Skills of Technical Presentations: A Guide for Professionals in
Business and Industry
James G. Gray, Jr.

The Management of Business-To-Business Advertising: A Working Guide for
Small to Mid-size Companies
Stewart Halsey Ross

Company Reorganization for Performance and Profit Improvement: A Guide for
Operating Executives and Their Staffs
Stanley B. Henrici

Foreign Multinational Investment in the United States: Struggle for
Industrial Supremacy
Sara L. Gordon and Francis A. Lees

ADVERTISING COMPLIANCE LAW

Handbook for Marketing Professionals and Their Counsel

JOHN LICHTENBERGER

Q

QUORUM BOOKS

NEW YORK • WESTPORT, CONNECTICUT • LONDON

Library of Congress Cataloging-in-Publication Data

Lichtenberger, John.
  Advertising compliance law.

  Bibliography: p.
  Includes index.
  1. Advertising laws—United States.   I. Title.
KF1614.L53   1986   343.73′082   85-31248
                        347.30382
ISBN 0-89930-122-3 (lib. bdg. : alk. paper)

Library of Congress Catalog Card Number: 85-31248
ISBN: 0-89930-122-3

First published in 1986 by Quorum Books

Greenwood Press, Inc.
88 Post Road West, Westport, Connecticut 06881

Printed in the United States of America

The paper used in this book complies with the
Permanent Paper Standard issued by the National
Information Standards Organization (Z39.48-1984).

10 9 8 7 6 5 4 3 2 1

This publication is not intended to provide legal advice.
Persons who need legal services should contact a duly
licensed professional.

CONTENTS

ADVERTISING
COMPLIANCE LAW

1.
FALSE, UNFAIR, AND DECEPTIVE ADVERTISING

The federal government's power to regulate advertising is found chiefly in the federal agency known as the Federal Trade Commission (FTC). The main ingredient in FTC's authority over advertising is Section 5 of the very important Federal Trade Commission Act (FTC Act). In sweeping language, that section declares "unfair or deceptive acts or practices in or affecting commerce" to be unlawful.[1] In addition to Section 5, other sections of the FTC Act govern advertising regulation. Section 12 forbids any "false advertisement" likely to induce the purchase of food, drugs, devices or cosmetics. And if an act or practice is a violation of Section 12, it is also a violation of Section 5.[2]

Section 15 defines a false advertisement, for purposes of Section 12, as one that is "misleading in a material respect." In determining whether an ad is misleading, Section 15 requires that the Commission take into account "not only representations made or suggested by statement, word, design, device, sound, or any combination thereof, but also the extent to which the advertisement fails to reveal facts material in the light of such representations or material with respect to consequences which may result from the use of the commodity to which the advertisement relates under the conditions prescribed in said advertisement, or under such conditions as are customary or usual."[3]

The Commission has a wealth of enforcement weapons in its ad compliance arsenal to use against alleged violators. Under Section 5(b), FTC can issue an administrative complaint against any "person, partnership, or corporation" which the Commission has reason to believe has been "using any unfair method of competition or unfair or deceptive act or practice in or affecting commerce."[4] The way this works in practice is that FTC proceeds against what it considers to be unfair or deceptive trade practices on a case-by-case basis. If FTC decides to issue a complaint in a particular matter, the person, partnership, or company that is the subject of the complaint has, essentially, two choices. It can either fight the complaint within FTC and, ultimately in the courts, or enter into a consent agreement with FTC containing a cease-and-desist order in which it agrees to halt or correct the practices challenged by the Commission.

WHAT YOU SHOULD KNOW ABOUT "DECEPTION"

Over the years, the extremely important term, "deception," has been defined in numerous FTC decisions. As a marketing professional or a legal advisor in this field, you should be aware of these decisions and how the reasoning used might apply to your particular advertising practices, or your client's practices. In doing so you will be better prepared in avoiding FTC scrutiny of your ads and the potential sanctions that could apply. For example, the cases show that there has to be a representation, omission, or practice likely to mislead consumers. (A strong minority at FTC would say that the Commission must find an act or practice having the "tendency or capacity" of misleading consumers.)[5] In its cases, FTC has found the following advertising practices to be "deceptive": false oral or written representations, misleading price claims, sales of hazardous or systematically defective products or services without adequate disclosures, and failure to disclose information about pyramid sales.[6]

The easiest situation to avoid is where a misrepresentation appears in the ad. You can avoid this problem by carefully scrutinizing your ad copy before it's published or aired and excising any representation—express or implied—that you, or experts you consult, know to be contrary to fact.

A harder "deception" situation involves misleading omissions. To avoid difficulties with FTC based on this ground, you should carefully review your ad copy to be certain that you've made all disclosures necessary to prevent your ad claims from being misleading. Be aware, however, that not every omission is deceptive—even if disclosure would benefit consumers. In deciding if an omission is deceptive, FTC looks at the overall impression created by your ad claim. For example, when you offer a product for sale, this creates an implied representation that it's fit for the purposes for which it's sold. If you fail to disclose that your product is not fit, that is a deceptive omission. An omission may also be deceptive if the representations you make aren't literally misleading; if those representations create among consumers a reasonable expectation or belief that's misleading without the omitted disclosure.[7]

As FTC noted in the Cigarette rule: "The nature, appearance, or intended use of a product may create an impression on the mind of the consumer . . . and if the impression is false, and if the seller does not take adequate steps to correct it, he is responsible for an unlawful deception."[8]

If your ad claims are not adequately substantiated, (i.e., they lack a reasonable basis), those claims are considered deceptive.[9] Reason: Most ads that make objective claims imply—and many expressly specify—that the advertiser possesses adequate substantiation for those claims. The claim would be rendered deceptive if the advertiser does not in fact possess that substantiation.

In addition, you should make sure that your ad contains all material information before your ad reaches its intended audience. If it doesn't, FTC may decide that your ad is deceptive. So be certain that your ad does not leave out important information. How can you tell if the information to be provided is important? One method: Ask yourself whether an ordinary consumer viewing or reading your ad needs to know that information to properly evaluate your product or service.

Another important piece of advice in reviewing your ad is don't be "part smart." That is, don't rest once you've examined all of the claims, express or implied, contained in your proposed ad. At that point, you should remember to examine the *entire ad* for possible deception. For example, in *American Home Products*, FTC noted that many challenged Anacin ads—when examined in their entirety—conveyed the message that its product's superiority had been proven. The important consideration, said FTC, "is the net impression conveyed to the public."[10] As the Third Circuit noted in the *American Home Products* decision:

The Commission's right to scrutinize the visual and aural imagery of advertisements follows from the principle that the Commission looks to the impression made by the advertisements as a whole. Without this mode of examination, the Commission would have limited recourse against crafty advertisers whose deceptive messages were conveyed by means other than, or in addition to, spoken words.[11]

The meaning of your advertising claims is, of course, very important since FTC must determine that a representation, omission, or practice has occurred. But how do you determine the meaning of your ad claims? If they are express claims, the meaning is generally evident. For example, "Product X Cures Baldness."

Implied claims pose more difficult problems. For these claims, you can frequently determine the meaning of the claim by examining the claim itself and evaluating such factors as the entire ad, the juxtaposition of various phrases in the ad, the nature of the claim, and the nature of the transaction. For example, in the landmark *Warner-Lambert* decision, the label contained this statement: "Kills Germs By Millions On Contact." This was immediately preceded by the following: "For General Oral Hygiene, Bad Breath, Colds, and Resultant Sore Throats." FTC concluded that by juxtaposing these two statements in close proximity to each other, the advertiser made the claim that since its product, "Listerine," can kill millions of germs, it can cure, prevent and ameliorate colds and sore throats.[12]

If the nature of your advertising claim involves safety, you should take extra care to make sure that your claim is accurate. As FTC noted in the *Firestone* decision, safety is "an issue of great significance to consumers. On this issue, the Commission has required scrupulous accuracy in advertising claims, for obvious reasons."[13]

What kinds of proof should you have on hand to show the meaning of your advertising claims? You should consider having consumer perception, or other surveys, expert opinions, copy tests, or any other reliable proof of consumer interpretation. Studying the decisions of the National Advertising Division (NAD) can tell you what kinds of proof that self-regulatory body considers acceptable. And NAD is conversant with the standards and decisions of FTC. And, of course, you should review, or have counsel review, the pertinent decisions of FTC prior to preparing any ad campaign where the meaning of your claims could be called into question.

NEW FTC ENFORCEMENT POLICY ON "DECEPTION"

In October 1983, FTC, by a 3-2 vote of its Commissioners, adopted a new enforcement policy in which it finds an act or practice deceptive "if there is a misrepresentation, omission, or other practice that is likely to mislead the consumer acting reasonably in the circumstances, to the consumer's detriment."[14] Under this new policy, three essential elements must be present before FTC will find deception has occurred.

First, "there must be a representation, omission or practice that is likely to mislead the consumer." Examples: false oral or written representations, sales of hazardous products without adequate disclosures, and failure to perform promised services.

The two dissenting Commissioners responded to the new enforcement policy by submitting their own sixty-three-page analysis of the law of "deception" to the House Committee on Energy and Commerce.[15] According to this dissenting view, there must be an act or practice that has the tendency or *capacity* to mislead consumers. In finding that such an act or practice has the tendency or capacity to mislead, under this minority view, the Commission needn't find that actual deception has occurred.

Second, FTC (as presently constituted) looks at the representation, omission, or practice from the viewpoint of a consumer acting reasonably in the circumstances. If the representation, omission, or practice affects, or is directed primarily to, a particular group, FTC examines reasonableness from that group's perspective. As the majority noted in its enforcement policy statement, "An interpretation may be reasonable even though it is not shared by a majority of consumers in the relevant class, or by particularly sophisticated consumers. A material practice that misleads a significant minority of reasonable consumers is deceptive."[16]

This "reasonable consumer" test is probably the most controversial of the three elements of FTC's enforcement policy. The dissenting Commissioners would express this portion of the test in terms of the act or practice complained of as having the capacity to mislead "substantial numbers" of consumers.[17] According to this viewpoint, previous FTC pronouncements and decisions have stated this test as "substantial segment,"[18] a "substantial percentage,"[19] "substantial numbers,"[20] or "some reasonably significant number"[21] of consumers.

What happens when you would like to target your ad claims to a specific group? In such cases, FTC will determine the effect of the claim on a reasonable member of that group. As an advertiser, you're not liable for every interpretation or action by a consumer. As FTC noted in *Heinz v. Kirchner*:

An advertiser cannot be charged with liability with respect to every conceivable misconception, however outlandish, to which his representations might be subject among the foolish or feeble-minded. Some people, because of ignorance or incomprehension, may be misled by even a scrupulously honest claim. Perhaps a few misguided souls believe, for example, that all 'Danish pastry' is made in Denmark. Is it therefore an actionable deception to advertise 'Danish pastry' when it is made in this country? Of course not. A representation does not become 'false and deceptive' merely because it will be unreasonably misunderstood by an insignificant and unrepresentative segment of the class of persons to whom the representation is addressed.[22]

You should be particularly careful when your advertising claims are directed to a "special audience" such as children or the elderly. Reason: FTC will take into consideration the age and nature of your ad's audience as well as the nature of your advertising claims. As the U.S. Supreme Court noted in its landmark decision involving attorney advertising: "The determination whether an advertisement is misleading requires consideration of the legal sophistication of its audience."[23] Accordingly, your advertising claims will be scrutinized much more closely if they're directed, say, to children than if they're directed to well-educated professionals such as doctors (e.g., prescription drug ads) or lawyers (e.g., law book ads). As FTC noted in its *Ideal Toy* decision, "False, misleading and deceptive advertising claims beamed at children tend to exploit unfairly a consumer group unqualified by age or experience to anticipate or appreciate the possibility that representations may be exaggerated or untrue."[24]

Regardless of which test FTC uses (i.e., "reasonable consumer" or "substantial number"), if you follow either with a common-sense approach, you'll go a long way in avoiding problems with FTC. For example, if your ad contains a false headline, (e.g., "Brown's Diet Mix will help you lose five pounds overnight"), accurate information in the remainder of the ad may not remedy the falsity. Reason: Whether you conclude that reasonable consumers or a substantial number of consumers may look only at the headline and not at the textual information, the result is the same: A distinct possibility of deception exists.

However, an opposite result may occur if the nature of your ad requires the consumer to read the text as well as the headline. In *D. L. Blair*, for instance, FTC decided that the ad's text corrected a possibly misleading headline. Reason: In order to enter the advertised contest, the consumer had to read the text, and the text eliminated any false impression of the headline.[25]

FTC cases also illustrate that you should avoid using fine print in the text of your written ad to correct possibly misleading impressions elsewhere in your ad. For example, in *Giant Food*, FTC concluded that a fine-print disclaimer did not correct a deceptive impression. Quoting with approval from the FTC Administrative Law Judge's finding, the Commission noted that, "very few if any of the persons who would read Giant's advertisements would take the trouble to, or did, read the fine print disclaimer."[26]

However, in *Beneficial Corp. v. FTC*, the Third Circuit reversed FTC's opinion that no qualifying language could eliminate the deception from using the slogan, "Instant Tax Refund."[27]

The cases are also clear on the point that accurate labeling generally will not cure deceptive advertising. However, FTC in its "Statement of Basis and Purpose for the Cigarette Advertising and Labeling Trade Regulation Rule" indicated that there are instances where label disclosures could cure the bad effects of "deceptive nondisclosure":

It is well settled that dishonest advertising is not cured or excused by honest labeling [footnote omitted]. Whether the ill-effects of deceptive nondisclosure can be cured by a disclosure requirement limited to labeling, or whether a further requirement of disclosure in advertising should be imposed, is essentially a question of remedy. As such it is a matter within the sound discretion of the Commission [footnote omitted]. The question of whether in a particular case to require disclosure in advertising cannot be answered by application of any hard-and-fast principle. The test is simple and pragmatic: Is it likely that, unless such disclosure is made, a substantial body of consumers will be misled to their detriment?[28]

In addition, if your ad contains "pro forma" disclaimers, this will not correct a deceptive claim contained in your ad. For example, in *Warner-Lambert*,[29] the challenged "Listerine" mouthwash ads contained claims that the product would prevent colds but was preceded by a statement that the product did not provide absolute protection against colds. FTC concluded that this was a pro forma statement that did not correct the false claim that Listerine prevents colds.

The lesson for advertisers that wish to, or have to, use disclosures or other qualifying language in their ads is clear: make sure such disclosures are conspicuous and understandable. To be on the safe side, you can try to comply with FTC's Statement of Enforcement Policy relating to disclosures applicable to television advertising.[30] However, these standards are very stringent and are not applicable to all print situations.

Are there certain types of claims that you can make in your ads without fear that FTC will take action against you? Yes. You may safely use "puffery" (i.e., obvious exaggerations) in your ads with little fear of FTC action. What is "puffery"? FTC defined it in the *Wilmington Chemical* case as "an expression of opinion not made as a representation of fact. A seller has some latitude in puffing his goods, but he is not authorized to misrepresent them or to assign to them benefits they do not possess [cite omitted]. Statements made for the purpose of deceiving prospective purchasers cannot properly be characterized as mere puffing."[31]

However, if you're going to use "puffery" in your ads, you should make sure that no reasonable consumer (or substantial numbers of consumers) will take those exaggerated claims seriously. For example, in its *Jay Norris* decision, FTC rejected an advertiser's contention that the words, "electronic miracle" in describing a television antenna was puffery. The Commission noted: "Although not insensitive to respondent's concern that the term miracle is commonly used in situations short of changing water into wine, we must conclude that the use of 'electronic miracle' in the context of respondent's grossly exaggerated claims would lead consumers to give added credence to the overall suggestion that this device is superior to other types of antennae."[32]

In addition, you're generally on safe ground if you make subjective advertising claims involving how your product tastes, looks, feels or smells. "Zappo Cola tastes great." "Fashion shirts look and feel terrific." "Cayman Clean Perfume Smells Like Paris in Springtime." These are all examples of such subjective claims.

The third element of deception under FTC's new enforcement policy is "materiality." As FTC stated in *American Home Products Corp*: "A misleading claim or omission in advertising will violate Section 5 or Section 12, however, only if the omitted information would be a material factor in the consumer's decision to purchase the product."[33]

The Commissioners that dissented from the enforcement policy did so in part because they feared that this element might be construed to require the Commission to find that consumers have suffered "actual injury" in order to find that deception had occurred. The enforcement policy defined a "material" misrepresentation or practice as "one which is likely to affect a consumer's choice of or conduct regarding a product. In other words, it is information that is important to consumers. If inaccurate or omitted information is material, injury is likely."

FTC views certain categories of information as presumptively material. For example, the Commission considers express claims and—under certain conditions—claims that significantly involve health and safety as presumptively material.

The first deception case decided by FTC since the announcement of its new enforcement policy was *Cliffdale Associates, Inc.*[34] In that case, the Commission ruled that ads claiming a product could "save [consumers] up to $200 a year on gasoline" were false and deceptive. The Commission decision upheld a 1982 administrative law judge's decision and a 1981 FTC complaint charging that Cliffdale Associates, Inc., made false performance claims and lacked a reasonable basis for other claims in its promotional materials for its product.

Using its new "deception" test, FTC found that the company had falsely claimed its product was a significant and unique new invention. Instead, FTC found the product to be "a simple airbleed device similar to many other such devices that have been marketed over the years."

FTC also found the company falsely claimed the product was needed on every car. FTC concluded that this claim was deceptive since it "would tend to induce all consumers . . . to buy the device. Those consumers who cannot in fact profit from the Ball-Matic will have relied on the representation to their detriment." The company's ads also claimed its product would give the typical driver gas savings of at least 20 percent. The Commission found this claim to be false.

FTC noted the device's performance capability was "difficult for consumers to evaluate themselves." Accordingly, FTC found consumers relied more heavily on the company's scientific evidence, and as a result, were likely to be injured by the claims.

FTC PROTOCOL

An important document that you should be aware of is a 1975 FTC "Protocol" on deceptive advertising. This "Deceptive and Unsubstantiated Claims Policy Protocol" contains a series of inquiries that the Commission staff should answer in pursuing advertising cases. This protocol took on renewed importance in 1981 after the newly installed FTC Chairman, James C. Miller, III, announced that the protocol would be a key document during his tenure at FTC.[35] We are reproducing this document for you in *full text* as Appendix 1A appearing at the end of this chapter.

FTC DECEPTION CASES CRITICIZED
BY FORMER CHAIRMAN

As part of his testimony to the House Subcommittee on Commerce, Transportation and Tourism on April 1, 1982, former FTC Chairman Miller listed a number of FTC cases that he criticized for their interpretation of deception. The cases contain staff analyses approved by the Chairman giving the reasons why these cases were, in his view, wrongly treated.[36]

Accordingly, these cases offer invaluable guidance to advertisers, ad agencies, and their legal counsel on the approach to deception by the former FTC chairman and his top staff.

Because of their importance, we are reproducing this list of cases and the accompanying analyses as submitted by Miller to the subcommittee as Appendix 1B appearing at the end of this chapter.

BATTLE OVER "UNFAIRNESS" DEFINITION

Former FTC Chairman Miller advocated a more specific statutory definition of "unfairness." His proposed definition would include three elements:

1. The consumer injury should be substantial;
2. The injury from the alleged unfair act or practice should outweigh its benefits; and
3. The harm must be one which consumers could not reasonably have avoided.

Miller believed that "unavoidable consumer injury" should be the *crucial* element in finding an action unfair. As you will recall, section 5 of the FTC Act includes a broad prohibition against "unfair" as well as against "deceptive" acts. Accordingly, under this sweeping authority, FTC can proceed in situations, including advertisements, where consumers are being treated "unfairly."

FTC has used its "unfairness" authority as the basis for many of its cease-and-desist orders as well as in numerous rulemaking proceedings. However, FTC generally also included allegations of deception and/or falsity in its complaints leading to such orders. And, "deception" generally accompanied unfairness as the basis for its proposed trade regulation rules in the advertising area. So it is hard to quantify just what impact a change along the lines Miller suggested would have in the ad compliance area, other than making FTC trade regulation rulemaking even harder to accomplish than it is now. Indeed, it was the furor over FTC's proposed rulemaking over children's advertising that strengthened the resolve of those politicians and others in the advertising community who called for FTC's authority to be reined in by, among other things, eliminating or vastly circumscribing FTC's unfairness authority.[37] In that rulemaking, FTC's staff had recommended, among other recommendations, a ban of all television ads aimed at children under eight years old. While the basis for that rulemaking was both "unfairness" and "deception," the argument that such ads were "unfair" was the only real basis on which to have such a ban since it would have been virtually impossible to prove that all ads aimed at children under eight were, somehow, per se deceptive. Ever since then, "unfairness" as a ground for FTC action has had less importance in the Commission's thinking. It appears that that trend will continue throughout the 1980s. Nevertheless, it will be interesting to note what action Congress ultimately takes, if any, on redefining "unfairness" and the impact that such a redefinition will have on the future actions of FTC.

It should be noted that in spring of 1985 bills were introduced in both the Senate and House, both of which contain similar language that would redefine "unfairness" under Section 5. The Senate version contains language quite similar to Miller's formulation and, not surprisingly, is favored by him. Under that version (S. 1078), Section 5 would be amended by adding this language:

The Commission shall have no authority under this section or section 18 to declare unlawful an act or practice on the grounds that such act or practice causes or is likely to cause substantial injury to consumers which is not reasonably avoidable by consumers themselves and not outweighted by countervailing benefits to consumers or to competition.

The main difference in the House version is that it would add "public policy" as a factor to be taken into account in determining whether an act or practice is unfair.

NOTES

1. FTC Act, Section 5(a)(1).

2. *Simeon Management Corp.*, 87 F.T.C. 1184, 1219 (1976), *aff'd* 579 F.2d 1137 (9th Cir. 1978); *Porter & Dietsch*, 90 F.T.C. 770, 873-74 (1977), *aff'd*, 605 F.2d 294 (7th Cir. 1979), *cert. denied*, 445 U.S. 950 (1980).

3. FTC Act, Section 15(a)(1).

4. FTC Act, Section 5(b).

5. See *Advertising Compliance Service*, Tab #4, False, Unfair, Deceptive, Article #11.

6. See, *Advertising Compliance Service*, Special Report #6, November 21, 1983, *Letter to Congress Explaining FTC's New Deception Policy*, page 3.

7. See, for example, *Firestone*, 81 F.T.C. 398, 451-52 (1972), *aff'd*, 481 F.2d 246 (6th Cir.), *cert. denied*, 414 U.S. 1112 (1973); *National Dynamics*, 82 F.T.C. 488, 549-50 (1973); *aff'd and remanded on other grounds*, 492 F.2d 1333 (2d Cir.), *cert. denied*, 419 U.S. 993 (1974), *reissued*, 85 F.T.C. 391 (1976). *National Comm'n on Egg Nutrition*, 88 F.T.C. 89, 191 (1976), *aff'd* 570 F.2d 157 (7th Cir.), *cert. denied*, 439 U.S. 821, *reissued*, 92 F.T.C. 848 (1978).

8. 29 Fed. Reg. 8324, 8352 (7-2-64).

9. See, *Advertising Compliance Service*, Special Report #6, page 3.

10. 98 F.T.C. 136, 374 (1981), *aff'd* 695 F.2d 681 (3d Cir. 1982).

11. 695 F.2d 681, 688 (3d Cir. 1982).

12. *Warner Lambert*, 86 F.T.C. 1398, 1489-90 (1975), *aff'd* 562 F.2d 749 (D.C. Cir. 1977), *cert. denied*, 435 U.S. 950 (1978).

13. 81 F.T.C. 398, 456 (1972), *aff'd* 481 F.2d 246 (6th Cir.), *cert. denied*, 414 U.S. 1112 (1973).

14. See, *Advertising Compliance Service*, Tab #4, False, Unfair, Deceptive, Article #10.

15. See, *Advertising Compliance Service, Tab* #4, False, Unfair, Deceptive, Article #11.

16. *Advertising Compliance Service*, Special Report #6, November 21, 1983. See also, *Heinz v. Kirchner*, 63 F.T.C. 1282 (1963).

17. *National Comm'n on Egg Nutrition*, 88 F.T.C. 89, 185 (1976), *enforced in part*, 570 F.2d 157 (7th Cir. 1977); *Jay Norris Corp.*, 91 F.T.C. 751, 836 (1978), *aff'd*. 598 F.2d 1244 (2d Cir. 1979).

18. *Statement of Basis and Purpose for the Funeral Industry Practices Rule*, 47 Fed. Reg. 42260.

19. *Benrus Watch Co., Inc. v. FTC*, 352 F.2d 313, 319-20 (8th Cir. 1965), *cert. denied*, 384 U.S. 939 (1966).

20. *Raymond Lee Organization, Inc.*, 92 F.T.C. 489, 649 (1978), *aff'd*, 679 F.2d 905 (D.C. Cir. 1980).

21. *The Kroger Co.*, 98 F.T.C. 639, 728 (1981), *modified*, 100 F.T.C. 573 (1982).

22. 63 F.T.C. 1282, 1290 (1963).

23. *Bates v. State Bar of Arizona*, 433 U.S. 350, 383 note 37 (1977).

24. 64 F.T.C. 297, 310 (1964).

25. 82 F.T.C. 234, 255-256 (1973).

26. 61 F.T.C. 326, 348 (1962).

27. 542 F.2d 611, 618 (3d Cir. 1976).

28. 29 Fed. Reg. 8325 (1964).

29. 86 F.T.C. 1398, 1414 (1975), *aff'd*, 562 F.2d 749 (D.C. Cir. 1977), *cert. denied*, 435 U.S. 950 (1978).

30. CCH Trade Regulation Reporter, ¶7569.09 (10-21-70).

31. 69 F.T.C. 828, 865 (1966).

32. 91 F.T.C. 751, 847 n.20 (1978), *aff'd*, 598 F.2d 1244 (2d Cir.), *cert. denied*, 444 U.S. 980 (1979).

33. 98 F.T.C. 136, 368 (1981), *aff'd* 695 F.2d 681 (3d Cir. 1982).

34. 49 Fed. Reg. 14087 et. seq., April 10, 1984; see also, *Advertising Compliance Service*, Tab #4, False, Unfair, Deceptive, Article #13.

35. See, *Advertising Compliance Service*, Tab #4, False, Unfair, Deceptive, Article #1; note that Commissioner Terry Calvani was named as Acting FTC Chairman, effective October 7, 1985, to replace the outgoing Chairman, James C. Miller III.

36. See, *Advertising Compliance Service*, Tab #4, False, Unfair, Deceptive, Article #7.

37. See, *Advertising Compliance Service, Tab* #16, Children's Ads, Articles #1-3.

Appendix 1A

FEDERAL TRADE COMMISSION, 1975 PROTOCOL: DECEPTIVE AND UNSUBSTANTIATED CLAIMS POLICY PROTOCOL

A. Consumer Interpretations of the Claim

1. List the main interpretations that consumers may place on the claim recommended for challenge, including those that might render the claim true/substantiated as well as those that might render the claim false/unsubstantiated.

2. Indicate which of these interpretations would be alleged to be implications of the claim for purposes of substantiation or litigation. For each interpretation so

indicated, state the reasons, if any, for believing that the claim so interpreted would be false/unsubstantiated.

B. Scale of the Deception or Lack of Substantiation

3. What is known about the relative proportions of consumers adhering to each of the interpretations listed above in response to Question 1?

4. What was the approximate advertising budget for the claim during the past year or during any other period of time that would reflect the number of consumers actually exposed to the claim? Is there more direct information on the number of consumers exposed to the claim?

C. Materiality

5. If consumers do interpret the claim in the ways that would be alleged to be implications, what reasons are there for supposing that these interpretations would influence purchase decisions?

6. During the past year, approximately how many consumers purchased the product* about which the claim was made?

7. Approximately what price did they pay?

8. Estimate, if possible, the proportion of consumers who would have purchased the product only at some price lower than they did pay, if at all, were they informed that the interpretations identified in response to Question 2 were false.

9. Estimate, if possible, what the advertised product would be worth to the consumers identified by Question 8 if they knew that the product did not have the positive (or unique) attributes suggested by the claim. If the claim can cause consumers to disregard some negative attribute, such as a risk to health and safety, to their possible physical or economic injury, so specify. If so, estimate, if possible, the annual number of such injuries attributable to the claim.

D. Adequacy of Corrective Market Forces

10. If the product to which the claim relates is a low-ticket item, can consumers ordinarily determine prior to purchase whether the claim, as interpreted, is true; or invest a small amount in purchase and then by experience with the product determine whether or not the claim is true? Does the claim relate to a credence quality, that is, a quality of the product that consumers ordinarily cannot evaluate during normal use of the product without acquiring costly information from some source other than their own evaluative faculties?

11. Is the product to which the claim relates one that a consumer would typically purchase frequently? Have product sales increased or decreased substantially since the claim was made?

12. Are there sources of information about the subject matter of the claim in addition to the claim itself? If so, are they likely to be recalled by consumers when they purchase or use the product? Are they likely to be used by consumers who are not aggressive, effective shoppers? If not, why not?

---

*Throughout, "product" refers to the particular brand advertised.

E. Effect on the Flow of Truthful Information

13. Will the standard of truth/substantiation that would be applied to the claim under the recommendation to initiate proceedings make it extremely difficult as a practical matter to make the type of claim? Is this result reasonable?

14. What are the consequences to consumers of an erroneous determination by the Commission that the claim is false/unsubstantiated? What are the consequences to consumers of an erroneous determination by the Commission that the claim is true/substantiated?

F. Deterrence

15. Is there a possibility of getting significant relief with broad product or claim coverage? What relief is possible? Why would it be significant?

16. Do the facts of the matter recommended present an opportunity to elaborate a rule of law that would be applicable to claims or advertisers other than those that would be directly challenged by the recommended action? If so, describe this rule of law as you would wish the advertising community to understand it. If this rule of law would be a significant precedent, explain why.

17. Does the claim violate a Guide (Editor's Note: A "Guide" contains FTC advice to an industry as contrasted with a formal rule.) or is it inconsistent with relevant principles embodied in a Guide?

18. Is the fact of a violation so evident to other industry members that, if we do not act, our credibility and deterrence might be adversely affected?

19. Is there any aspect of the advertisement—e.g., the nature of the advertiser, the product, the theme, the volume of the advertising, the memorableness of the ad, the blatancy of the violation—which indicates that an enforcement action would have substantial impact on the advertising community?

20. What, if anything, do we know about the role advertising plays (as against other promotional techniques and other sources of information) in the decision to purchase the product?

21. What is the aggregate dollar volume spent on advertising by the advertiser to be joined in the recommended action?

22. What is the aggregate volume of sales of the advertised product and of products the same type?

G. Law Enforcement Efficiency

23. Has another agency taken action or does another agency have expertise with respect to the claim or its subject matter? Are there reasons why the Commission should defer? What is the position of this other agency? If coordination is planned, what form would it take?

24. How difficult would it be to litigate a case challenging the claim? Would the theory of the proceeding recommended place the Commission in a position of resolving issues that are better left to other modes of resolution, for instance, debate among scientists? If so, explain. Is there a substantial possibility of whole or partial summary judgment?

25. Can the problem seen in the ad be handled by way of a rule? Are the violations widespread? Should they be handled by way of a rule?

H. Additional Considerations

26. What is the ratio of the advertiser's advertising expense to sales revenues? How, if at all, is this ratio relevant to the public interest in proceeding as recommended?

27. Does the claim specially affect a vulnerable group?

28. Does the advertising use deception or unfairness to offend important values or to exploit legitimate concerns of a substantial segment of the population, whether or not there is direct injury to person or pocketbook, *e.g.*, minority hiring or environmental protection?

29. Are there additional considerations not elicited by previous questions that would affect the public interest in proceeding?

Appendix 1B

LIST OF CASES AND STAFF ANALYSES AS SUBMITTED BY FTC CHAIRMAN JAMES C. MILLER III TO HOUSE SUBCOMMITTEE ON COMMERCE, TRANSPORTATION AND TOURISM ON APRIL 1, 1982

I. CLAIMS ON WHICH THE COMMISSION PREVAILED

Kroger Co., D. 9102 (9/25/81)

Kroger's advertising described the results of its "Price Patrol," in which homemakers surveyed prices of 100 to 150 items at local supermarkets. The Commission conceded "that the evidence does not dispute Kroger's basic argument that its prices were frequently below or equal to those of its competitors." Nevertheless, based on its own expertise, without any other evidence of the ad's meaning, the Commission held that the ads were deceptive because they implicitly represented that the surveys were "methodologically sound" and "statistically projectible."

Commissioner Patricia Bailey dissented on the meaning of the ads. She noted that Kroger made a point of emphasizing the informality of the surveys. She wrote, "the notion that these surveys were 'methodologically sound' and therefore 'prove' an overall 'projection' of lower prices is simply, in my view, an artificial construct imposed by the majority [of the Commissioners] on the ads in question." On the merits of bringing this case, she wrote, "I fear that the majority opinion will chill the development of useful comparative price advertising, especially among retail grocers, which is extremely useful to the public, particularly in times of high inflation."

Block Drug Company, 90 F.T.C. 893 (1977)

The FTC challenged claims that Poli-Grip would help denture wearers eat problem foods, such as apples, without discomfort or embarrassment. This product is cheap, frequently purchased, and easy for consumers to evaluate for themselves. When these three facts are present, the FTC is not needed to police the marketplace, because advertisers cannot make enough money from deception to recoup their investment in the advertising. As Commissioner Mayo Thompson said in his dissent, "it is inconceivable to me that any denture wearer who applied Poli-Grip or Super

Poli-Grip and bit into a red apple and then saw his dentures smiling back at him would ever purchase the Gripper again.''

Ford Motor Co., 87 F.T.C. 756 (1976)

The headline of the challenged ad claimed that "All 5 Ford Motor Co. small cars got over 26 mpg." The ads stated that mileage varies according to maintenance, equipment, total weight, driving habits, and so forth, and added that no two drivers, or even cars, are exactly alike. Despite these disclaimers, the Commission found an implied claim that the *average* driver would get the advertised mileage. The Commission found this claim based solely on its own expertise, and without considering a survey conducted by Ford.

Levitz Furniture Corporation, 88 F.T.C. 263 (1976)

A discount furniture store ran ads that claimed "New Reduced Prices," and "Levitz Furniture actually lowers prices." The Commission alleged that the ads claimed consumers would save from Levitz's regular price. As former Commissioner Pitofsky wrote in criticizing the Commission for bringing these fictitious pricing cases, "as long as consumers are accurately informed of the offering price, they can make sensible decisions, and the transactions may still be at prices lower than could be obtained at most other outlets in the marketing area." 90 *Harvard Law Review* 661 (1977) at 688.

Nagle, Spillman & Bergman, Inc., 88 F.T.C. 244 (1976) and *Morton-Norwich Products, Inc.*, 86 F.T.C. 299 (1975)

In these cases, the Commission challenged claims for two salt substitutes. Both companies claimed that their products, substituting potassium chloride for sodium chloride, were appropriate for those who wanted to decrease their salt intake. None of the ads mentioned potassium. Nonetheless, the Commission found that the ads were deceptive because they failed to mention that the product should not be used by those on a potassium-restricted diet.

In *Nagle*, the Commission also challenged a claim that the product "tastes like salt." Not only is this claim inherently subjective, but because the product is cheap and frequently purchased, consumers can easily evaluate whether it tastes like salt.

General Motors Corp., 85 F.T.C. 17 (1975)

GM advertised that *Road and Track* magazine found the Vega to be the best handling passenger car ever built in the U.S. The Commission interpreted GM's claim to mean that Vega *really* is the best handling car. Because the Commission apparently felt that *Road and Track* magazine was not adequate substantiation, GM could not substantiate the broader claim the Commission inferred from the ad. The result of the order in this case is that consumers are deprived of learning through advertising valuable opinion information from reputable publications.

Spiegel, Inc., 82 F.T.C. 20 (1973), 494 F.2d 59 (7th Cir. 1974), cert denied 419 U.S. 896 (1974)

In its advertising circulars, Spiegel offered products on 30 days "free trial" or at a "percentage off." These offers were subject to the customer meeting credit qualifi-

cations, a requirement mentioned only in small print and stated in the Spiegel catalogue. Spiegel required the customer to submit credit-related data with the order.
The Commission, over the dissent of Commissioner Miles Kirkpatrick, concluded
that the ads created the impression that the offer was unconditional when actually it
depended on the customer's credit rating. When the appellate court upheld the Commission, Judge Pell, in dissent, wrote that the Commission had found "a detriment
to the public interest in the situation of deadbeats being deceived into thinking they
are going to receive a free trial of, or discount on, merchandise which they could not
realistically purchase on either a cash or a deferred basis."

Brite Mfg. Co., 65 F.T.C. 1067 (1964), 347 F.2d 477 (D.C. Cir. 1965)

Brite involved watch bands that were imported largely from Japan, and so marked
on the back. Based on its own expertise, the Commission found that there was a
preference among Americans for domestic watches and that it was deceptive to fail
to disclose the foreign origin of the watches prior to sale.

Dannon Milk Products, Inc., 61 F.T.C. 840 (1962)

Dannon's advertising described yogurt as "Nature's perfect food that science made
better." Although Dannon argued that this was mere puffing, the Commission
found that the claim that a food is perfect "concerns nutrition," and is therefore a
factual claim. The Commission challenged this claim because a person could not
subsist on a diet of yogurt alone.

Mohawk Ref. Co., 54 F.T.C. 1071 (1958), 263 F.2d 818 (3d Cir. 1959), see also Kerron, 54 F.T.C. 1035 (1958), 265 F.2d 246 (10th Cir. 1959)

The point-of-merchandise materials and labels did not make any claims alleged to be
false, but they failed to disclose that the oil being sold was refined from previously
used oil rather than virgin crude oil. Although the evidence showed that re-refined
oil was *as satisfactory* for lubrication as virgin crude oil, the Commission held that
the failure to disclose that the oil was re-refined was deceptive.

Liggett & Myers Tobacco Co., 55 F.T.C. 354 (1958)

In this case, a cigarette company claimed that its product had a taste that was
"always milder." The hearing examiner dismissed this charge as mere puffing and
said that there was no public interest in litigating the case. The Commission reversed
and found that in the context of the ad, the "milder" claim suggested that it was less
irritating in a physical sense, and, not just milder to taste or smell. Under either
interpretation, consumers can determine for themselves whether this cigarette is
milder.

Gelb, 33 F.T.C. 1450 (1941), aff'd as modified, 144 F.2d 580 (2d Cir. 1944)

The Commission sued a manufacturer that claimed its hair coloring product was
permanent because it was feared that some consumers might believe it would color
hair that had not yet grown out. The Court of Appeals noted that "it seems scarcely
possible that any user of the preparation could be so credulous as to suppose that
hair not yet grown out would be so colored." Nonetheless, it upheld the Commission's order.

Sebrone Co., 34 F.T.C. 1126 (1942), aff'd 135 F.2d 676 (7th Cir. 1943)

A deodorant that claimed to "kill strongest odors" was challenged as false by the Commission because it only masked, and did not destroy, odors. Deodorants are an inexpensive, frequently purchased product, and consumers can easily determine for themselves whether they are satisfied with the product.

II. CLAIMS ON WHICH THE COMMISSION LOST ON APPEAL

The courts have frequently stated that the meaning of an ad is a matter committed to the discretion of the Commission. As former Commissioner Pitofsky wrote, "this modest-sounding rule is a principal reason that the Commission has managed to prevail in the appellate courts in the overwhelming majority of its [advertising] decisions that have been appealed." 90 Harvard Law Review 661 (1977) at 667-78.

The following cases provide a welcome sign that the courts are no longer deferring to the Commission completely. Nonetheless, it is not at all clear that the courts will impose a significant check regarding deception. Even if they do, constraints will emerge only on an *ad hoc* basis, at considerable expense and time to all concerned.

Standard Oil Co. of California, **84 F.T.C. 1401 (1974), modified 577 F.2d 653 (9th Cir. 1978)**

This case involved claims that a gasoline additive, F-310, would reduce air pollution. The Commission interpreted a visual demonstration, featuring black smoke from a car's exhaust without F-310 added, then clear exhaust after F-310 was used, as a claim that the additive would "cause the disappearance of virtually 100 percent of exhaust emission pollutants." The Court of Appeals reversed this finding, stating "we do not think that any television viewer would have a level of credulity so primitive that he could expect to breathe fresh air if he stuck his head into a bag inflated by exhaust, no matter how clean it looked."

Trans World Accounts, Inc., **90 F.T.C. 350 (1977), modified, 94 F.T.C. 141, further modified, 94 F.T.C. 1051, aff'd in part and remanded in part 594 F.2d 212 (9th Cir. 1979)**

This case involved letters sent by a debt collection agency urging immediate payment and stating failure to comply may result in immediate commencement of litigation by our client. The Commission found that the letters were deceptive because they threatened imminent legal action when no such action was contemplated. Commissioner Collier dissented, writing that "may" means legal action is possible, not probable. He noted, "[t]he majority's decision effectively regulates the word 'may' out of respondents' vocabulary." The Court upheld the finding of liability, but reversed the Commission's restrictions on the use of the word "may."

III. CLAIMS ON WHICH THE COMMISSION DISAGREED WITH THE STAFF

In these cases, the Commission issued a complaint that was later rejected either by an administrative law judge, or by the Commission itself on appeal. Although the staff ultimately did not prevail, the mere fact that the Commission thought there was reason to issue a complaint illustrates the current problems with the deception standard. Tens of thousands of dollars were spent regarding these complaints—in the case of the Children's Advertising rule-making, which was based on both unfairness and deception, over $1,000,000—that would not have been spent had a better statutory definition of deception existed.

California Milk Producers Advisory Board, 94 F.T.C. 429 (1979)

The complaint challenged an advertising slogan that "every body needs milk." The Commission, in issuing the complaint, interpreted the claim to mean that milk is essential for all individuals, even those who are allergic to milk, and that it is beneficial in large and unlimited quantities. The administrative law judge agreed with the interpretation of the ads, but concluded that since less than one percent of the population was allergic to milk, there was no public interest in proceeding.

Jay Norris, 91 F.T.C. 751 (1978), aff'd as modified 598 F.2d 1244 (2d Cir. 1979)

One of the claims the Commission challenged was the claim that nylon socks were "guaranteed to wear forever in normal use." The complaint alleged that these claims meant that the socks were literally indestructible and would last forever. The Administrative Law Judge dismissed this allegation. He held that the ad claimed that the socks would last a long time, and that if they wore out, Jay Norris would replace them. This portion of the decision was not appealed to the Commission.

Bristol-Myers Co., 85 F.T.C. 688 (1975)

The complaint in this case challenged advertisements that depicted Dry Ban as clear and dry when it was applied in contrast to another leading brand, that was oily and sticky. The complaint interpreted these ads to mean that Dry Ban was "a dry spray that is not wet when applied to the body." On appeal from the Administrative Law Judge's initial decision upholding the charges, the Commission concluded that the ads claimed only that the product was drier than competing brands. The Commission dismissed the complaint. As Commissioner Mayo Thompson noted in his concurring opinion, "[i]f the American consumer has no more serious problem than the possibility of being deceived as to the relative 'dryness' of his underarm deodorant, he is in much better shape than I had been led to suppose at the time I joined this agency."

Firestone Tire and Rubber Co., 81 F.T.C. 398, aff'd 481 F.2d 246 (6th Cir. 1973)

The Commission's complaint alleged, among other things, that the tire name "Safety Champion" implied that these tires were safer than all other tires. A consumer survey conducted by the company showed that only 1.4% would perceive the claim alleged in this complaint. Nonetheless, the Administrative Law Judge enjoined the use of the term because he interpreted it as representing that the tires were free from defects and safe under all conditions of use. The Commission reversed the prohibition against the use of the term, finding that "Safety Champion" does not represent that the tire is safer than all other tires.

2.
ADVERTISING SUBSTANTIATION

You're prepared to defend your advertising against FTC charges that your claims are false, unfair or deceptive. But is that good enough? No. The Federal Trade Commission can challenge your ad as illegal if you didn't have proof (i.e., "substantiation") on hand that your claims were true *before* your ad was printed or broadcast. This is known as the advertising substantiation doctrine and, while this doctrine has been under extensive review over the past four years, it remains as one of the lynchpins of advertising regulation in the United States.

How does this doctrine work in practice? If you make factual claims in your ads about your product's attributes or performance capabilities, you have to have proof on hand *before* that ad runs that substantiates your claims. Let's say your ad contains the price claim, "Our prices are the lowest among the five leading brands." Assume further that your prices *are* the lowest among the five leading brands. Would your ad be sheltered from FTC scrutiny? No. FTC would ask you what proof you had on hand *before* your ad ran substantiating this claim. If you didn't have such proof—in the form of a survey, for example—FTC could bring a complaint against you, even if you could later prove that claim to be true.

LESSONS FROM THE PFIZER DECISION

The reasoning behind FTC's advertising substantiation doctrine is found in the landmark case, *In re Pfizer, Inc.*[1] In *Pfizer*, FTC had challenged advertising by Pfizer, Inc. for its product, "UN-BURN," a nonprescription product recommended for use on minor burns and sunburn. Typical of the radio and TV advertising challenged by FTC were the following ads:

New Un-Burn actually anesthetizes *nerves* in sensitive sunburned skin. Un-Burn relieves pain *fast*. Actually *anesthetizes nerves* in sensitive sunburned skin.

Sensitive skin. . . . Sunburned skin is sensitive skin. . . . Sensitive sunburned skin needs . . . UN-BURN. New UN-BURN contains the same local anesthetic doctors often use. . . . Actually anesthetizes nerves in sensitive sunburned skin. I'll tell you what I like about UN-BURN. It's the best friend a blonde ever had! . . . I'm a blond . . . and I know what it means to have sensitive skin. Why I'm half afraid of moon burn! That's why I'm mad about UN-BURN. It stops sunburn pain in less time than it takes me to slip out of my bikini. That's awfully nice to know when you're the sensitive type. . . .[2]

FTC's complaint charged that Pfizer did not substantiate these advertising claims (i.e., "anesthetizes skin" and "stops sunburn pain") by having on hand "adequate and well-controlled scientific studies or tests prior to the making of such statements."

In that case, FTC concluded that for an advertiser to make a claim without possessing a "reasonable basis" to support that claim was unfair since that would make consumers take a risk as to whether the claim was true. As FTC noted in *Pfizer*:

Given the imbalance of knowledge and resources between a business enterprise and each of its customers, economically it is more rational, and imposes far less cost on society, to require a manufacturer to confirm his affirmative product claims rather than impose a burden upon each individual consumer to test, investigate, or experiment for himself. The manufacturer has the ability, the know-how, the equipment, the time and the resources to undertake such information by testing or otherwise—the consumer usually does not.[3]

As an advertising compliance planner, what concrete lessons can you learn from *Pfizer*—and the body of law on substantiation that followed—in formulating or reviewing advertising copy so as to be sure your ad claims are substantiated? There are several.

First, you should determine exactly what claims your ad contains. Keep in mind the possibility that consumers seeing or hearing your ad may discern different, and even additional, claims than the ones you intend. Try to adopt their perspective. And remember that *each* claim (depending on the nature of the claim) may have to be substantiated.

Second, consider the type of claims made. Are the claims mainly appeals to taste (such as the availability of your product in different sizes or colors) or "puffing" claims? If so, such claims would not have to be substantiated. However, if your ad makes factual claims about your product's specific attributes or performance characteristics, then you would have to substantiate those claims.

Third, if your claims must be substantiated, you must determine how much substantiation is enough to provide a "reasonable basis." Under *Pfizer*, this varies from case to case since it depends on an interplay of five relevant factors:

1. *The type and specificity of your ad claim* (e.g., safety, efficacy, dietary, health, medical). The more specific your advertising claim, the more substantiation you'll need.

2. *The type of product you're advertising.* If you make factual claims for drugs, food or a potentially hazardous consumer product, you'll have to have on hand greater substantiation than for other types of products.

3. *The possible consequences of a false claim.* If you make claims for a product that may be hazardous, you'll have to have much greater substantiation than for nonhazardous products, particularly if your claim concerns safety. For example, let's say you ran an ad for a stepladder that claims to be "Dependable. Durable. Safe for all home uses." There is a substantial amount of litigation, and law, involving products liability relating to stepladders. Moreover, there is a substantial body of literature as to effective safety testing for this particular product. FTC would presume that you were aware of this before advertising and had conducted sufficient testing prior to running your ad.

4. *The degree of reliance by consumers on your claim.* This means that if the potential buyers of your product cannot verify your claims by themselves, you'll need to supply greater substantiation for your claims. For example, if you advertise the greater technical superiority of your personal computer, you'll need to have greater substantiation since few consumers would be in a position to verify whether this was true or not.

5. *The type and accessibility of proof adequate to form a reasonable basis for making a particular claim.* For example, let's say you advertise a diet aid and the particular claims you make are about an ingredient in that product about which reams of articles and studies have been conducted. In such a case, you'll need to have on hand the most pertinent of those articles and studies as well as your own tests or studies to show to the FTC if it asks you for substantiation.

In addition to these five factors, FTC will also consider (1) how much it costs, or would cost, to develop substantiation for the claim, and (2) the amount of substantiation that experts in the field would consider reasonable.

RECENT CONTROVERSY

In October 1981, FTC Chairman James C. Miller III, vowed that FTC would review the Commission's advertising substantiation policy.[4] He cited a potential "chilling effect" on advertisers and costs for advertiser and consumer alike from the program. His statements about the policy were widely disseminated by the media and caused widespread confusion, and criticism, both from within the Commission and from the advertising community itself.[5]

In November 1982, Miller circulated among the FTC Commissioners a draft questionnaire on the advertising substantiation program.[6] This draft questionnaire was the forerunner of a later request for comments from the public on the ad substantiation program.[7]

In order to reach a consensus on the ad substantiation project, Chairman Miller later modified his earlier views on ad substantiation. In an exclusive interview with *Advertising Compliance Service* on November 3, 1982, Miller said, "It's almost axiomatic that if you're trying to achieve truthful advertising you have to have advertisers substantiate their claims."[8]

After an extensive review of the ad substantiation program, FTC ended up pretty much where it had started by unanimously reaffirming its commitment to that program in the summer of 1984. According to an FTC policy statement on the program issued at that time, "a firm's failure to possess and rely upon a reasonable basis for objective claims constitutes an unfair and deceptive act or practice in violation of Section 5 of the FTC Act." FTC emphasized that it "intends to continue vigorous enforcement of this existing legal requirement that advertisers substantiate express and implied claims, however conveyed, that make objective assertions about the item or service advertised."[9]

Nevertheless FTC did adopt several "refinements" in its policy to foster better enforcement at a lower cost. These refinements include:

- Seeking substantiation from companies on an individual basis instead of using industrywide "rounds," which involve publicized inquiries with similar demands for substantiation to advertisers within a specific industry;
- Considering both the consequences of a false claim and the benefits of a true claim when deciding if advertisers and advertising agencies had adequate substantiation; and
- Retaining the discretion, in the following circumstances, to consider evidence developed *after* an advertiser makes a claim: (1) During the pre-complaint stage to decide whether there is a public interest in proceeding against a firm; (2) When deciding the appropriate scope of an order; and (3) When assessing the reasonableness of an advertiser in relying on the prior substantiation it did have.

AVOIDING PROBLEMS WHEN USING SURVEYS

If you plan to use surveys in your ads or to substantiate factual advertising claims, you're well advised to become familiar with FTC's current standards of reviewing surveys.[10] Based on an analysis of FTC policy, here are some hazards to avoid if you plan to use a survey in an ad or to substantiate a claim:

- Does any reference in a survey in your ad imply a measure of precision you don't intend or that may be misleading? Be careful to explain or clarify your survey's limitations.
- Make sure your ad doesn't contain literally truthful statements based on survey results that may convey implied claims your survey can't support.
- Be sure you don't imply a survey is nationally projectable if it isn't. *Example*: If you use a nonprojectable survey in a national ad campaign without a disclosure or other language to prevent the implication of national projectability.

Also, make sure your survey passes muster in these three ways:

• It should be competently—and accurately—analyzed.

• It should relate to the ad and support the claim for which it is offered as evidence.

• It should have a methodology experts would regard as appropriate for the circumstances; in most cases this methodology should be designed by experts.

And, of course, your ad shouldn't overstate survey results or exaggerate them.

Unfortunately, there's no single formula you can use to develop a survey methodology that guarantees FTC acceptance. FTC views of methodology—along with the adequacy of the response rate and the other mechanics of conducting the survey—depend on the circumstances.

Surveys you offer to substantiate claims of health and safety will be subjected to the greatest scrutiny. If your surveys try to substantiate the medical properties of your product, these surveys will be held to "scientific" standards of proof. Example: In its *American Home Products*[11] decision, FTC found that tests conducted to substantiate superiority claims for Anacin allegedly failed by:

• not producing statistically significant results;

• using an aspirin-caffeine combination instead of Anacin for the tests against plain aspirin when the compound could have behaved differently from Anacin; and

• failing to distinguish between different forms of pain.

In its *AHP* opinion, FTC quoted approvingly the legislative history of the Federal Food, Drug and Cosmetic Act, saying, "We are more strict with the advertising of foods, drugs, devices, and cosmetics because their effect is direct and their use might endanger life." FTC went on to note that the U.S. Supreme Court's decision in *McNeilab, Inc. v. American Home Products Corp.* "took into account the fact that claims had a bearing on matters of public health."[12]

Almost every survey implies that the answers given by its sample are projectable to a larger group. However, the specific issue of national projectability is important if you're conducting a national advertising campaign.

This is especially true if you use phrases like "nationwide survey" or "national test winner." When R. J. Reynolds challenged Lorillard's claim that Triumph cigarettes were "National Smoker Study Winners," a federal judge found "that the percentages used, as derived from a mall intercept study, do not constitute national statistics as represented." He said a mall intercept study "as such" was not "an unreasonable basis for comparative advertising." It failed, however, to provide national projectability.

The validity of your survey's results depends on an adequate response rate to your survey. Basically, this means you should get enough responses so that your survey contains a fair sample of the group (e.g., doctors) that you've chosen. The following factors influence FTC's approach to your surveys:

- *Nature of your product*: You should ask if it would be too expensive for a consumer to learn by trial and error. Would it be too dangerous?
- *Nature of your claim*: If you make beauty or other subjective claims, you may get by with lower response rates than if you make health and safety claims.
- *Nature of the population studied*: You should be aware that some populations— specific professions, for example—traditionally give low response rates.
- *Medium of the survey*: You should understand that each form of survey has a different response rate that is considered acceptable.
- *Inducement*: Ask: Were the subjects paid to respond? FTC may expect a higher response if you provide an inducement.

Many surveys are capable of varying interpretations; indeed, many are designed to provide ambiguous results. But advertisers should be careful not to misinterpret results, or to make them appear what they are not: For example, the word "win" should not be used to mean "better than expected" or "just as good."

Other points to consider:

Tests that may be appropriate to substantiate a product claim, or to be the basis of a campaign, may not be appropriate bases for comparative claims.

You may overcome legitimate limitations in the usefulness of survey results—especially those inherent in the survey design—by placing disclosures in your ads, or by using other language that prevents consumers from inferring claims that the surveys cannot support.

The form of your disclosure can vary. However, you should be wary of relying on fine print to remedy possible deception, and should never rely on it to correct serious deception or falsehood.

The status of the law—and of FTC policy—regarding surveys is still emerging. Advertisers who plan to use surveys in their ads or to substantiate them are therefore well advised to become familiar with the standards found in pertinent FTC cases.

CONTINUITY AND CHANGE

One of the most important actions taken by FTC during the Chairmanship of James Miller III was the issuance of two parallel decisions involving Bristol-Myers Co. and Sterling Drug, Inc. in July 1983.[13] These orders completed the Commission proceedings in the landmark analgesic cases, which began in 1973 with complaints against Bristol-Myers, Sterling Drug, and American Home Products.[14] The complaints charged that the companies made false and unsubstantiated claims about their products' ingredients, efficacy, safety, and ability to relieve tension.

In *American Home Products*,[15] which involved advertising for Anacin and Arthritis Pain Formula, the Commission issued a final order in 1981. In that case, the Commission required that for any comparative efficacy or freedom from side effects claim for analgesics, substantiation consisting of two well-controlled clinical studies, as defined in the order, was necessary. The Commission required that in the absence of two well-controlled clinical tests to support the claim, the advertisement must disclose that the claim had not been proven or that there was a "substantial question" as to its validity. This order was predicated on the theory that when an advertisement makes a claim about the effectiveness or freedom from side effects of analgesic products, consumers expect the claim to be substantiated by the type of scientific evidence which experts would require to validate such a claim.

The scientific community, and Food and Drug Administration regulations regarding the safety and efficacy of new drugs, require at least two well-controlled studies because replication reduces the possibility that the results are due to chance and reduces the effect of flaws in the design of any one study. The evidence in the *Bristol-Myers* case indicated that scientists consider replication especially important for clinical studies for over-the-counter analgesics because of the subjective nature of the participants' responses and because of the presence of other variables which are difficult to quantify but could influence test results.

The Commission's opinion in *American Home Products* was written by Michael Pertschuk shortly before Miller became FTC Chairman and before the appointment of George Douglas, President Reagan's second appointee to the Commission. The *Bristol-Myers* and *Sterling Drug* opinions were written by Commissioner David Clanton and were the first major FTC opinions in consumer protection matters under the new administration. These opinions diverged from *American Home Products* in two primary respects.

First, the Commission reversed the "substantial question" doctrine of *American Home Products*. In *Bristol-Myers* (which involved advertising for Bufferin, Excedrin, and Excedrin PM) and in *Sterling Drug* (which involved advertising for Bayer Aspirin, Cope, Vanquish, and Mydol) the Commission prohibited comparative efficacy or freedom from side effects claims without the support of at least two well-controlled clinical studies *only when the advertising expresses or implies that the claim has been established or proven*. Claims of therapeutic performance or freedom from side effects which do not say or imply that they have been scientifically established must be supported only by competent and reliable scientific evidence. The

Commission found that well-controlled clinical tests would be a reasonable basis for these claims, but the Commission left open the possibility that a lesser amount of evidence might also provide a reasonable basis.

Second, the *Bristol-Myers* and *Sterling Drug* decisions narrowed the requirement of aspirin disclosure from what had been required in *American Home Products*. In *American Home Products*, the FTC order had required disclosure that Anacin and Arthritis Pain Formula contain aspirin, when advertising made any performance claim for these products. In *Bristol-Myers* and *Sterling Drug*, the disclosure of aspirin content is only required in advertising which compares the analgesic ingredients of a product that contains aspirin with the analgesic ingredients of another product that also contains aspirin. The orders also prohibit the misrepresentation of the identity of any analgesic ingredient in the products.

Undoubtedly, if the Commission's orders are upheld on appeal, a recurring issue in the future will be whether a claim is an express or implied establishment claim, subject to a higher standard of proof than a nonestablishment claim. In a dissenting opinion, Commissioner Patricia Bailey observed: "The lines drawn by the majority providing guidance as to when such [establishment] claims are present are exceedingly fine." The *American Home Products* decision was appealed and upheld by the Court of Appeals in all significant respects. FTC's decisions in *Bristol-Myers* and *Sterling Drug* are significant for the advertising community because of what they reflect in terms of change and continuity. In terms of change, the decisions reflect an effort on the part of the Miller Commission to make final orders more narrow and more precise than were the orders of the Pertschuk Commission. In terms of continuity, the Commission's opinions— which are lengthy and merit careful reading by those involved in advertising regulation—reflect a reaffirmation by the Commission of the basic principles of advertising law. In these opinions, the Commission has expressed its adherence to the following basic principles:

- Interpreting advertising claims is not a mystical process; it involves the exercise of common sense and good judgment.

- The Commission can determine the meaning of an ad without resorting to assessments of consumer perception or other expert testimony. But when consumer perception studies on the meaning of an ad have been introduced, this evidence must be considered by the Commission in reaching its conclusion. This evidence assists the Commission in reaching a sound decision. There may be instances where claims cannot be inferred from an examination of the ads on their face; in such cases, the Commission may need to resort to consumer evidence.

- When the Commission interprets an ad, it must consider the net impression that the ad makes on consumers. An ad may violate the law if an implied claim is not properly substantiated, even though the ad's statements, taken literally, are true. The Commission may not, however, inject novel meanings into ads and then strike them down as unsubstantiated; ads must be judged by the impression they make on reasonable members of the public.

- If an ad conveys more than one meaning to reasonable consumers, and one of those meanings is false, the ad may be condemned.
- In order for claims to be considered false or deceptive in violation of the FTC Act, they must be material to the purchase decision; that is, the claims must be the type on which consumers are likely to rely in deciding to purchase a particular good or service.

The Commission recognized that there is a category of claims which do not require substantiation: This consists of "puffing" claims, which are not capable of measurement or which consumers would not take seriously. Examples cited by the Commission are an advertisement touting a foreign sports car as "the sexiest European," and an advertisement for Bayer Aspirin stating that "Bayer works wonders."

An interesting issue in the *Sterling Drug* case was whether it is a violation of the FTC Act for a company to make mutually inconsistent claims. Contemporaneously, Sterling Drug claimed that:

1. Bayer Aspirin is as effective for the relief of headache pain as any other non-prescription analgesic;
2. Vanquish is a more effective reliever of headache pain than Bayer aspirin;
3. Bayer Aspirin will cause stomach upset no more frequently than will any other nonprescription analgesic;
4. Vanquish will cause less stomach upset than unbuffered aspirin;
5. Bayer Aspirin is as effective a reliever of nervous tension headache as any nonprescription analgesic; and
6. Cope is more effective for the relief of nervous headache tension than any other nonprescription analgesic.

Obviously, all these claims cannot be true.

The complaint charged that making these inconsistent, contemporaneous claims was a violation of Section 5 of the FTC Act. The Commission found that these claims had, in fact, been made by Sterling Drug, but declined to find a violation on the grounds that (1) a reasonable basis does not determine whether a claim is actually true, and (2) that it is theoretically possible that two inconsistent claims can both be substantiated with a reasonable basis.

The Commission's decision on this issue can provide comfort to those in the media who are concerned with inconsistent claims made by different advertisers; the Commission has determined that where each claim is adequately substantiated, the advertiser's burden (and, presumably in turn, the media's burden) has been met.

The Commission has made it abundantly clear, in *Bristol-Myers* and *Sterling Drug*, that it continues to adhere to the basic *Pfizer* doctrine that advertisers must have adequate substantiation for claims before making them. The Commission expressed its adherence to the principle established in *Pfizer* that the evidence required to constitute a reasonable basis depends on a variety of factors, including:

1. the type and specificity of the claim made;
2. the type of product;
3. the possible consequences to consumers on the claim; and
4. the type and accessibility of evidence adequate to form a reasonable basis for making the particular claim.

OTHER SOURCES

Before reviewing your ads to determine the adequacy, or need, for prior substantiation, don't forget to examine the role of the Better Business Bureaus' National Advertising Division (NAD). Ever since the demise of the National Association of Broadcasters's advertising codes and their enforcement body, the Code Authority, NAD's ad compliance role has increased significantly. The monthly decisions issued by the NAD in its Case Reports continue to provide guidance to the industry.

Serving as the advertising industry's self-regulatory agency, NAD evaluates the accuracy of national print and broadcast advertising. Since NAD keeps up-to-date on the latest FTC developments on advertising, its decisions can be a very helpful source of information about what type of ad substantiation is acceptable to substantiate factual advertising claims. (For more details about NAD and its role in ad substantiation, turn to Chapter 4 of this book. The role of the networks in ad substantiation is examined in Chapter 5.)

NOTES

1. 81 F.T.C. 23 (1972).
2. 81 F.T.C. at 57.
3. 81 F.T.C. at 62.
4. See, *Advertising Compliance Service*, Tab #5, Substantiation, Article #2 and Tab #17, Food, Drugs & Cosmetics, Article #1.
5. See, *Advertising Compliance Service*, Tab #5, Substantiation, Article #3.
6. See, *Advertising Compliance Service*, Tab #5, Substantiation, Article #7.
7. See, *Advertising Compliance Service*, Tab #5, Substantiation, Article #8 and Special Report #2, March 21, 1983.
8. See, *Advertising Compliance Service*, Tab #2, General Articles, Article #11.
9. See, *Advertising Compliance Service*, Tab #5, Substantiation, Article #12.
10. This section is adapted from the two-part article, "Avoiding Problems When

Using Surveys in Your Ads,'' by William H. Feldman, *Advertising Compliance Service*, Tab #5, Substantiation, Articles #4 and 5.

11. FTC Dkt. No. 8918, 9-9-81.

12. 501 F.Supp. 517 (S.D.N.Y.) 1980.

13. This section was adapted from the two-part article, ''Current Developments in Advertising Regulation,'' appearing in *Advertising Compliance Service*, Tab #2, General Articles, Articles #34 and 35, by Jeffrey S. Edelstein, an associate with Hall, Dickler, Lawler, Kent & Howley, and the former Director of Broadcast Standards and Practices of the American Broadcasting Company.

14. *Bristol-Meyer's Co. et al.*, FTC Dkt. #8917, #7-5-83; *Sterling Drug, Inc. et al.*, FTC Dkt. 8919, 7-5-83.

15. 98 F.T.C. 136 (1981), *aff'd*, 695 F.2d 681 (3d Cir. 1982).

3.
WHAT YOU SHOULD KNOW ABOUT COMPARATIVE ADVERTISING

Comparative advertising occurs when your competitor's product or service is named in your ad and compared unfavorably to your product or service. As popular as this form of advertising is today, this wasn't always so. In fact, comparative advertising's popularity is a relatively recent phenomenon.

Before the 1970s, nearly all advertisers viewed comparative advertising with a mixture of fear and disdain. They couldn't see any tangible benefit in comparing their products to their competitors products. Why give your competitors a "free ride," they reasoned. Moreover, they feared that these ads might confuse consumers or even create sympathy for their competitors —the last thing they wanted their advertising campaign to accomplish. But most of all, these advertisers feared that they would be sued if they used comparatives. Reason: A competitor might claim the comparative ad unlawfully disparaged its product.

HISTORY

This historical reluctance to name competitors in ads was bolstered by the then-prevailing opinion of ad industry self-regulatory bodies. The Council of Better Business Bureaus' National Advertising Division (NAD), the National Association of Broadcasters (NAB), and two out of the three networks believed that the use of comparative advertising would likely lead to disparagement and deception. Moreover, the Federal Trade Commission (FTC)—the chief national regulator of advertising—did nothing to encourage comparative advertising (as it later did in the 1970s). As a result, comparative advertising was rare, particularly on television.[1]

The anticomparative advertising attitude of advertisers began to change after the spectacular success of the Avis, "We Try Harder," advertising campaign.[2] Avis used that advertising campaign to tell consumers that since it was only "number two" in the rental car business, the company's philosophy was to "try harder" than "number one," a clear reference to Hertz, the leading rental car company. Avis's "We Try Harder" ad campaign had a successful five-year run "and by the end of its first year, Avis reported a net profit for the first time in fifteen years."[3]

The early development of comparative advertising was also aided by a shift in attitude in two other key groups: government and consumers. The neutral stance of the federal government, and particularly the Federal Trade Commission, started to change in the late 1960s. This, in turn, was caused by the rise in consumerism in the late 1960s and early 1970s. The Commission conducted several studies to determine whether comparative advertising would benefit consumers. FTC's conclusion —it would. FTC's strongly pro-comparative advertising position was eventually codified in 1979. Specifically, FTC policy "encourages the naming of, or reference to competitors, but requires clarity, and, if necessary, disclosure to avoid deception of the consumer. Additionally, the use of truthful comparative advertising should not be restrained by broadcasters or self-regulation entities." ("FTC Policy Statement Regarding Comparative Advertising.") (See Appendix 3A at the end of this chapter for the full text of this important Commission policy statement.)

As a result of FTC pressure, the networks made a dramatic change of course. NBC decided in 1971 to allow comparative ads; CBS and ABC followed suit in 1972. Before this, comparative advertising was banned on CBS and ABC.[4] (See Appendixes 3B and 3C at the end of this chapter for the full text of the ABC and NBC Comparative Advertising Guidelines.)

Other key players in the ad compliance arena followed with their own comparative advertising guidelines. The American Association of Advertising Agencies (4A's) issued its "Policy Statement and Guidelines for Comparative Advertising" in 1974. The 4A's Guidelines acknowledged that comparative advertising, if used "truthfully and fairly," gives consumers useful information. Nevertheless, the Guidelines warn that comparative advertising "can distort facts" and give consumers "information that misrepresents the truth." (For the full-text reproduction of these guidelines, turn to Appendix 3D at the end of this chapter.)

Another extremely important ad compliance player at the time was the National Association of Broadcasters (NAB). Its NAB Code, a codification of voluntary advertising standards for television and radio, was amended, effective April 1, 1975, to provide comparative advertising guidelines for broadcasters. However, the Code was suspended permanently by NAB in 1982 in the wake of a federal district court ruling that one of the code standards (not involving comparative advertising)[5] violated the Sherman Antitrust Act.[6]

CURRENT STANDARDS

As a marketing professional, you need to know the current standards or guidelines for acceptable comparative advertising. If your company, or client, plans to launch a comparative advertising campaign on network television, it is imperative that you study each of the network's Comparative Advertising Guidelines. (See, e.g., Appendixes 3B and 3C.) Regardless of the medium on which your ads will appear, you must also have a sound working knowledge of (1) the Lanham Act and the important comparative advertising cases involving that federal statute, (2) the decisions on comparative advertising of the Council of Better Business Bureaus's National Advertising Division (NAD) and its appellate arm, the National Advertising Review Board (NARB), and (3) the guidelines, regulations and decisions of the Federal Trade Commission involving comparatives.

The remainder of this chapter will examine these important areas and what you need to know about each one.

THE LANHAM ACT

Whether you're an attorney or a marketing professional, you should be aware of the growing body of case law involving comparative advertising. This knowledge can not only alert you to possible comparative advertising offenses by competitors, but enable you to craft comparative advertising campaigns that could withstand scrutiny by the courts.

This body of law has become much more important in recent years as FTC has become much less of a force in advertising regulation. Once a formidable presence in advertising compliance, FTC was hit by a powerful Congressional effort during the late 1970s to curtail what its critics called excessively zealous regulation. This Congressional attack dovetailed with a new Reagan-appointed Commission in the 1980s that openly advocated a scaled-back regulatory approach.

Nature abhors a vacuum and so, apparently, does advertising law. Thus, while FTC's advertising compliance ardor has cooled, there has been a significant increase in actions to remedy false and misleading advertising under Section 43(a) of the Lanham Trademark Act.[7] Once a sleeping giant in comparative advertising law, this 1946 federal statute has increased dramatically in importance over the past decade. Accordingly, you should understand this important federal law and its contribution to comparative advertising law's body of cases. Reason: It has been interpreted by the courts to provide a private cause of action for false comparative advertising.

This statute forbids the "false description or representation" of goods. Specifically, Section 43(a) provides that:

Any person who shall affix, apply, or annex, or use in connection with any goods or services, or any container or containers for goods, a false designation of origin, or any false description or representation, including words or other symbols tending falsely to describe or represent the same and shall cause such goods or services to enter into commerce, and any person who shall with knowledge of the falsity of such designation of origin or description or representation cause or procure the same to be transported or used in commerce or deliver the same to any carrier to be transported or used, shall be liable to a civil action by any person doing business in the locality falsely indicated as that of origin or in the region in which said locality is situated, or by any person who believes that he is or is likely to be damaged by the use of any such false description or representation.

Although this statute became effective on July 5, 1947, the first important decision involving comparative advertising wasn't decided until 1954. In that year, the Third Circuit Court of Appeals rejected the then-prevailing notion that Section 43(a) was limited to trademark or "passing off" cases where a marketer misrepresented an attribute of its product that had been exclusively identified by consumers with a competitor's product. In *L'Aiglon Apparel, Inc. v. Lana Lobell, Inc.*,[8] a dress maker brought suit under the Lanham Act against a dress retailer for "fraudulent and injurious use of a picture" of the dressmaker's more expensive dress in the dress retailer's advertising. The Third Circuit ruled that the dress maker's complaint did come under Section 43(a).

Nevertheless, Section 43(a) remained largely dormant until relatively recently.[9] There are a variety of factors that caused this. As we've seen, comparative advertising was a little-used advertising tool until around fifteen years ago. (And courts have uniformly held that this statute only applies to comparative advertising.) Also, until the mid 1970s, FTC's role as the nation's chief watchdog over fraudulent, deceptive, or misleading advertising also meant that aggrieved competitors were also frequently protected from such ads by that agency. Thus there was no need for advertisers to choose litigation under Section 43(a), an often costly and time-consuming alternative.

More recently, a "bootstrap" effect can be observed in respect to Section 43(a) cases. As the amount of Lanham Act litigation has increased, advertisers, and their counsel, have become increasingly aware of the powerful potential of this federal statute.

Who May Sue Under Section 43(a)

Only competitors or persons with a direct commercial interest have standing to sue under Section 43(a) of the Lanham Act.[10] The courts have so far almost universally held that consumers do not have standing to sue under this section.[11]

Nevertheless, your product or service does not have to be in direct competition with a competitor's product or service to give you standing to sue. In *Dallas Cowboys Cheerleaders v. Pussycat Cinema*,[12] for example, the cheerleaders' organization which performs at Dallas Cowboys' football games was deemed to have standing to sue under Section 43(a). That case involved a pornographic film, "Debbie Does Dallas," in which an actress was pictured in the film and in ads wearing a uniform "strikingly similar to that worn by the Dallas Cowboys Cheerleaders." The plaintiffs in that case had charged that the film and its ads misappropriated their trademarks and service marks and deceptively implied that the film was associated with their organization. They alleged that this damaged their reputation and caused injury to them as a commercial enterprise.

Essential Elements of a Section 43(a) Case

As legal counsel for a marketer of a consumer product, it has come to your attention that a competitor has launched a stinging comparative advertising campaign against your client's product. How do you determine whether your client has a cause of action against the competitor for its ad campaign? You can find the essential elements of a false advertising action under Section 43(a) in the landmark decision of *Skil Corp. v. Rockwell International Corp.*[13] What this case says you have to do is prove that:

1. The defendant (in this example, your client's competitor) made a false statement of fact about its own product in its comparative advertisements;
2. The competitor's ads "actually deceived or have the tendency to deceive a substantial segment" of those people that saw or heard the ads;
3. This deception is "material," that is likely to influence buying decisions;
4. The competitor caused its "falsely advertised" products to enter interstate commerce; and
5. Your client "has been or is likely to be injured" as a result of these ads, in the form of direct diversion of sales from your client to the competitor, or by a diminishing of the goodwill consumers associate with your client's product.

Limitations on the Use of Section 43(a)

As we've seen, the first element of a section 43(a) case is proof that the defendant made a false statement of fact about its *own* product. (See *Bernard Food Industries, Inc. v. Dietene Co.*)[14] Let's say your competitor made false claims in its ads that your product was not effective for its intended use. Would you have a cause of action under Section 43(a) against the competitor for the false claims? No. You could not sue your competitor in this situation—regardless of the extent of your potential damages. Reason: The competitor in this example did not make a false statement of fact about its product, only about your product. (Nevertheless, you might be able to sue your competitor under state law for disparagement.)[15]

However, you should be aware that this limitation has been construed very narrowly by the important Second Circuit Court of Appeals in *Vidal Sassoon, Inc. v. Bristol Myers Co.*[16] In this case, comparative ads for Bristol Myers' "Body on Tap" shampoo allegedly misled consumers into believing that this product was superior to Vidal Sassoon's product. The Second Circuit rejected this argument of Bristol Myers: that Vidal Sassoon had failed to state an adequate Section 43(a) claim as it alleged "only misstatements concerning the test results and the manner in which the tests were conducted, not the 'inherent quality' " of the shampoo. The Second Circuit said that:

While we recognize that §43(a) encompasses only misrepresentations with reference to the 'inherent quality or characteristic' of defendant's product [citation omitted], we are nevertheless convinced that Judge Stewart was correct in concluding that Sassoon would probably succeed in showing that the intent and total effect of the advertisements were to lead consumers into believing the Body on Tap was competitively superior, surely a representation regarding its 'inherent quality.'

Section 43(a) and Implied Claims

Modern advertising is more sophisticated and technologically advanced than ever—particularly on television. One result: implied claims are much more common today than in the past. Accordingly, a growing problem confronting the courts is how to grant companies relief from damaging implications found in their competitor's ads. Often, these implications are subtly enhanced by the wizardry of modern camera techniques, skillful editing and technological flourishes.

However, Section 43(a) of the Lanham Act was adopted almost forty years ago—well before modern advertising techniques came into being. Unquestionably, therefore, this statute is more suited to enabling courts to fashion relief to advertisers from *express* claims. An express claim is one that's directly and distinctly stated in the ad. A court needs only to examine the ad to find such a claim. It doesn't have to require proof of what the ad means to consumers.

For example, let's say a television commercial for "Sorex" a throat lozenge, opens with a man in bed in pajamas speaking with a raspy voice, saying "This sore throat pain is killing me." His wife says, "Why suffer? Take Sorex," and hands him a lozenge. The scene shifts to the product while an announcer exclaims that "Sorex" contains "four times as much hexapentathol, an anti-sore throat ingredient, as the leading brand." The commercial ends with the man, dressed up in suit and tie, singing a duet with his wife at the piano, his raspiness completely gone. After the singing ends, the man exclaims, "I don't know what I'd do without you, dear." His wife responds "Me—and 'Sorex.' "

In our example, there was an express claim that "Sorex" contained "four times as much hexapentathol as the leading brand." But let's assume that that statement is true and assume further that hexapentathol only plays a minor role in the relief of sore throat pain. Let's also assume that "Sorex" is demonstrably inferior to the leading brand in curing sore throats. The leading brand contains other ingredients more efficacious in the reduction of sore throat pain. If Section 43(a) were limited to express claims, the advertiser of the leading brand would not be entitled to relief in this situation. Reason: The ad did not expressly claim that "Sorex" was better than the leading brand at relieving sore throat pain or even that it significantly lessened sore throat pain. All the ad said was that it contained more of one "anti-sore throat ingredient" than the leader, a true statement.

Nevertheless, most consumers would probably say that the ad made implied claims that the product will cure sore throats and that this ability to do so is based on the fact that it contains hexapentathol. Since this ingredient is four times more prevalent in "Sorex" than in the leading brand, the further implication is that it is superior to the leader in relieving sore throat pain.

Fortunately for advertisers beset by such false and misleading advertisements, the courts have extended the Lanham Act's reach to such implied claims. In *American Home Products Corp. v. Johnson & Johnson*,[17] makers of the acetaminophen-based pain reliever, "Tylenol," successfully enjoined American Home Products Corp., maker of the aspirin-based pain reliever, Anacin, from making advertising claims implying superiority when the proof showed the two analgesics to be equally effective. In that case, the Second Circuit concluded that when deciding if an ad is false and misleading under Section 43(a) of the Lanham Act, it is appropriate for the court to examine an ad in its entirety, including both express *and* implied claims.

But how does a court go about establishing that an implied claim was in fact made by an ad? As the Second Circuit noted in *American Home Products Corp.*, the court must examine consumers' reactions, in the form of consumer perception data, to reveal how consumers perceived the challenged ad:

That Section 43(a) of the Lanham Act encompasses more than literal falsehoods cannot be questioned. Were it otherwise, clever use of innuendo, indirect intimations, and ambiguous suggestions could shield the advertisement from scrutiny precisely when protection against such sophisticated deception is most needed. It is equally well established that the truth or falsity of the advertisement usually should be tested by the reactions of the public.[18]

As the cases amply illustrate, you would be well advised to have consumer research data whenever implied claims are made in your advertisements.

While this data does not have to be nationally projectable or methodologically perfect,[19] it must be reliable and probative. The relevant test is not whether consumers can later remember your ad or a particular claim, but the immediate message perceived by consumers. That's why you should use *consumer preception tests* (which measure consumer's understanding of what the ad says) rather than *recall studies* (which measure how well consumers remember an advertisement or a particular implied claim) to analyze ads containing implied claims.

It should be noted, however, that in cases under the Federal Trade Commission Act, the Commission does not have to use consumer perception data to interpret an ad's implications.[20] Reason: The Federal Trade Commission, as the nation's premiere advertising regulatory body, is deemed to possess sufficient expertise to analyze the implications of an ad.

Remedies Available Under Section 43(a)

There are several remedies available to a competitor aggrieved by a false or misleading comparative ad. It can seek preliminary and/or permanent injunctive relief, money damages, a "corrective advertising" remedy, and even attorney's fees. However, the most important remedy, as revealed in the vast majority of Lanham Act cases, is injunctive relief, and particularly the preliminary injunction. The key reason: The aggrieved party's most immediate concern is to stop the dissemination of the offending false comparative ad. The easiest way to do that under Section 43(a) is to seek a preliminary injunction to prevent further harm and preserve the status quo until trial. If successful, a plaintiff may obtain a permanent injunction after trial. Essentially, a plaintiff seeking a preliminary injunction would have to show (1) the likelihood of success on the merits, (2) the likelihood of irreparable injury, and (3) that the balance of hardships favors the plaintiff.

In *Johnson & Johnson v. Carter-Wallace, Inc.*,[21] the Second Circuit rejected the defendant's theory that a plaintiff seeking an injunction in such cases must prove actual loss:

The statute demands only proof providing a reasonable basis for the belief that the plaintiff is likely to be damaged as a result of the false advertising. The correct standard is whether it is *likely* that Carter's advertising has caused or will cause a loss of Johnson sales, not whether Johnson has come forward with specific evidence that Carter's ads actually resulted in some definite loss of sales. . . . Contrary to Johnson's argument, however, the likelihood of injury and causation will not be presumed, but must be demonstrated.[22]

Money damages are a much more difficult matter. In *Johnson & Johnson*, the Second Circuit said the award of money damages "would require more proof." The Eighth Circuit has found Section 35 of the Lanham Act[23] to be the exclusive remedy in Section 43(a) cases.[24] The problem with this approach is that Section 35 refers only to cases involving registered trade-marks. In any event, monetary damages are usually not pursued as the main goal of the aggrieved party is to halt the allegedly deceptive ad campaign.

Corrective advertising, as a measure of damages, would probably be in the form of an award of that amount of money necessary to overcome linger-ing impressions in the minds of consumers caused by the offending compara-tive advertising campaign.[25]

In the "Battle of the Burgers," McDonald's Corporation brought a Lanham Act action against its arch-rival, the Burger King Corporation. Among other things, McDonald's sought a "corrective advertising" remedy that, if ultimately approved by the court, would have required Burger King to engage in corrective advertising "to dispel the continuing and lingering effects on the public of the . . . false and misleading representations."[26] However, the parties settled their differences quietly out of court, so no further judicial elucidation of this measure of damages came out of this liti-gation. But its appearance in this major comparative advertising lawsuit may well be a harbinger of things to come.

Largest Lanham Act Award

While monetary and other damages are available under the Lanham Act to a party injured by a comparative advertising campaign, they are infre-quently pursued.[27] The aggrieved party in such cases has generally been content in having halted the offending ads by means of injunctive relief. The time-consuming nature of pursuing damages as well as the difficulty of proof are factors militating against pursuing the case further.

Nevertheless, a recent case illustrates that persistence can pay off big for an advertiser aggrieved by an allegedly deceptive comparative advertising campaign. In November 1984, Judge Earl Carroll of the United States District Court for the District of Arizona followed up his preliminary injunction issued against the Jartran Corporation in 1981 with a huge $40 million damage judgment for violation of the Lanham Act and for unfair competition.[28]

U-Haul International filed the action on June 16, 1980, suing Jartran, Inc.; Jar Corporation; James A. Ryder, the owner of 85 percent of Jartran's stock; and Jartran's advertising agency (which independently settled the case).

James A. Ryder was the former president of Ryder International, the noted truck rental firm. In the mid-1970s Ryder had been displaced as the guiding light of the company that bears his name. Rather than remain in the background, Ryder decided to form his own truck-rental firm. At first, Jartran leased vehicles to commercial enterprises, but this business pro-gressed slowly. Jartran then decided to enter the self-move rental business—a change in corporate strategy that would bring it directly into conflict with the plaintiff. Jartran was faced with the problem that most of its equipment was being delivered at Detroit, Michigan, from two large truck manufacturers.

Jartran, rather than deadhead the equipment to its various agencies, decided to launch a major comparative advertising campaign to induce persons from the economically-depressed Detroit area to use Jartran's vehicles while moving elsewhere. Jartran ran over two thousand ads between mid-1979 and the end of 1980. Jartran spent $6 million on what became a national campaign, which the court found to be phenomenally successful. According to Judge Carroll, gross revenues for Jartran rose from $3 million in 1979 to $95 million in 1981 as a result of the advertising campaign.

According to Judge Carroll's opinion, the effects on the plaintiff were just as dramatic. In 1979, U-Haul had almost all of the self-move, household goods trailer rental business and about 60 percent of the same type of truck rental business; its chief competition was James Ryder's old firm. While it was true that U-Haul had to incur some unusual expenses in the late 1970s due to a change in distributorships from service stations to centralized equipment facilities, this decline, according to the court's opinion, was about $49 million sharper than predicted. For the first time, U-Haul found itself against a competitor that actually took business away from it, rather than merely increasing the market.

Basically, the challenged ads had three themes: (1) That Jartran's trucks were better than those on the market: "Why Rent A Truck That May Deliver Only 5 MPG? Jartran Guarantees You 10 MPG or More." Also, "Jartran can rent you lightweight, well balanced trailers that are easy to hook up." (2) Another ad was headlined, "U-Haul it to San Francisco . . . $1131/Jartran it to San Francisco . . .$499"; (3) Finally, there was the statement "Nobody can rent you a truck like Jartran can." Plaintiff sought both damages and a preliminary injunction under Section 43(a) of the Lanham Act.

The defendants argued in both the preliminary injunction and damages actions that the disputed statements were mere puffery and that, in any event, the Lanham Act was limited to so-called "palming off" or "passing off" and did not embrace false statements of fact.[29] In his opinion on the preliminary injunction Judge Carroll swept these contentions aside. Citing *McNeilab Inc. v. AHP Corp.*,[30] the court found that the Lanham Act encompassed not only actually false statements of origin but also other misstatements as well as in the words of *McNeilab*, "innuendo, indirect intimations, and ambiguous suggestions . . ."

The Arizona court went on to find that the kinds of statements Jartran made in (1) and (2) above were false, although he refused to issue an injunction against the "nobody rents trucks" theme on the basis that this slogan was in fact puffery. Of course, to establish a cause of action under the Lanham Act it is necessary to establish not only the falsity of the ads, but also that the plaintiff is somehow damaged by the false ads. Hence, U-Haul introduced testimony from experts that, according to Judge Carroll, established that consumers in the Phoenix area perceived that the Jartran ads referred to U-Haul. The judge's issuance of the preliminary injunction was deemed proper by the Ninth Circuit.

In reaching a damages award in November 1984, the Court elaborated on its findings in respect to the misleading nature of the advertising claims. The court found that Jartran's price comparison ads were misleading for it arrived at the advertised price for its equipment by establishing a promotional rate. It then used U-Haul's basic rate for comparison, plus the applicable distribution fee—a temporary surcharge to regulate rentals in areas in which there is an actual build-up of equipment. Since U-Haul imposed distribution fees in less than 5 percent of its moves, and since surveys showed that in actuality most of Jartran's transactions exceeded the advertised rates, the claims were false, particularly in light of the fact that U-Haul had a policy of meeting the competition's prices. Thus, Judge Carroll concluded, "Jartran's comparative claim, that Jartran could save the consumer big money to almost any city on truck and trailer rentals was false, deceptive and misleading."

In arriving at a damage judgment, the judge found that U-Haul did not have to segregate the effects of Jartran's entrance as a legitimate competitor from that of its false advertising. The court noted that it would arrive at an award for actual damages of $20 million by either of two routes: (1) the estimate of an economist that plaintiff lost in excess of $22 million as a result of the Jartran ad campaign and (2) Carroll's own estimate that the ad campaign had cost Jartran $6 million to launch and that U-Haul had spent $13.4 million to counter the campaign.

The court noted that under the Lanham Act, "a Court may award additional damages, up to three times the amount awarded for actual damages, 'according to the circumstances of the case.' "[31] The court added that this case's circumstances make such an award appropriate and so granted additional damages of $20 million, for a total of $40 million. In addition, the court granted U-Haul a permanent injunction "restraining Jartran, its agents, servants, officers and all those in privity with it from publishing the price comparison, equipment performance, or miles-per-gallon advertisements found to be false and deceptive." Calling it an "exceptional case," the Court further ordered that U-Haul was entitled to reasonable attorneys fees in an amount to be determined by the Court.

OTHER AVENUES OF RELIEF

As we've seen, Section 43(a) of the Lanham Act can be a valuable tool for an advertiser injured by a competitor's comparative ad campaign. However, you should be aware that other, less-costly, alternatives for redress in such cases exist. You can, for example file a complaint with the

(1) Council of Better Business Bureaus's National Advertising Division (NAD), (2) three major networks, or (3) Federal Trade Commission. Each of these alternatives has its advantages—and disadvantages. The following sections analyze the benefits and pitfalls of each choice.

THE NAD/NARB SYSTEM

The most important advertising industry self-regulatory mechanism is the National Advertising Division (NAD) of the Council of Better Business Bureaus and its appellate branch, the National Advertising Review Board (NARB). NAD monitors national print and broadcast advertising and also receives complaints about the truth or accuracy of national advertising from consumers and competitors.

Since 1972, the NAD/NARB system has experienced a growing number of challenges involving comparative advertising. In 1984, for example, there were forty-eight competitor challenges as opposed to forty-six such challenges in 1983. Moreover, competitor challenges represented 45 percent of NAD's cases in 1984, as compared to 42 percent of its cases in 1983.

Indeed, competitor challenges surpassed NAD's own efforts in 1984. NAD monitoring in 1984 resulted in thirty-three challenges, some 31 percent of its case load. This was only the third time in its fourteen-year history in which competitive challenges equalled or surpassed NAD's own efforts. (Nineteen eighty-two was the first year in which competitive challenges equalled NAD's own efforts.)[32]

These figures illustrate not only the increasing usage of comparative advertising in national advertising. They show too the growing willingness of aggrieved competitors to call on the NAD/NARB system for redress. The main advantage of doing so is undoubtedly cost. If NAD decides to review a challenged ad, that self-regulatory body absorbs the costs—estimated at around $1,500 per decision—and not the challenger.[33] Accordingly, a competitor can often succeed in removing a misleading comparative advertising campaign from national print or broadcast media—and without the potentially high costs of litigation. However, a challenger may *voluntarily* incur costs in connection with an NAD challenge; NAD's own resources are pressed to the limit by its case load. That self-regulator appreciates all the expert help it can get. So if you challenge a competitor's comparative ad campaign, it will be a valuable resource to NAD if you analyze your competitor's claims and give NAD the results of tests and other data to support your challenge.

Before launching a challenge at NAD, you should consider whether you wish to give your data to the Division. Reason: NAD has a strict rule that data you give to NAD about a challenged ad must also be given to the advertiser whose ad is challenged. So it's advisable that you analyze that data first to make sure you don't give your competitor proprietary information or confidential material.[34]

On the other hand, NAD will allow you to request that your identity remain confidential. In NAD's experience, however, these challenges are usually not as clearly defined as "open challenges" since, for example, they lack support from experimental data.[35]

In deciding whether to litigate or bring an action before NAD, another factor to consider is time. And time generally is a key consideration in comparative advertising cases. If you go the Lanham Act route, you can, in an appropriate case, obtain such quick judicial relief as a temporary injunction. If time is less of a factor, NAD may well be the most appropriate forum for you. In any event, roughly 98 percent of all NAD cases are settled within one year, 76 percent within nine months, 58 percent within six months, and 23 percent within the first three months.[36]

Another apparent advantage of litigation over the NAD/NARB process is the fact that the relief obtained in court is backed up by the broad power of a court order. That of course is not true with decisions rendered by NAD or NARB since compliance is completely voluntary with the advertiser. Nevertheless, in NAD's fourteen years of existence no advertiser that participated in the NAD/NARB process has failed to accept that regulatory body's decision.

If you're planning to challenge a competitor's comparative advertising campaign—or planning to launch such a campaign—it can be extremely helpful to study NAD's decisions involving comparative ads. The following twenty cases were chosen from two categories—claims NAD deemed proper (i.e., substantiated) and claims that the advertiser agreed to modify or discontinue because of concerns raised by NAD.

Comparative Ad Claims Substantiated

In the following ten cases, NAD concluded that advertisers had successfully substantiated their comparative advertising claims.

1. *Gulf Oil Corp.* This investigation involved a charcoal starter. The following comparative ads appeared in magazines. They were challenged by NAD but were ultimately deemed to be substantiated by that self-regulatory body: "Bargain-brand charcoal lighters often give you more than you bargained for. Like odors and extra smoke that can ruin the taste of your food. . . . Unlike bargain brands, Gulf Lite uses a special clay filtering process to eliminate odors and impurities."

The advertiser was able to substantiate successfully these ads by showing NAD test results involving "bargain brands" (i.e., defined as products priced ten cents below Gulf Lite). These tests showed that these brands vary with fluctuations in market supply of solvents and make more smoke when lit.

In comparison, Gulf's charcoal starter is made with a consistent blend of ingredients and uses clay filtration to reduce impurities. The link between these impurities and tainted flavors in cooked foods has been established by taste tests, according to the advertiser. It submitted smoke photos and test data to NAD to back up this claim.[37]

2. *General Mills, Inc.* In a case involving chocolate chip granola bars, NAD concluded that the following comparative advertising claim was substantiated: ". . .more chocolate chips than any other granola bar! [with an asterisk referring to a footnote]: Based on a per ounce comparison to other national brands."

This claim was made for Nature Valley Chocolate Chip Chewy Granola Bars in newspaper inserts and was also shown on the product package featured in the ad.

The advertiser successfully substantiated the claim by showing NAD the results of comparative testing conducted before launching the reformulated product and again after the introduction of a third brand. NAD's review of this data confirmed the presence of substantially more chocolate chips, by weight, than competing products.[38]

3. *SCM Corp./Glidden Coating & Resins Div.* This case involved comparative claims for an oil stain product. Again, NAD concluded that these claims had been substantiated. Specifically, a magazine ad showed that Glidden Oil Stain kept its color and water repellency in contrast to two leading brands after being subjected to simulated weathering. Similarly, TV ads for the product showed beads of water on seven boards, each stained with a leading brand of oil stain. Only the bead on the Glidden stained board was unabsorbed after standing.

The advertiser's method for successfully substantiating its claims: It gave NAD results of exterior and simulated weathering tests showing Glidden's superior performance. The tests had been conducted on exposed exterior test fencing, on boards placed in weatherometers subjected to controlled exposure to ultraviolet light and moisture, and by application of a water absorption test. The tests were conducted in accordance with federal specifications.[39]

4. *Richardson-Vicks, Inc.* Magazine ads for the product Cremacoat Throat Coating Cough Medicines made these comparative claims: "Cremacoat coats irritated throats. It soothes better, so you cough less than with conventional cough syrup . . . Relieves coughs significantly better, and four years of development and clinical testing proved it."

NAD agreed that the claims were successfully substantiated after the advertiser did the following: It showed NAD summaries of three clinical trials in which one Cremacoat formula was compared with a leading cough syrup containing the same active ingredient but lacking the highly viscous ingredient unique to Cremacoat. These tests showed Cremacoat offered increased relief from coughing.[40]

5. *United States Borax & Chemical Corp.* Television commercials compared Borateem to all-fabric bleaches for warm-water washes and made this claim: "The Borax Bleacher. . . . It's made to whiten, brighten and remove

stains in warm water.'' Magazine ads claimed: ''Bleaches whiter. Bleaches brighter. Bleaches safely.'' and displayed similar statements on the principal panel of the product label. The manufacturer of a leading dry bleach challenged the advertising and label claims. Its basis: Borateem contains no recognized bleach ingredient similar to the hypochlorite of liquid bleach or the perborate of dry bleach.

The advertiser didn't dispute the competitor's statement that Borateem lacks bleach. The advertiser noted that Borateem contains enzymes (stain removers) and fluorescent agents (whiteners/brighteners) and that Borateem gave superior results in controlled tests against leading brands of dry bleaches. Reason: The dry bleach ingredient does not work as well in warm water as in hot.

NAD's conclusion: The advertiser had successfully substantiated its claims.[41]

6. *Block Drug Co.* In this NAD case, a manufacturer of a leading denture cleanser challenged Block Drug Company's television commercial in which denture users contrasted the minty fresh taste of Dentu-Gel with the ''tablet taste'' of denture soaks.

NAD's decision: The advertiser successfully substantiated its claim after showing the self-regulatory agency details of three research studies. These studies showed that (1) most users customarily rinse or brush the soaked dentures before replacement in the mouth; (2) a major stated reason for rinsing or brushing dentures after soaking was to get rid of the taste of the soak; and (3) users preferred the aftertaste of Dentu-Gel to that of their customary denture soaks.[42]

7. *McCulloch Corp.* A comparative advertising campaign that appeared in magazine ads said: ''A logsplitter that's half the size and half the price of comparable gas powered logsplitters. This electric brute packs 10 tons of hydraulic splitting power. So it can split a cord of oak in just 2 hours. For about 15¢ worth of electricity.'' ''Get a saw for a penny. . . . So for one extra penny, we'll include an electric McCulloch chain saw. Electromac 12 (a $95.99 value) when you buy a Woodmate 1.''

To successfully substantiate these claims, the advertiser showed NAD the weight and list price of comparable gas-powered logsplitters. Other research data confirmed that the Woodmate I exerted 10 tons of splitting power and, in a series of field tests, one operator split a cord of oak in approximately two hours for the kilowatt cost claimed.[43]

8. *Beatrice Foods Co./Martha White Inc.* Comparative television commercials made these claims for Martha White Jim Dandy Boil-In-Bag Quick Grits: ''Grits that gives you the convenience of instant and the rich creamy flavor of quick grits . . . with the natural, hearty, corn flavor you don't get with instant and with no messy pan to clean.''

A competitor questioned the taste claim and argued that viewers might wrongly assume the final phrase applied to instant cereals.

NAD's conclusion was that "the commercial was unlikely to confuse viewers in respect to the convenience of instant grits and that the claims were substantiated."[44]

9. *Sterling Drug, Inc./Glenbrook Labs*. Magazine ads made these claims: "Nothing gives you more relief than Bayer." ". . . [E]xtra-strength Tylenol contains 50% more medicine than Bayer . . . but no more relief." ". . . [A] new medical study conducted at a leading university shows the amount of pain reliever in extra-strength Tylenol is no more effective for headaches than Bayer."

NAD sought substantiation for these claims, including comparison tests and the medical study referred to in the ad. After reviewing the evidence, NAD concluded the claims were substantiated.[45]

10. *Posner Laboratories, Inc*. These comparative claims appeared in magazines: "Posner Perfect Performance is better than the leading no-lye relaxer! Better Conditioning; [a]n independent test proves it! Hair is more manageable, better conditioned, easier to comb! Better Feel: . . . Better Body & Sheen." Similar claims were made in television spots. A competitor questioned the comparative claims.

The advertiser successfully substantiated its claims by submitting to NAD the details of two independent, comparative studies of Perfect Performance and the leading relaxer. In both studies, the products were tested on forty panelists. The conditioning effects were professionally evaluated and results showed a preference for Perfect Performance.[46]

Comparative Ad Claims Modified or Discontinued

You have seen how advertisers were successfully able to defend their comparative advertising campaigns that had been challenged, by competitors and others, before NAD. The following ten cases involving comparative advertising have been selected from NAD Case Reports. They are summarized below as examples of instances where the advertiser ultimately agreed to modify or discontinue these claims. (It should be noted, however, that NAD policy is that such modification or discontinuance of ads "is not to be taken as an admission of impropriety on any advertiser's part. In some cases, advertisers have voluntarily changed or discontinued advertising in cooperation with NAD's self-regulatory efforts. Other advertisers have discontinued challenged claims for their own reasons but have agreed not to run them again without furnishing appropriate substantiation.")[47]

11. *Mobil Oil Corp*. One of the most visually striking and effective televised comparative ads in recent years is the Mobil ad that shows the labels of twenty-four competitive products in succession while claiming: "The best engine protection you can give your car . . . Do you know how many of these motor oils would love to make this claim? Well one can. Mobil 1."

In addition, radio ads claimed: ". . . the best engine protection you can give your car compared to ordinary oils . . . the oil that saves you gas." A competitor brought the claims to NAD's attention and asked if Mobil had proof of superiority against virtually every domestic motor oil.

Mobil's explanation for its claims: As a purely synthetic oil, Mobil 1 could outperform any conventional oil. However, the competitor suggested to NAD that consumers wouldn't realize the ad simply compared synthetic and mineral oils or that the claim only applied to one of Mobil's oils. The challenger also questioned Mobil's superior performance claims under typical driving conditions.

The ad industry self-regulator concluded that the advertiser hadn't substantiated Mobil 1's superior protection claim. Its recommendation: The television commercial should spell out that any proven advantages existed under extreme conditions. Accordingly, Mobil told NAD that the claim "the best engine protection you can give your car" has been eliminated from the ad. The new audio says, "Do you know which of these oils gives you the best engine protection under the toughest driving conditions—sub-zero cold or blazing heat? This one. Mobil 1."[48]

12. *Colgate Palmolive Co.* A comparative ad that appeared on television and in other media cited the large number of lemons used in reformulated lemony Ajax and made these claims for the product: "Got real lemon juice," "more cleaning power (as a burst on the label)," "works better than all leading dishwashing liquids," "clean up the greasiest dishes." Combinations of the same claims were noted in a coupon promotion, newspaper advertising, and on the label.

A competitor had the new product analyzed and showed its results to NAD as well as the results of a plate-washing test to dispute claims that Ajax (1) has enough lemon juice to enhance its performance, and (2) is superior to the leading brands.

The advertiser responded by saying that performance claims were based on an increase in the detergent ingredients and results of a comparative dishwashing test. The test entailed combining results from separate washings, first with dishes soiled with shortening, the second with spaghetti sauce. "Judged by the persistence of suds in the wash water, new Ajax was superior to eight leading brands," according to NAD.

NAD "questioned the ad claim for overall superiority and the emphasis on grease-cutting power. While the results established a clear superiority in the spaghetti sauce washing test, new Ajax was not as effective for dishes soiled with shortening."

In addition, the advertiser acknowledged that there hadn't been any increase in the level of lemon juice used in the new Ajax. To settle the challenge, the advertiser proposed several revisions to the current commercial. For example, it would remove the "more cleaning power" burst from the bottle label (used in conjunction with visual or audio references to lemon juice), modify the overall superiority claim (to limit it to spaghetti sauce residue) and contract the performance claim to "clean up all these dishes." In addition, the new ads wouldn't overstate the quantity or cleaning efficacy of the lemon juice ingredient.[49]

13. *Campbell Soup Company*. Television ads made the following comparative claims:

In Swanson chicken broth you get 50 percent more chicken than in the leading brand. Imagine what our richer, fuller flavor can do for your favorite recipes. Hearty chicken soup has never tasted heartier. You can taste the richer flavor in gravy and stuffing. From elegant sauces to stir-fry dishes, with Swanson chicken broth you can taste the difference . . . [—Y]ou get richer, fuller flavor.

The advertiser took these steps to back up its claims: It showed NAD analyses of protein, creatinine, and fat content of both brands to back up its higher-chicken-content claim. And it provided NAD with the details of a blind taste test to support the taste claims.

NAD agreed the test results showed Swanson broth contains more lean chicken meat than does the competitor's brand. NAD said, however, the comparative claim was not backed up for total chicken ingredients (i.e., lean meat plus chicken fat). As to the taste test, NAD agreed the results clearly supported the claim that consumers can taste the difference. But it was less certain, said NAD, that this difference can be attributed to Swanson's richer, fuller flavor. And no data was presented to substantiate claims that the difference was evident in complex recipes.

While disagreeing with NAD's analysis, the advertiser agreed to take NAD's views into account for future ads. That settled this investigation.[50]

14. *Kraft, Inc.* In this investigation of televised comparative ads, the advertiser's proof fell short of convincing NAD. The ads in question:

Real cream. That's what makes La Creme Whipped topping different than those Cool Whip toppings. See, La Creme is made with real cream. They're not. And there's no mistaking that rich real cream taste of La Creme. Real cream. Real cream taste. [Magazine ads included the claims]: One farm-fresh taste of La Creme whipped topping, and you'll never top your holiday pumpkin pie with anything else. You'll see there's nothing like the taste of real cream.

A competitor questioned whether the amount of cream, as an ingredient in cream cheese, would substantiate claims for real-cream taste and content.

The advertiser denied that it had said cream was the "predominant or only ingredient." It showed NAD sensory evaluation data of consumer and expert panels in an attempt to substantiate these ads.

NAD examined an older challenge involving the same product.[51] In that case, NAD sided with the advertiser in concluding that claims its product contained "real dairy ingredients" were substantiated.

Since that time, however, the advertiser introduced claims for "real cream" and strengthened the taste claims. NAD agreed that the sensory evaluation data proved that enough cream is present to substantiate claims for real-cream taste. Nevertheless, NAD expressed concern that the TV ad might tend to overemphasize the cream content.

While the advertiser disagreed with this position, it agreed to modify the ads consistent with NAD's opinion "in the interest of resolving the controversy."[52]

15. *Cooper Laboratories/Coopervision, Inc.* A competitor challenged these comparative advertising claims involving contact lenses: ". . . [T]he world's leading extended-wear lens" and "My doctor told me I'd find Permalens more comfortable—there's more water in them than in any other lens." The claims appeared in TV commercials.

The advertiser tried to back up its "world's leading extended-wear lens" claim by giving NAD certain "composite data" including a survey of selected U.S. eye-care professionals. However, NAD concluded, that this data did not substantiate the claim.

As to the "water content" claim, the advertiser conceded that some specialized lenses have higher water content than Permalens. It agreed to modify the claim.[53]

16. *Lever Brothers Co.* When you say your product is the "only" one to have a particular quality or attribute, it's a comparative ad comparing your product to all other such products. In the following television commercial, these comparative claims appeared: "Imperial Light. It's the only light spread with 25 percent fewer calories than regular margarine, no cholesterol, and Imperial's great buttery flavor."

A competitor challenged this claim. Its reason: It also markets a spread containing 25 percent fewer calories than margarine.

The advertiser ultimately agreed to revise the ad by deleting the word, "only."[54]

17. *National Car Rental System, Inc.* In another case involving a claim of being "the only" one, it turned out that the words "one of" preceding this claim had inadvertently been left out. Specifically, newspaper ads made these claims: "Chances are you'll never need it. But if you do, only National gives you access to 24-hour road service from Amoco Motor Club—the world's largest full-service motor club."

The American Automobile Association challenged the claim "world's largest," whether measured by numbers of contract garages, clubs and branch offices, membership or member services.

The advertiser conceded that the qualifying words "one of" were left out of the challenged ad, and that this omission would be corrected in future ads.[55]

18. *Abbott Laboratories.* Television ads made these comparative claims: "There's good, there's better, and there's Blue, Selsun Blue, the best

dandruff shampoo money can buy. . . . Clinical testing among leading brands proved it worked best.''

Magazine ads made similar claims.

A competitor challenged these comparative claims. Its reason: A second independent study failed to confirm the results of the first study.

NAD's conclusion: Comparative claims made about dandruff treatments do not require support from two independent studies. NAD recommended, however, that the advertiser delete such claims as ''the best . . . money can buy'' or ''simply works the best.'' Reason: The test was limited in scale and medically-oriented, and so did not take into account all the factors that make one shampoo more satisfactory to individuals when used regularly. The advertiser agreed to make these modifications in its ads.[56]

19. *Scott Paper Company.* A comparative advertising campaign that opened on television, radio and print made these claims: ''Thicker than the pop-up wipes, bigger than the other leading folded wipe, so each cushion sheet has the right combination to clean baby better. . . . No wonder more mothers use Baby Fresh Wipes.''

The advertiser used both objective (i.e., a lab test for perianal cleansing) and subjective (i.e., a national tracking study), evidence to substantiate its claims.

However, NAD questioned the lab tests' relevance. Reason: They were developed for adult-use patterns and the results were inconclusive. Accordingly, the self-regulatory body recommended that Scott modify its claim to disclose that it was based on a recent consumer survey. The advertiser maintained the validity of its laboratory test; however, it agreed to modify future ad claims accordingly.[57]

20. *Conair Corp.* NAD contended that the following comparative ad implied superior performance against competitive products: ''We didn't get to be number one in hair dryers just by spouting out a lot of hot air. We're number one because our hair dryers are more powerful. More versatile. More durable.''

The advertiser said its ad meant that it was ''more powerful, more versatile, and more durable'' than *its own* previous models. Accordingly, it didn't have any substantiation data in relation to competitors. The advertiser agreed that in future ads it wouldn't imply superiority against competitors.[58]

Conclusions

Cases 1-10 illustrate the many techniques advertisers use to substantiate their comparative advertising claims. In Case 3, for example, the advertiser successfully substantiated its comparative ads for an oil-stain product with exterior and simulated weathering tests that showed the product's superior performance. In Case 4, the advertiser did so by showing NAD summaries of three clinical trials that substantiated its comparative claims. The theme of all of these cases is that your comparative advertising campaign can withstand an NAD challenge so long as you prepare *beforehand* by, for example, conducting, or having conducted, appropriate research, studies and tests. Cases 11-20, on the other hand, illustrate many of the pitfalls for the advertiser who, in good faith, obtains substantiation for its comparative claims, but that substantiation is deemed insufficient by NAD. In Case 18, for example, NAD found that the test the advertiser used to substantiate its comparative claims about dandruff shampoo was limited in scale and medically-oriented. NAD concluded that this resulted in a claim that did not take into account all factors that make a shampoo more satisfactory to consumers when used on a regular basis.

BBB's Code of Advertising

In addition to studying the NAD/NARB cases, you should also examine those sections of the Better Business Bureaus' "Code of Advertising" pertaining to comparative advertising. For example, Section 13, "Superiority Claims—Comparatives—Disparagement," states that:

A. Truthful comparisons using factual information may help consumers make informed buying decisions, provided:
   1. all representations are consistent with the general rules and prohibitions against false and deceptive advertising;
   2. all comparisons that claim or imply, unqualifiedly, superiority to competitive products or services are not based on a selected or limited list of characteristics in which the advertiser excels while ignoring those in which the competitors excel;
   3. the advertisement clearly discloses any material or significant limitations of the comparison; and
   4. the advertiser can substantiate all claims made.
B. Advertising which deceptively or falsely disparages a competitor or competing products or services should not be used.[59]

If you wish to make comparative price and/or savings claims in your ads, the BBB Code offers guidance for such situations as well.[60] Additionally, the Better Business Bureau has issued advertising and selling standards for particular industries, including automobile rental,[61] home insulation,[62] carpet and rugs,[63] home improvement[64] and residential swimming pools.[65] These standards contain parallel language to the BBB Code concerning comparative advertisements.

Child-Directed Comparative Ads—Guidelines

If you wish to make comparative advertising claims in ads directed to children, you should also be aware of the Guidelines of NAD's Children's Advertising Review Unit (CARU).[66] CARU's position is that it may be hard for a youngster to understand comparative advertising. CARU's guidelines say such claims, when used in child-directed ads, "should be based on real product advantages" that children can understand. These guidelines make the following specific recommendations:

1. Comparative advertising should provide factual information. Comparisons should not falsely represent other products or previous versions of the same product.
2. Comparative claims should be presented in ways that children understand clearly.
3. Comparative claims should be supported by appropriate and adequate substantiation.[67]

ACTIONS BEFORE FTC

Another alternative you have to either litigation or an NAD complaint is to bring an action before the Federal Trade Commission (FTC). Comparative advertising found to be deceptive is a violation of Section 5 of the Federal Trade Commission Act.[68] However, FTC at its best proceeded slowly and comparative advertising abuses generally lend themselves to more expeditious treatment. Moreover, the Commission has been less aggressive in recent years than it was during its heyday, the activist seventies. So advertisers increasingly perceive FTC as a poor alternative to litigation or some form of self-regulatory avenue, such as NAD/NARB or the networks.

Nevertheless, FTC has decided a number of important comparative advertising cases in recent years. One of the most important of these decisions is *The Kroger Co.*[69] In that case, a large grocery chain ran a weekly series of ads that compared the overall prices of its items with those of competitors. Kroger generally won the survey and claimed this survey showed that it was cheapest overall to shop at Kroger. However, FTC ruled that the advertised survey was not a reliable statistical sampling; meanwhile, Kroger conducted an internal survey that was reliable. This survey demonstrated that while Kroger was lowest priced in dry grocery items (the only ones used in the Price Patrol survey), it was not as competitive on meats and produce.

Thus, in 1981 FTC ordered Kroger to stop running the Price Patrol ads unless:

1. Kroger made its survey in a competent and reliable manner with either random surveys or surveys made in a truly representative way; and
2. The items chosen for comparison were either identical or substantially similar.

Kroger was also ordered not to let those employees responsible for pricing merchandise know which items would be chosen for a Price Patrol survey. Additionally, Kroger was required to prominently disclose in its ads whether any major food categories were omitted from the sampling.

Kroger appealed FTC's decision to the Eleventh Circuit Court of Appeals. Meanwhile, the Commission voted to eliminate certain of the Kroger order's requirements. The only provisions of the order left intact: the requirements that Kroger's pricing employees not know what items would be picked for an ad survey and that Kroger conspicuously disclose if it systematically left out any product category from the Price Patrol. In addition, the order was limited to a two-year period, that expired on December 31, 1984.[70]

In *American Home Products Corp. v. FTC*,[71] FTC had ordered AHP to cease and desist from making certain allegedly deceptive advertising claims for its drug products. Specifically, the Third Circuit affirmed FTC's finding that AHP had misrepresented its product to the public by saying its analgesic product, Anacin, was "medically-proven" best for headache pain, and by implying that medical journal articles substantiated the claim that Anacin offered better headache relief. However, the Commission had discovered no reliable scientific tests to back up the statement that Anacin was better. But its public reaction tests showed the public believed, after viewing Anacin ads, that Anacin had been in some way medically proven superior.

FILING A COMPLAINT WITH THE NETWORKS

Most of the media attention in recent years has focused on the court battles over comparative advertising. Accordingly, we've seen the "Battle of the Burgers," in which McDonalds' and Wendy's brought suit against Burger King for its comparative advertising campaign involving, among other things, the claim of consumer preference for "flame-broiling" over "frying."[72] In addition, there were the "Orange Juice Wars,"[73] the "Battle of the Shampoos,"[74] and the "War of the Analgesics."[75]

Less well publicized, however, are the battles that take place each day in challenges before the networks involving comparative advertising. If you plan to advertise on one of the networks or wish to challenge a competitor's TV commercial, you should be aware that each network has a very extensive Department of Broadcast Standards and Practices. These departments review all commercials prior to their being aired.

Until fairly recently, the National Association of Broadcasters's Code of Good Practices (NAB Code) set the standards for advertising that were generally used by the networks in deciding whether to clear an ad for airing. However, the NAB Code was suspended on March 10, 1982 after a successful Justice Department antitrust action against certain Code sections not directly related to comparative ads.[76] The Code was never reinstated which means that station owners must make their own decisions on comparative advertising.[77] Accordingly, the networks' own advertising guidelines and clearance procedures have taken on a greater significance following the demise of the NAB Code. (See Appendices 3B and 3C for ABC's and NBC's comparative advertising guidelines.)

What can you do if you learn about a comparative advertising campaign by your competitor appearing on television that you believe disparages your product or is false, misleading or deceptive? You should be aware that each one of the major networks has "challenge procedures," methods by which you may challenge the offending ad and, if successful, remove it from the air. Challenges made by competitors are far from rare. Indeed, most challenges are competitor challenges and the vast majority of commercials challenged involve comparative ads. For example, 93 percent of the commercials challenged at ABC in 1981 involved comparative advertising.[78] (See Chapter 5 of this book for more information on advertising and the broadcast media.)

NOTES

1. *Advertising Compliance Service*, Tab #6, Comparative Ads, Article #1, Feldman, "Comparative Advertising and the Modern Regulatory Approach" (1982), p. 1.

2. See, Lee, "Comparative Advertising, Commercial Disparagement and False Advertising," 71 Trademark Reporter 620 (1981); Giges, "Comparative Ads: Battles That Wrote Do's and Dont's, Advertising Age 59 (September 29, 1980); *Advertising Compliance Service*, Tab #6, Feldman, "Comparative Ads and the Modern Regulatory Approach" (1982), p. 1.

3. Lee, "Comparative Advertising, Commercial Disparagement and False Advertising," at page 621.

4. Lee, "Comparative Advertising, Commercial Disparagement and False Advertising," at page 621, FN2.

5. It was the NAB Television Code's multiple product standard—which forbids advertising more than one product in a commercial that lasts under sixty seconds—that was held to violate the Sherman Antitrust Act. (Ed.)

6. *U.S. v. National Association of Broadcasters*, Civ. Action #79-1549, U.S. District Court for District of Columbia, Opinion of Greene, J. on cross-motion for summary judgment, March 3, 1982.

7. 15 U.S.C. §1125(a).

8. 214 F.2d 649 (U.S. Ct. of Appls., 3d Cir.), 1954.

9. For a discussion of the history of actions for false and/or misleading advertising under Section 43(a) of the Lanham Trademark Act see, e.g., Comment, "The Present Scope of Recovery for Unfair Competition Violations Under Section 43(a) of the Lanham Act," 58 Nebraska L. Rev. 159 (1979); Derenberg, "Federal Unfair Competition Law at the End of the First Decade of the Lanham Act: Prologue or Epilogue?" 32 N.Y.U. L. Rev. 1029 (1957).

10. This principle was established in *Colligan v. Activities Club of New York, Ltd.*, 442 F.2d 686 (2d Cir. 1971), *cert. denied*, 404 U.S. 1004 (1971). See also: *Florida ex rel. Broward County v. Eli Lilly & Co.*, 329 F. Supp. 364 (S.D. Fla. 1971).

11. However, see *Arneson v. Raymond Lee Organization, Inc.*, 333 F. Supp. 116 (C.D. Cal. 1971), where the U.S. District Court for the Central District of California ruled that consumers do have standing to sue under Section 43(a).

12. 467 F.Sup. 366 (S.D.N.Y. 1979), *aff'd*, 604 F.2d 200 (2d Cir. 1979).

13. 375 F. Supp. 77 (U.S. Dist. Ct., N.D. Ill., E.D.), 1974.

14. 415 F.2d 1279 (7th Cir. 1969), *cert. denied* 397 U.S. 912 (1970).

15. *Advertising Compliance Service*, Tab #8, Remedies (Private), Article #7, Donegan, "Can the Federal Courts Fill FTC's Role as Advertising Regulator?" (1983), p. 3.

16. 661 F.2d 272 (2d Cir. 1981).

17. 577 F.2d 160 (2d Cir. 1978). See also, Stiner, "The Lanham Trade-Mark Act Offers Relief for Implied Advertising Claims: *American Home Products Corp. v. Johnson & Johnson*," 11 Conn. L. Rev. 692 (1979).

18. 577 F.2d at 165 (2d Cir. 1978). See also: *American Home Products Corp. v. Abbott Laboratories*, 522 F. Sup. 1035 (S.D.N.Y. 1981); *McNeilab, Inc. v. American Home Products Corp.* 501 F. Supp. 517 (S.D.N.Y. 1980); *American Brands, Inc. v. R. J. Reynolds Tobacco Co.* 413 F. Supp. 1352 (S.D.N.Y. 1976).

19. If a comparative ad contains a misrepresentation of test results or if the survey has methodological flaws, a court may find the use of such results deceptive. See, e.g., *Philip Morris, Inc. v. Loew's Theatres, Inc.*, 511 F. Supp. 855 (S.D.N.Y. 1980); *R. J. Reynolds Tobacco Co. v. Loew's Theatres, Inc.*, 511 F. Sup. 867 (S.D.N.Y. 1980).

20. See, e.g., *FTC v. Colgate Palmolive Co.*, 380 U.S. 374 (1965) and *Resort Rental Car System, Inc. v. FTC*, 518 F.2d 962 (9th Cir. 1974), *cert. denied*, 423 U.S. 827 (1975).

21. 631 F.2d 186 (2d Cir. 1980).

22. 631 F.2d at 190 (2d Cir. 1980).

23. 15 U.S.C. §1117.

24. See, *Metric & Multistandard Components v. Metrics Inc.*, 635 F.2d 710 (8th Cir. 1980); See also *Toro Co. v. Textron, Inc.*, 499 F.Supp. 241 (D. Del. 1980).

25. See, *Durbin Brass Works, Inc. v. Schuler*, 532 F.Supp. 41 (E.D. Mo. 1982).

26. *McDonald's Corp. v. Burger King Corp.*, U.S. Dist. Ct. (So. Dist. of Fla., Miami Div.), Civ. Action No. 82-2005, *Complaint*, 9-23-82.

27. This section is adapted from the article in *Advertising Compliance Service*, Tab #8, Remedies (Private), Article #9, Healy, "Judge Grants Largest Award Under Lanham Act."

28. *U-Haul International, Inc., v. Jartran, Inc.*, No. Civ. 80-454, U.S. District Court for the District of Arizona (Phoenix), *final decision* filed November 27, 1984; *preliminary injunction* in 522 F.Supp. 1238, *aff'd* 681 F.2d 1159 (9th Cir., 1982).

29. *Samson Crane Co. v. Union Nat. Sales*, 87 F.Supp. 218 (D. Mass. 1949), *aff'd mem.*, 180 F.2d 896 (1st Cir. 1950).

30. 501 F.Supp. 517 (S.D.N.Y. 1980).

31. 15 U.S.C. §1117.

32. *NAD Case Report* 1/15/85.

33. *NAD Case Report* 7/15/83; see also, *Advertising Compliance Service*, Tab #3, Self-Regulation, Article #34. The figure of $1,500 does not include expenses incurred by the advertiser or the complainant.

34. *Advertising Compliance Service*, Tab #3, Self-Regulation, Article #47, p. 1.

35. *Advertising Compliance Service*, Tab #3, Self-Regulation, Article #50, p. 1.

36. Based on 1983 figures. See *Advertising Compliance Service*, Tab #3, Self-Regulation, Article #50, p. 2.

37. *NAD Case Report* 12/17/84; see also, *Advertising Compliance Service*, Tab #3, Self-Regulation, Article #56, p. 1.

38. *NAD Case Report* 9/17/84; see also, *Advertising Compliance Service*, Tab #3, Self-Regulation, Article #53, p. 1.

39. *NAD Case Report* 9/17/84; see also, *Advertising Compliance Service*, Tab #3, Self-Regulation, Article #53, p. 1.

40. *NAD Case Report* 12/15/83; see also, *Advertising Compliance Service*, Tab #3, Self-Regulation, Article #40, p. 2.

41. *NAD Case Report* 2/15/83; see also, *Advertising Compliance Service*, Tab #3, Self-Regulation, Article #42, p. 2.

42. *NAD Case Report* 11/15/83; see also, *Advertising Compliance Service*, Tab #3, Self-Regulation, Article #38, p. 2.

43. *NAD Case Report* 1/17/83; see also, *Advertising Compliance Service*, Tab #3, Self-Regulation, Article #27, p. 2.

44. *NAD Case Report* 10/17/83; see also, *Advertising Compliance Service*, Tab #3, Self-Regulation, Article #37, p. 1.

45. *NAD Case Report* 10/17/83; see also, *Advertising Compliance Service*, Tab #3, Self-Regulation, Article #37, p. 1.

46. *NAD Case Report* 3/15/84; see also, *Advertising Compliance Service*, Tab #3, Self-Regulation, Article #43, p. 3.

47. This cautionary statement appears in every NAD Case Report before its listing of cases in which advertising has been modified or discontinued. It also cautions: "Reports may not be used for promotional purposes." See, e.g., *NAD Case Report* 12/16/85, p. 41.

48. *NAD Case Report* 8/15/84; see also, *Advertising Compliance Service*, Tab #3, Self-Regulation, Article #51, p. 2.

49. *NAD Case Report* 12/15/82; see also, *Advertising Compliance Service*, Tab #3, Self-Regulation, Article #24, p. 1.

50. *NAD Case Report* 10/17/83; see also, *Advertising Compliance Service*, Tab #3, Self-Regulation, Article #37, p. 2.

51. *News from NAD* 12/15/81; see also, *Advertising Compliance Service*, Tab #3, Self-Regulation, Article #5, p. 2.

52. *NAD Case Report* 2/15/83; see also, *Advertising Compliance Service*, Tab #3, Self-Regulation, Article #28, p. 2.

53. *NAD Case Report* 2/15/84; see also, *Advertising Compliance Service*, Tab #3, Self-Regulation, Article #42, p. 3.

54. *NAD Case Report* 12/17/84; see also, *Advertising Compliance Service*, Tab #3, Self-Regulation, Article #56, p. 2.

55. *NAD Case Report* 8/15/83; see also, *Advertising Compliance Service*, Tab #3, Self-Regulation, Article #35, p. 2.

56. *NAD Case Report* 9/15/83; see also, *Advertising Compliance Service*, Tab #3, Self-Regulation, Article #36, p. 2.

57. *NAD Case Report* 11/17/83; see also, *Advertising Compliance Service*, Tab #3, Self-Regulation, Article #27, p. 2.

58. *NAD Case Report* 9/15/82; see also, *Advertising Compliance Service*, Tab #3, Self-Regulation, Article #19, p. 3.

59. *Code of Advertising*, Better Business Bureau, Section 13, p. 11.

60. *Code of Advertising*, Better Business Bureau, Section 1, p. 2-3.

61. Better Business Bureau, *Standards for Automobile Rental Advertising*, October 1983, Publication No. 24-189.

62. Better Business Bureau, *Standards for Home Insulation Materials: advertising and selling*, October 1980, Publication No. 24-138.

63. Better Business Bureau, *Standards for Carpet and Rugs: advertising and selling*, Issued January 1978, Publication No. 24-143.

64. Better Business Bureau, *Standards of Practice for the Home Improvement Industry*, Revised September 1981, Publication No. 311-25131.

65. Better Business Bureau, *Standards for Residential Swimming Pools: advertising and selling*, Issued April 1978, Publication No. 24-148.

66. *Self-Regulatory Guidelines for Children's Advertising*, Third Edition, 1983.

67. *Self-Regulatory Guidelines for Children's Advertising*, p. 8, "Comparative Claims."

68. 15 U.S.C. §§41-77.

69. 98 F.T.C. 689 (1981), modified 100 FTC 573 (1983).

70. See *Advertising Compliance Service*, Tab #6, Comparative Ads, Article #4, Healy, "Comparative Advertising: An Update" (1984).

71. 695 F.2d 681 (3d. Cir. 1982).

72. This case was, apparently, quietly settled out of court by the parties. See: *Wendy's International, Inc. v. Burger King Corporation*, U.S. District Ct. (So. Dist. of Ohio, Eastern Div.), *Complaint*, Civil Action No. C-2-82-1175, filed 9-27-82. *McDonald's Corporation v. Burger King Corporation*, U.S. District Court (So. Dist. of Fla., Miami Div.), *Complaint*, Civ. Action No. 82-2005-CIV-EPS, filed 9-23-82; See also *Advertising Compliance Service*, Tab #8, Remedies (Private), Article #4, "Lanham Act Is Key Weapon in Battle of Burgers."

73. *The Coca-Cola Co. v. Tropicana Products, Inc.*, #82-7422, (2d Cir. 1982); see also *Advertising Compliance Service*, Tab #8, Remedies (Private), Article #5, "The Lanham Act Phenomenon: Another Round."

74. *Vidal Sassoon v. Bristol-Myers Co.*, 661 F.2d 272 (2d Cir. 1981); see also *Advertising Compliance Service*, Tab #8, Remedies (Private), Article #5, "The Lanham Act Phenomenon: Another Round."

75. *American Home Products v. Johnson & Johnson*, 577 F.2d 160 (2d Cir. 1978); See also *Advertising Compliance Service*, Tab #6, Comparative Ads, Article #1, Feldman, "Comparative Advertising and the Modern Regulatory Approach."

76. *U.S. v. National Association of Broadcasters*, Civ. Action #79-1549, U.S. Dist. Court for Dist. of Columbia, Opinion of Greene, J. on cross-motion for summary judgement, March 3, 1982. See also *Advertising Compliance Service*, Tab #14, Broadcasting, Article #1, "NAB Suspends Code in Reaction to Federal Court Ruling."

77. For a more complete discussion of these procedures, turn to Chapter 5, *Broadcasting*.

78. *Advertising Compliance Service*, Tab #14, Broadcasting, Article #6, Edelstein, "Challenging Network Commercials," p. 1.

Appendix 3A
FEDERAL TRADE COMMISSION POLICY STATEMENT
REGARDING COMPARATIVE ADVERTISING

1. *Introduction*. The Commission's staff has conducted an investigation of industry trade associations and the advertising media regarding their comparative advertising policies. In the course of this investigation, numerous industry codes, statements of policy, interpretations, and standards were examined. Many of the industry codes and standards contain language that could be interpreted as discouraging the use of comparative advertising. This Policy Statement enunciates the Commission's position that industry self-regulation should not restrain the use by advertisers of truthful comparative advertising.

2. *Policy Statement*. The Federal Trade Commission has determined that it would be of benefit to advertisers, advertising agencies, broadcasters, and self-regulation entities to restate its current policy concerning comparative advertising. [For purposes of this Policy Statement, comparative advertising is defined as advertising that compares alternative brands on objectively measurable attributes or price, and identifies the alternative brand by name, illustration or other distinctive information.] Commission policy in the area of comparative advertising encourages the naming of, or reference to competitors, but requires clarity, and, if necessary, disclosure to avoid deception of the consumer. Additionally, the use of truthful comparative advertising should not be restrained by broadcasters or self-regulation entities.

3. The Commission has supported the use of brand comparisons where the bases of comparison are clearly identified. Comparative advertising, when truthful and nondeceptive, is a source of important information to consumers and assists them in making rational purchase decisions. Comparative advertising encourages product improvement and innovation, and can lead to lower prices in the marketplace. For these reasons, the Commission will continued to scrutinize carefully restraints upon its use.

   A. *Disparagement*. Some industry codes which prohibit practices such as "disparagement," "disparagement of competitors," "improper disparagement," "unfairly attaching," "discrediting," may operate as a restriction on comparative advertising. The Commission has previously held that disparaging advertising is permissible so long as it is truthful and not deceptive. In *Carter Products, Inc.*, 60 F.T.C. 782, *modified*, 323 F.2d 523 (5th Cir. 1963), the Commission narrowed an order recommended by the hearing examiner which would have prohibited respondents from disparaging competing products through the use of false or misleading pictures, depictions, or demonstrations, "or otherwise" disparaging such products. In explaining why it eliminated "or otherwise" from the final order, the Commission observed that the phrase would have prevented respondents from making truthful and non-deceptive statements that a product has certain desirable properties or qualities which a competing product or products do not possess. Such a comparison may have the effect of disparaging the competing product, but we know of no rule of law which prevents a seller from honestly informing the public of the advantages of its products as opposed to those of competing products. 60 F.T.C. at 796.

Industry codes which restrain comparative advertising in this manner are subject to challenge by the Federal Trade Commission.

B. *Substantiation.* On occasion, a higher standard of substantiation by advertisers using comparative advertising has been required by self-regulation entities. The Commission evaluates comparative advertising in the same manner as it evaluates all other advertising techniques. The ultimate question is whether or not the advertising has a tendency or capacity to be false or deceptive. This is a factual issue to be determined on a case-by-case basis. However, industry codes and interpretations that impose a higher standard of substantiation for comparative claims than for unilateral claims are inappropriate and should be revised.

[(Sec. 5, 38 Stat. 719, as amended; 15 U.S.C. §45). (44 Fed. Reg. 47328 & 47329, August 13, 1979)].

Appendix 3B

AMERICAN BROADCASTING COMPANY ADVERTISING GUIDELINES

COMPARATIVE ADVERTISING

Truthful and fair comparative advertising can provide consumers with useful information and aid them in making a rational choice between competitive products or services.

These guidelines apply to the evaluation of commercials which name or otherwise identify, directly or indirectly, competitive products or services.

1. Identification

   The identification of competitive products or services shall be in accordance with the following Guidelines:

   A. Competitive products or services must be accurately and clearly identified.

   B. Identification of a competitive product or service shall be for comparison purposes. Identification may not be used solely to upgrade the advertised product or service by associating it with a competitive product or service if such association creates a deceptive or misleading impression.

   C. False or misleading disparagement of competitive products or services shall not be used. Falsely claiming that a competitive product or service has little or no value (i.e., "ashcanning") is not permitted.

2. Claims

   A. Comparisons and demonstrations shall be based on specific differences between the products or services advertised, comparing similar or related properties or ingredients, dimension to dimension, feature to feature.

B. When aspects of products or services are compared as to performance, they must be significant and meaningful to consumers.

C. When comparative claims are based solely on consumer preference, professional preference, or sales data, such claims shall not create an impression of comparable or superior effectiveness or performance.

D. Claims, demonstrations, and other representations must include all information necessary for their proper understanding by the average consumer. Inadequately qualified language, "dangling comparatives," and similar references are not permitted.

E. Superiority Claims

Commercials using superiority claims — those generally incorporating the terms "better" or "best" or words of similar effect which are not specifically qualified — can cause public confusion and lessen confidence in advertising when those claims are false, misleading, or not properly substantiated.

1) Objective claims generally deal with performance, efficacy, sales, preference, mileage, taste, and other tangible attributes which are measurable and verifiable. These claims must be supported by adequate substantiation before they can be approved.

    An absolute superiority claim which can only be supported if qualified must be so qualified. For example, an advertiser may not claim that its car gets the best gas mileage of any car on the market if its mileage is only better than that of American cars.

    Taste claims which give the impression of being objective rather than simply being personal opinion must be supported by competent taste testing data.

2) Goal/promise claims express commitments or objectives established by the advertiser for its product, service, or company. These claims generally cannot be verified and are acceptable as long as it is clear that they are simply the advertiser's self-made goals or promises. An example is: "We promise to do our best." However, if the claim appears to be an objective statement of improvement (e.g., "Our service is better than it used to be."), the claim must be supported.

3) Subjective/puffery claims are subjective statements of personal preference or other hyperbolic claims that cannot be verified. An example is: "When I wear X, I feel that I look my best." Another example is: "Y is the most terrific game around." These types of claims are generally not capable of verification since they deal with subjective preferences or hyperbole; they cannot be proved or disproved. They are generally acceptable without support as long as the clear net impression that they are likely to make upon the viewing public is subjective personal preference or puffery. However, puffery claims become subject to substantiation whenever they make representations of fact which are capable of being verified. An advertiser's claim that his laundry detergent is the most effective in America for removing stains can and must be substantiated.

    An unsupported or misleading objective claim is not acceptable even though it is phrased in subjective terms. A commercial claiming that, in the advertiser's opinion, its watch is the most accurate money can buy, is unacceptable if the advertiser lacks support for the claim. Merely expressing an opinion cannot transform an objective, verifiable claim into puffery. Also unacceptable are subjective superiority claims which are obviously false (e.g., an advertiser claiming that one line of its product is, in its opinion, the finest ever manufactured, when it manufactures a higher-grade, more expensive line).

4) The manner of execution can affect interpretation of a superiority claim. Copy which appears as puffery in script or storyboard form, when improperly executed, can come across as an objective claim when produced, and vice versa. Therefore, care must be taken in execution to avoid a net impression which is unacceptable under these guidelines.

5) Of course, the prohibitions in children's advertising of competitive/comparative/superiority claims remain in effect.

F. Price Comparisons

Because retail price is subject to constant change, as well as fluctuation from outlet to outlet, comparisons of retail price may not be utilized in comparative advertising unless (1) the compared prices accurately, fairly, and substantially reflect the actual prices of the products at the retail level during the period the commercial is broadcast and within the entire geographical area in which the advertising is broadcast; and (2) the copy discloses that the consumer should expect some variation from outlet to outlet.

G. The overall impression created by comparative advertising must be accurate.

3. Support of Claims

A. Product and consumer testing relevant to comparative claims must be conducted in accordance with generally accepted scientific and technical procedures and must be determined by the Department of Broadcast Standards and Practices as adequate for the purposes of the comparison.

B. Test findings must be significant, in accordance with recognized standards of statistical validity.

C. The advertiser has the burden of establishing that it has exercised due diligence to determine the test used as proof of any comparative claim is fair and accurate.

D. Where applicable, government, industry, or other established standards shall be used to determine the appropriateness of material used as substantiation.

E. Material used as substantiation shall take into account:

1) the purpose for which the products or services are intended,

2) the manner in which they are normally used by the consumer, and

3) individual label instructions.

F. The nature and limitations of the tests relied upon must be clearly disclosed to the Department of Broadcast Standards and Practices.

G. Demonstrations, graphic techniques, and reproductions or displays of research tests must not cause the consumer to reach an erroneous conclusion about the respective merits of the products compared.

H. Advertising copy claims must fairly and accurately reflect the empirical data upon which they are predicated.

(Reprinted with permission of American Broadcasting Companies, Inc.)

Appendix 3C

NATIONAL BROADCASTING COMPANY
DEPARTMENT OF BROADCAST STANDARDS

COMPARATIVE ADVERTISING GUIDELINES

NBC will accept comparative advertising which identifies, directly or by implication, a competing product or service. As with all other advertising, each substantive claim, direct or implied, must be substantiated to NBC's satisfaction and the commercial must satisfy the following guidelines and standards for comparative advertising established by NBC:

1. Competitors shall be fairly and properly identified.

2. Advertisers shall refrain from disparaging or unfairly attacking competitors, competing products, services or other industries through the use of representations or claims, direct or implied, that are false, deceptive, misleading or have the tendency to mislead.

3. The identification must be for comparison purposes and not simply to upgrade by association.

4. The advertising should compare related or similar properties or ingredients of the product, dimension to dimension, feature to feature, or wherever possible by a side-by-side demonstration.

5. The property being compared must be significant in terms of value or usefulness of the product or service to the consumer.

6. The difference in the properties being compared must be measurable and significant.

7. Pricing comparisons may raise special problems that could mislead, rather than enlighten, viewers. For certain classifications of products, retail prices may be extremely volatile, may be fixed by the retailer rather than the product advertiser, and may not only differ from outlet to outlet but from week to week within the same outlet. Where these circumstances might apply, NBC will accept commercials containing price comparisons only on a clear showing that the comparative claims accurately, fairly and substantially reflect the actual price differentials at retail outlets throughout the broadcast area, and that these price differentials are not likely to change during the period the commercial is broadcast.

8. When a commercial claim involves market relationships, other than price, which are also subject to fluctuation (such as but not limited to sales position or exclusivity), the substantiation for the claim will be considered valid only as long as the market conditions on which the claim is based continue to prevail.

9. As with all other advertising, whenever necessary, NBC may require substantiation to be updated from time to time, and may re-examine substantiation, where the need to do so is indicated as the result of a challenge or other developments.

(Exerpt of "NBC Broadcast Standards for Television" courtesy of The National Broadcasting Co. Inc. © 1985 The National Broadcasting Company, Inc. All Rights Reserved.)

Appendix 3D

POLICY STATEMENT AND
GUIDELINES FOR COMPARATIVE ADVERTISING

The Board of Directors of the American Association of Advertising Agencies recognizes that when used truthfully and fairly, comparative advertising provides the consumer with needed and useful information.

However, extreme caution should be exercised. The use of comparative advertising, by its very nature, can distort facts and, by implication, convey to the consumer information that misrepresents the truth.

Therefore, the Board believes that comparative advertising should follow certain guidelines:

1. The intent and connotation of the ad should be to inform and never to discredit or unfairly attack competitors, competing products or services.

2. When a competitive product is named, it should be one that exists in the marketplace as significant competition.

3. The competition should be fairly and properly identified but never in a manner or tone of voice that degrades the competitive product or service.

4. The advertising should compare related or similar properties or ingredients of the product, dimension to dimension, feature to feature.

5. The identificaion should be for honest comparison purposes and not simply to upgrade by association.

6. If a competitive test is conducted it should be done by an objective testing source, preferably an independent one, so that there will be no doubt as to the veracity of the test.

7. In all cases the test should be supportive of all claims made in the advertising that are based on the test.

8. The advertising should never use partial results or stress insignificant differences to cause the consumer to draw an improper conclusion.

9. The property being compared should be significant in terms of value or usefulness of the product to the consumer.

10. Comparatives delivered through the use of testimonials should not imply that the testimonial is more than one individual's thought unless that individual represents a sample of the majority viewpoint.

The Committee on Improving Advertising of the American Association of Advertising Agencies recommended to the Board of Directors a new Policy Statement and Guidelines for Comparative Advertising which were approved by unanimous vote on February 23, 1974.

The purpose of the new Statement and Guidelines is for guidance of creative and account management people in 4A agencies working with their clients.

By the way of background, the Board of Directors of the 4A's issued a Policy Statement on Comparative Advertising on February 15, 1966 which was subsequently updated on February 19, 1969.

Both the 1966 and the revised 1969 Policy Statements tended to "discourage" comparative advertising.

However, the Committee on Improving Advertising and the Board of Directors accept the fact that comparative advertising is now a reality. All three networks accept it. The Federal Trade Commission encourages it. Some major advertisers use it.

The Guidelines take into consideration the Board's feeling that extreme care is needed when using comparative advertising.

> Stanley Tannenbaum
> Chairman
> Committee on Improving Advertising

April, 1974

(Reprinted by permission of the American Association of Advertising Agencies, Inc.)

4.
SELF-REGULATION
OF ADVERTISING

The regulation by the federal government of advertising in America reached its zenith in the mid-1970s. At that time, the Federal Trade Commission (FTC) was clearly the nation's number one advertising compliance watchdog. Its impact on the advertising community had grown exponentially under a series of activist chairmen and by dint of such expansive legislative initiatives as the Magnuson-Moss Warranty-Federal Trade Commission Improvement Act of 1975.[1]

In the late-1970s, however, FTC's direction began to change and change dramatically, towards less authority in policing the marketplace. A massive, and highly effective, lobbying campaign to limit FTC's powers was launched by such business trade groups as the National Association of Manufacturers (NAM) and such industries as the funeral industry. After protracted battles over reauthorization measures, Congress responded with legislation curbing some of FTC's vast powers. Despite these battles, FTC retains enormous potential power over the marketplace and over advertising. However, the advent of a new breed of Reagan-appointed Commissioners—beginning with the appointment of Chairman James C. Miller III in late 1981 (whose chairmanship lasted around four years) portends a further diminution of the role of FTC in ad compliance regulation for at least the remainder of the 1980s.

With the declining involvement of FTC in various aspects of ad compliance, there has been a parallel increase in importance in three major areas: (1) ad industry self-regulation, (2) private lawsuits, and in particular suits involving Section 43(a) of the Lanham Act, and (3) somewhat greater state regulation of deceptive advertising. This chapter focuses on those mechanisms devised by the ad industry to regulate voluntarily advertising compliance within the advertising community, and particularly on the ad industry's key self-regulatory mechanism, the National Advertising

Division (NAD)/National Advertising Review Board (NARB) of the Council of Better Business Bureaus, Inc.

OVERVIEW

The advertising industry has evolved a variety of self-regulatory mechanisms to handle the voluntary regulation of advertising. The main agency of self-regulation, NAD/NARB, was created in July 1971 by the American Advertising Federation (AAF), American Association of Advertising Agencies (4 A's), Association of National Advertisers (ANA), and the Council of Better Business Bureaus (BBB).

NAD is the investigative branch. It launches inquiries, determines the issues, collects and evaluates data, and makes the initial finding as to whether challenged advertising claims are substantiated. When NAD can't agree that the substantiation is satisfactory, it negotiates with the advertiser for modification or permanent discontinuance of the ads. NARB is the appellate wing of the NAD/NARB system. If an advertiser doesn't agree with a NAD decision, the advertiser can appeal that decision to NARB.

A relatively new program of local advertising self-regulation was established by AAF and BBB in 1981. Under this program, Advertising Review Committees (ARC) are available to local Better Business Bureaus for consultation and advice.

Each of the major networks—American Broadcasting Company, Columbia Broadcasting System, and National Broadcasting Company—has its own advertising guidelines and broadcast standards and practice departments, which review all televised commercials before they're aired. (The networks' self-regulatory system is examined in Chapter 5 of this book.)

Until recently, the National Association of Broadcasters's Code of Good Practice (NAB Code) formed the basis for these departments' review of the commercial material submitted to them. However, the NAB Code was suspended on March 10, 1982 following a successful suit by the Justice Department on antitrust grounds. The Code was never reinstated.

NAD/NARB

One effect of FTC's retrenchment and the demise of the NAB Code has been to elevate the importance of the NAD/NARB system. If you're a national advertiser, or represent one, you should familiarize yourself with the workings of this key self-regulatory body.

Essentially, NAD's role in the NAD/NARB system is that of investigator. As part of its investigatory mission, NAD systematically monitors national television, radio, and print ads. The results of such investigations are often "cases," basically more in-depth inquiries into ads containing a claim or claims that may be questionable (i.e., not adequately substantiated). In these "cases," NAD examines all available information pertaining to a particular challenged claim or claims.

NAD's conclusion as to whether a particular ad claim was satisfactorily substantiated or not is published each month in a report called the "NAD Case Report." This Report is divided into two main categories: "Advertising Substantiated" and "Advertising Modified or Discontinued." Let's say that your ad was the subject of an NAD "case" and has now reached a conclusion. If your case appears in the "Advertising Substantiated" portion of the Report, it means NAD concluded that you were successfully able to substantiate your ad claims. You did this, no doubt, by showing NAD results of tests, studies or other data you had on hand *before* the challenged ad was run. And these data persuaded NAD that your ad claims were supported. On the other hand, if your case appears in the "Advertising Modified or Discontinued" portion of the Report, it means that NAD and you could not agree that your substantiation was satisfactory. If this were to occur, NAD would negotiate with you to have you modify or permanently discontinue the challenged ad. If the controversy still is not settled, you or NAD may appeal the matter to NARB, NAD's appellate body, for final decision. If NARB rules against you, do you have to comply? No. Compliance with NAD/NARB decisions is strictly voluntary. Nevertheless, in the fourteen years of NAD/NARB's history not one advertiser taking part in an NAD inquiry followed by an NARB appeal has failed to follow the decision.

Incidentally, NAD would provide you and your ad agency with a draft copy of the Case Report before it's published to give you a chance to correct matters of fact. Moreover, you could add a brief "Advertiser's Statement," so long as it's factual and nonpromotional, if you so desire.

In addition to its own investigatory efforts, NAD receives cases from a variety of other sources, including competitors, Better Business Bureaus, consumers, consumer groups, and trade associations. In fact, these other sources account for around two-thirds of NAD's cases.[2]

Indeed, a major trend in recent years has been the increase of competitor challenges at NAD. In fact, in 1984 such challenges surpassed NAD's own efforts. Competitive challenges in 1984 resulted in forty-eight challenges or 45 percent of NAD cases. Meanwhile, NAD monitoring resulted in thirty-three challenges or 31 percent of cases.[3] This was only the third time in NAD's fourteen-year history when competitor challenges equalled or surpassed NAD's own efforts.[4]

Does NAD pursue every complaint referred to it? No. It declines most complaints. NAD lists the following as among the reasons NAD would turn down a complaint:

1. If it concerns local advertising or business practice such as prompt delivery of goods, the most appropriate self-regulatory organization to handle the problem is the Better Business Bureau located in the same area as the advertiser's head

office. Ninety percent of the complaints received from individual members of the public belong in this category. They are handled by referral . . .

2. Questions related to the basic performance of products and services, label claims and directions, matters of taste, and political and issue advertising are not within NAD's mandate.

3. Advertising addressed to a business, professional or select audience with specialized knowledge of the subject matter is inappropriate for review by NAD.

4. Where possibly unlawful business practices are involved or the advertiser belongs to the very small minority unresponsive to self-regulation. NAD refers complaints to the appropriate government agency.

5. NAD will not initiate an inquiry involving advertising which is the subject of litigation by the FTC or another government agency.[5]

If your advertising is challenged by NAD, how do you go about "winning" your case? NAD doesn't approach its procedures as win-lose situations. Rather, the self-regulatory body will look at your ad in terms of whether there is adequate *prior* substantiation. In other words, the groundwork for successfully substantiating your ad claims should have been laid *before* your ad aired or was published. (Nevertheless, NAD will consider substantiation developed after the ad was aired or published under certain circumstances.)[6]

Accordingly, it's highly advisable that you have on hand prior to advertising such substantiating data as laboratory studies, consumer tests, market research, product demonstrations, or market share data. Here are some examples of substantiation that *have* passed muster with NAD:

• A television comparative advertising campaign for Sprite was challenged by a competitor, the Seven-Up Company. The campaign included this claim, among others: "Recently, an independent research firm ran a taste test between Sprite and 7-Up. And the taste people chose most often was the taste of Sprite . . ." The advertiser successfully substantiated this and other similar claims by showing NAD the results of a "paired-comparison test" of people saying they preferred Sprite, as well as two other tests.[7]

• An advertiser successfully substantiated its comparative ad claims for a fabric softener sheet. It did so by showing NAD the results of "comparative laboratory laundering tests" and "consumer-rated, at-home, sequential trials."[8]

• The following magazine ads were also substantiated to NAD's satisfaction: "There's not much difference in the way men's underwear looks when it's new. It's only after repeated washings and dryings that you begin to notice the difference. That's when Fruit of the Loom underwear's outstanding quality begins to show." The ads also claimed: ". . . the fabric in our briefs is 50 percent stronger than the number two brand," "America's largest selling underwear."

The advertiser successfully substantiated these claims, among others, by showing NAD: (1) market-share data to substantiate its leading-status claim and the identity of the "number two brand," and (2) the results of independent laboratory tests on teeshirts and briefs as evidence that Fruit of the Loom's "bursting strength" was greater than its competitor's product by over 50 percent.[9]

Once NAD enters the scene, how long does it take to process a case? That depends, in large measure, on the complexity of the issues involved. In 1983, 58 percent of NAD's reported cases were settled within six months, 76 percent within nine months, and 98 percent within one year. However, a substantial percentage of cases are settled even faster: Twenty-three percent of reported cases in 1983 were settled within three months.[10]

As should be evident by the discussion so far, NAD's hallmark is its case-by-case approach. It does not issue industry-wide pronouncements that would have significant impact on substantial segments of industry. (If it did, it could face such antitrust problems as confronted the NAB Code.) Accordingly, advertisers and ad agencies can gain insight into what is acceptable substantiation by studying the cases that affect their particular type of claim. An analysis of hundreds of cases over the years reveals many important trends. The following section examines ten of the most important such trends at NAD and includes examples of each trend taken from NAD decisions.

Comparative Advertising

Since the early 1970s, comparative advertising has experienced tremendous growth, becoming a favored ad technique of many advertisers and ad agencies. Nevertheless, the careless use of this valuable advertising tool can be costly. A relatively recent comparative advertising campaign, for example, will cost one advertiser $40 million, if the decision is ultimately upheld on appeal.[11]

If you plan to launch a comparative advertising campaign (or one has been launched against your company), you should study the comparative advertising cases brought under Section 43(a) of the Lanham Act. (See Chapter 3.) In addition, you should also follow those NAD cases—and there are many—that involve comparative advertising. Following are three examples.

1. A comparative advertising campaign for detergent pads appearing in magazine ads included this headline: "S.O.S. and Brillo you're all washed up." The ads made these claims: "New *steel-less* wool Panhandl'rs with super grease-cutting detergent clean and shine like steel wool, but last five times longer. Without rusting, splintering or scratching!" In addition, television commercials claimed that the pads "clean and shine like steel wool but last longer because they don't rust, splinter or easily fall apart."

NAD concluded that the claims for cleaning and shining performance and increased longevity in comparison with steel wool pads were substantiated. The advertiser succeeded in convincing NAD that these claims were substantiated by showing NAD the results of a series of lab and practical-use tests that used "typical" cookware surfaces, such as stainless steel and aluminum.

However, when asked by NAD to substantiate the nonscratch claim in magazine ads, the advertiser told NAD that it had withdrawn this claim from further use. Accordingly, the inquiry was terminated.[12]

2. Comparative ads for frozen shrimp appeared in newspapers. These ads included the following claims: "Introducing the U.S. Grade A Shrimp." "Of all major brands, only High Liner shrimp carries the coveted U.S. Grade A Shield." Point-of-sale ads made similar claims: "Of all major brands, only High Liner cooked shrimp meets stringent U.S. Grade A standards."

One of the advertiser's major competitors questioned the Grade A exclusivity claims since this company was also qualified to use the Shield.

This case reached a settlement once the advertiser agreed that it would not (1) include claims using the word "only," or (2) imply exclusivity concerning the Grade A certification.[13]

3. A comparative ad campaign for chocolate chip granola bars used newspaper insets and featured a product package that displayed this claim: ". . . more chocolate chips than any other granola bar!" with an asterisk referring to a footnote, "Based on a per ounce comparison to other national brands."

After reviewing the results of comparative testing, NAD concluded that the product contained substantially more chocolate chips, by weight, than competing products. Accordingly, the ad industry self-regulatory body concluded that the challenged claim in this case had been substantiated.[14]

Safety Claims

If you make claims involving safety in your ads, you should be prepared to have those claims be given much greater scrutiny by NAD than most other forms of advertising. Since so much more is at stake when safety claims are present in an ad, you should be extra certain that you have on hand adequate substantiation *prior* to advertising. The following are two such examples of NAD cases.

1. Magazine ads for a flea collar made these claims:

Revolutionary Breakthrough. . . . Now there is a safe, sure, 100% herbal way to be rid of fleas and ticks with confidence. Safe and gentle enough, so that you may even use it, as directed, on kittens and puppies. . . . Plastic strip flea collars may contain powerful synthetic chemicals. . . . Lifetime Flea Collar contains only organic herbal ingredients. . . . Hand crafted with genuine leather, wood and ceramic ornaments. . . .

Part of the data reviewed by NAD in this case were a sample product and label. The advertiser told NAD that its claims were based on information used by the Environmental Protection Agency (EPA) to support the registration of its product. EPA told NAD that product registration was completed once proof of performance wasn't required. In addition, EPA said the safety evaluation was based on past submissions of similar products. EPA generally disallows product safety claims when contradicted by label cautions, and EPA regs don't allow safety claims for registered products. NAD referred these unresolved safety issues to the advertiser.

The case was settled after the advertiser told NAD that future ads would reflect NAD's concerns.[15]

2. In one recent case, there was no problem whatsoever with the advertiser's substantiation. Nor did NAD allege that the advertiser's ads deceive or mislead consumers in any way. Nevertheless, the advertiser wasn't aware of one easily overlooked problem area in its ads: the safety implications of the ads. Here's what happened:

Television commercials for an amusement park showed passengers waving their hands while riding a roller coaster instead of keeping their hands inside the cars. Later ads again showed passengers on another ride with their hands in the air. NAD's Children's Advertising Review Unit (CARU) was concerned that children might imitate these practices with possibly injurious results.

The advertiser told NAD that these ads were already discontinued. Nevertheless, the advertiser said it would "notify the agencies responsible for advertising of all Six Flags Amusement Parks to avoid showing behavior which may encourage unsound safety habits."[16]

Implied Claims

You've gone through a great deal of time and expense to make sure all of the direct claims in your ad are substantiated. But have you considered all the implications of your ads? If your ads also make any implied claims, these claims must also be substantiated, as in the following two cases.

1. An advertising campaign for pet food had this theme: "We're helping pets live longer, healthier lives." An ad for Cat and Kitten Chow made these claims: "Nutrition that helps cats live healthier, longer lives. Maybe that's why veterinarians recommend them both."

NAD agreed that a survey submitted by the advertiser substantiated the 6-to-1 preference claim. However, NAD recommended the advertiser modify the wording of the ad "to avoid implying that the veterinarians opinions are based on Purina's nutritional advantages over other complete and balanced brands."

The advertiser agreed to modify the claims based on NAD's recommendations and the basic principle that optimum nutrition can help pets live longer and healthier lives.[17]

2. In this case, a television commercial compared Light n'Lively with real mayonnaise: "Light n'Lively gets the same richness from real eggs . . . its delicate taste from a secret blend of seasonings. . . . Try new Light n'Lively Reduced Calorie Mayonnaise from Kraft. The taste is for real." Newspaper ads claimed: "Light n'Lively Reduced Calorie Mayonnaise is made from real eggs and delicate seasonings, and so is regular mayonnaise. But there's less oil."

NAD questioned the implication in both ads that Light n'Lively is blended from the same ingredients as real mayonnaise, even though label ingredients include food starch, artificial flavoring, and added coloring. NAD's concern: "that the *net impression* of the advertisments conflicted with the use of ingredients barred, by tradition and FDA regulations, from real mayonnaise."

The advertiser disagreed with NAD. Nevertheless, it agreed to take NAD's views into account if it sues similar claims in future ads.[18]

"Up To" Claims

NAD frequently challenges savings claims that include the terms "up to" (e.g., save "up to" 40 percent). Reason: These claims often contain a misleading emphasis on the maximum savings that can be achieved.

1. Newspaper ads for a long-distance telephone service made these claims: "All around you, other businesses have been cutting their interstate long distance costs by up to 50% with Sprint . . . Because now with Sprint you can call anywhere in America."

Similar claims appeared in a television commercial and in magazine ads. NAD questioned whether the percentage savings claim should instead have been expressed as a range.

The advertiser noted that a promotional mailing piece included a comparative long-distance cost chart showing the costs of selected, individual calls by Sprint and AT&T for certain representative cities. Savings in that mailer were expressed in terms of a range of 20 percent to 55 percent.

Moreover, the advertiser told NAD its "up to 50%" claim had been withdrawn from broadcast ads and appropriate modifications had been made to print ads.[19]

2. An advertiser did successfully substantiate its "up to" savings claim in an ad involving the sale of jewelry and watches. That ad said, "Save up to 33⅓%. Special ruby, sapphire or emerald and diamond collection." The offer was available for ten days. A similar ad had quoted various "up to" savings claims on watches and jewelry.

In addition, the advertiser told NAD it had modified recent ads to express percentage reductions as a range, for example, "We're rolling back original prices 20% to 50%."[20]

Use of the Word "Free"

If you use, or plan to include, a "free" offer in your ads, you should be aware that NAD scrutinizes such ads very carefully. It wants to be sure that what is offered is really free, as for these two cases in point.

1. NAD concluded that use of the word "free" appearing in the following newspaper ads was proper:

Fight rising energy costs with a Trane High efficiency central air conditioner . . . and free gas furnace. To get your free Trane Ambassador gas furnace (E models), purchase a Trane Elite (TX models, 2-3 ton) or Executive (TD models, 3½-5 ton) central air conditioner, and installation services for both air conditioner and furnace, from your participating Trane dealer. Purchase and installation must be between September 4 and October 19, 1984. Call your participating Trane dealer.

The advertiser substantiated this claim by explaining to NAD how its program worked. NAD also took into account the "established business practice which holds that an offer of 'free' merchandise conditional upon a purchase should be for a specified limited time, with no increase in the normal price of the merchandise or alteration in its quality, and with clear disclosure of terms."[21]

2. Newspaper ads for an airline service included the following claim: "Upgrade yourself to first class. Free." A competitor challenged the ads. Its charge: Air One offered only a one-class service to passengers at one price and didn't upgrade its passengers for "free."

The advertiser resolved this case by informing NAD that the "upgrade yourself free" claims were discontinued and that it has no plans to use these claims in future ads.[22]

Precision in Language

Your ad compliance outlook will benefit greatly if you make sure the language appearing in your ads is precise and directly to the point. As the following two cases illustrate, if your ad claims are not completely accurate because of the use of imprecise or ambiguous language, your ad can be successfully challenged before NAD.

1. In a case involving car rentals, ads failed to include specific language telling consumers about the limited availability of certain car models. NAD received complaints from consumers that after they met requirements for advance registration of advertised car models, counter clerks told them the

cars were unavailable and consumers had to rent more expensive models.

The advertiser told NAD the problem was the result of the overwhelming popularity of the offer and incorrect actions by inexperienced counter personnel.

The advertiser agreed that future ads would include specific language telling consumers about the limited availability of the offers, when appropriate.[23]

2. NAD challenged the following televised ad claims for a vitamin and mineral supplement: "Spartus, with every essential vitamin and mineral in the U.S. RDA and more . . . Spartus with electrolytes essential for muscle action . . . Spartus, every essential vitamin and mineral, and more." Similar claims wre made in print ads. A competitor challenged these claims.

NAD ultimately agreed with the challenger that the claim, "every essential vitamin and mineral, and more," was inaccurate. Its reason: The formulas lacked several nutrients essential for humans for which no U.S. RDA has been defined. In addition NAD said the claim that "Spartus" contains all nutrients for which U.S. RDA's are established may be confusing, since the basic formula doesn't contain iron.

The advertiser told NAD the television commercial was discontinued and said it would modify print ads to consider NAD's concerns.[24]

Using Government Standards

Advertisers love to say that their product complies with applicable government standards, particularly if their product complies and other products do not. Moreover, if your product has the government's imprimatur on it, your ads are more likely to withstand NAD's scrutiny, as the following cases illustrate.

1. An advertiser made the following claims in newspaper ads: "Introducing Holly Farms 5-7 lb. naturally self-basting roaster . . . So naturally juicy it bastes itself while it cooks." The advertiser made similar claims on radio. In addition, the package label identified the chicken as "Naturally self-basting."

The advertiser told NAD the roaster is a special breed, distinguished from a broiler chicken. It noted that long-term experience shows good results in oven roasting without basting. In addition, the advertiser said the U.S. Department of Agriculture (USDA) approved the "self-basting" claim. Accordingly, NAD concluded the claims had been substantiated.[25]

2. The following television commercials featuring Frank Perdue were challenged: "Government standards would allow me to call this a Grade A chicken. But my standards wouldn't. This chicken is skinny. . . . The fact is, my graders reject 30% of the chickens government graders accept as Grade A."

The advertiser successfully substantiated these claims by showing NAD monthly records through 1983 to show that about 80 percent of incoming chickens were classified as USDA Grade A but only 56 percent of these were graded acceptable for packaging as whole chickens. In fact, the advertiser distributed only 45 percent of the total as whole chickens. This was confirmed by the advertiser's regular monthly quality audit.[26]

Nutritional Claims

Because the health of the audience is at stake, NAD pays particularly close attention to ads containing nutritional claims. So if you advertise a food, beverage, or vitamin/mineral product, you should take extra care to be sure your ads comply with all federal, state, and local regulations, industry standards, and are fully substantiated. Two cases in point illustrate some of the things NAD looks for in such cases:

1. Television commercials displayed Yoo-Hoo, a chocolate beverage, along with other canned sodas. An announcer asked, "Which of these leading soft drinks gives you nutrition with vitamin A, vitamin B_2, Vitamin C, Vitamin D, niacin, calcium, potassium and a little bit of protein?" The words "6% protein" appeared on screen. The advertiser made similar claims in a radio ad.

The advertiser proved that Yoo-Hoo contained the five claimed vitamins and the mineral calcium at 10 percent of the U.S. Recommended Daily Allowance (U.S. RDA). NAD questioned the claims for potassium and protein in both advertising labeling. NAD's reason: The product contained only 25 mg. of potassium, "an insignificant proportion" of the 2,000-6,000 mg. recommended by the Food and Nutrition Board of the National Academy of Sciences. Protein was present at about 1% by weight, or 6% of the US RDA.

The advertiser told NAD that it had reformulated its product to contain 240 mg. of potassium. In addition, the advertiser agreed to remove protein claims on the label and in advertising to comply with the Food and Drug Administration's (FDA) labeling standards.[27]

2. This case involved magazine ads for bananas that showed a list of nutrients including: "Complex Carbohydrates & Natural Sugars—23 mg." "Potassium—317 mg. to revitalize your muscle power and maintain body fluid balance," and "Low in calories—only 90." A footnote explained that, "Nutritional statistics are for a 100 gram peeled banana (3.5 oz.)." NAD questioned (1) the accuracy of the 23 mg. claim for carbohydrates and sugars, (2) the claim that potassium can revitalize muscle power, and (3) the absence of a simple description of serving size.

The 23 mg. claim, apparently, was a typographical error. (The ad should have read "23 gm.") The Association argued that the ad accurately described the general role of potassium in the body. And the Association noted that its nutritional facts were taken from recent analyses.

NAD maintained its view that the ad may have overstated a banana's dietary contribution. NAD also felt a more practical serving size (e.g., "a 7-inch banana") would be helpful. The Association agreed to consider NAD's concerns in future ads.[28]

Child-Directed Ads

If you do any advertising that is—or may be construed as being—directed to children, you should be aware of NAD's Children's Advertising Review Unit (CARU). CARU scrutinizes child-directed advertising to make sure they do not mislead children or have the potential for harming children in any way. As many of CARU's cases—and the *Self-Regulatory Guidelines for Children's Advertising*—often show, what would be considered acceptable for adult-directed ads is not always deemed appropriate for children, as illustrated in the following cases.

1. In a recent case involving a video game, CARU examined a child-directed television commercial showing a young boy sitting up in bed holding a pocket video game, and saying "Let's face it, being sick is better than being in school." The commercial went on to list the benefits of the electronic game, and concluded: "And the built-in alarm tells you when it's time to get more sympathy." "You've got to milk a good thing for all it's worth."

CARU's problem with the ad was not with any of the claims made. The self-regulatory body's difficulty was with the "attitude toward school expressed" and "the suggestion of using illness to take advantage of a parent offering support."

How the case was resolved: The advertiser—after receiving several consumer complaints and conducting further market research—decided to discontinue this ad permanently.[29]

2. One of the most popular toys during the last Christmas season was the type that can be transformed from one type of toy to another. CARU challenged television commercials for such toys, called "Transformers Action Figures," because they lacked separate purchase data and contained dramatically heightened visual and sound effects. CARU's concern: Children's imagination might be exploited "by stimulating unreasonable expectations of product quality or performance."

In one particular case, the advertiser of these toys told CARU that two of three questioned ads had been permanently discontinued, and a third commercial was modified because of CARU's concern that the film techniques might blur the distinction between dramatic and straightforward depiction of the toy.[30]

Energy-Savings Claims

A trend that started during the energy crisis of the mid 1970s, was the introduction of a host of products advertised as energy-savers. As the energy crisis diminished, so too did the number of such ads scrutinized by NAD. Nevertheless, NAD continues to keep abreast of energy savings claims. And, should an energy crisis again occur, NAD's handling of these cases would prove illustrative as to what NAD looks for in this area.

1. In a relatively recent case, NAD challenged the following magazine ad:

Ameri-Therm is the thermally actuated vent damper that's proven in millions of locations. Saves up to 15% on fuel bills. Preferred choice of American homeowners. Thermally actuated to operate efficiently with no wires, electricity or other power source.

NAD was concerned over the close proximity of the claims "Proven in millions of locations," and "Preferred choice of American homeowners," in the ad. NAD feared that consumers might get a misleading impression of experience with the brand in the United States. The advertiser agreed to take NAD's recommendations into account when preparing new ads.[31]

2. NAD concluded that claims appearing in dealer brochures for energy-saving windows were substantiated. The challenged claims:

The skillful engineering and careful construction of every Binning's Vinyl-Prime Solid Vinyl Replacement Window offer an economical answer to window-related energy loss and fuel costs. Since vinyl has superior thermal performance characteristics, these windows act as exceptional thermal insulation.

To substantiate the claims, the advertiser showed NAD the results of comparative thermal performance testing of a Vinyl-Prime window versus wood and aluminum frame windows, conducted by independent testing firms. The results showed the product was more energy-efficient in thermal insulation than the other window types tested. Other technical data verified resistance to air flow results in fuel savings.[32]

Information from NAD/NARB

It is a shame that entirely too many advertisers do not get to know very much about NAD until they receive a letter that begins, "Dear ***, Your advertising has recently come to the attention of the National Advertising Division . . . " In addition to its *NAD Case Report*, NAD has a wealth of pamphlets and other materials that can serve as valuable guides to advertisers and ad agencies *before* their ads are challenged. In fact, knowledge attained by regularly reading the NAD Case Reports and studying the various materials available from NAD can help *avoid* such challenges. Here is just a partial list of what's available from NAD:

- *Better Business Bureau, Code of Advertising*;
- Dear_____, *Your advertising has recently come to the attention of the National Advertising Division . . .* (an NAD Guide for Advertisers and Ad Agencies);
- *Identifying Competitors in Advertising* (National Advertising Review Board);
- *Advertising Self-Regulation and Its Interaction with Consumers* (National Advertising Review Board);
- *Self-Regulatory Guidelines for Children's Advertising* (Children's Advertising Review Unit);
- *An Eye on Children's Advertising* (Children's Advertising Review Unit);
- *Children and Advertising, An Annotated Bibliography*;
- *Standards for Automobile Rental Advertising* (BBB);
- *Standards for Carpet and Rugs—advertising & selling* (BBB);
- *Standards of Practice for the Home Improvement Industry* (BBB);
- *Standards for Home Insulation Materials—advertising & selling* (BBB);
- *Standards for Residential Swimming Pools—advertising & selling* (BBB).

If you would like copies of these or other available materials, or would like to regularly receive the *NAD Case Report*, contact NAD at: National Advertising Division, Council of Better Business Bureaus, Inc., 845 Third Avenue, New York, NY 10022. Telephone (212) 754-1358.

SELF-REGULATION OF BUSINESS-TO-BUSINESS ADS

There has been a great deal written in the business press and elsewhere about the self-regulatory aspects of advertising to consumers. However, very little has been written about a major source of advertising—business-to-business ads. These advertisements are generally for hard goods, such as steel, and are generally directed to corporate purchasing departments or other company executives who may influence a company's buying decision.

The key organization to know in this area is the Business Professional Advertising Association (B/PAA). As of March 1985, the B/PAA has some 4,500 members located in thirty-seven market areas across the United States. This 63-year-old organization was formerly known as the Association of Industrial Advertisers (from 1959-1974) and the National Industrial Advertiser's Association (1922-1974). It has had its present name since 1974.

The B/PAA has established a Code of Ethics to which each B/PAA member agrees to abide. This Code is designed to give guidance to members in the preparation, sale or acceptance of any form of "business communications" (e.g., advertising, direct mail, trade shows). (The B/PAA Code of Ethics is reproduced in full text as Appendix 4A at the end of this chapter.)

According to Ronald L. Coleman, B/PAA's Managing Director, over $2.3 billion were spent in 1984 by advertisers in trade publications, making it the main form of business-to-business advertising. Catalogue advertising is the second largest, followed by direct mail and trade shows. However, Coleman noted that in his thirteen years with B/PAA, "We have not had a major problem in the business area with ethics. Most of the [advertising] claims have been in the consumer package goods area."[33] What will the B/PAA do in cases where there are disputed advertising claims? (See Appendix 4B for the full text of the procedure B/PAA uses to review such claims.)

The companies generally are able to settle their differences prior to utilizing that method, according to Coleman. When B/PAA does send the offending company a letter expressing its opinion, it does so "as an independent organization giving its point of view."

If you would like more information about this group, you can contact them at: Business Professional Advertising Association, 205 E. 42nd Street, New York, NY 10017. Telephone: (212) 661-0222.

CHILDREN'S ADVERTISING AND SELF-REGULATION

During the high point of the Federal Trade Commission's regulatory fervor in the mid-1970s, it looked as if child-directed ads would undergo fundamental regulatory change. In 1978, FTC staff proposed, among other things, a ban on (1) all television commercials aired at children under eight, and (2) television commercials for sugared products, geared to the eight-to-twelve year olds. After an intense industry lobbying effort, this effort was ultimately blunted in 1980 when Congress voted to end FTC's authority to regulate children's advertising.

The defeat of these proposals, however, does not mean that an advertiser is free to advertise its products to children in any manner it chooses. If anything, that defeat placed even more importance on the existing self-regulatory mechanisms already in place for children's advertising.

One of these mechanisms is, of course, the network standards and guidelines for children's advertising (see Chapter 5). The other key self-regulatory mechanism is NAD's Children's Advertising Review Unit (CARU). This agency oversees the important "Children's Advertising Guidelines," in existence since 1972. Their goal is to encourage truth and accuracy in children's advertising. (Because of the importance of these guidelines, they are reproduced in full text as Appendix 4C.)

OTHER SOURCES

You should also be aware that there are other important sources of advertising self-regulation. Each of the networks has its own advertising guidelines (to be discussed in depth in Chapter 5 of this book). In addition, both the American Advertising Federation (AAF) and the American Association of Advertising Agencies have relevant standards or principles that are worth knowing. AAF's "Advertising Principles of American Business," were adopted by AAF's Board of Directors March 2, 1984. The full text of these principles is as follows:

Advertising Principles of American Business

1. Truth
   Advertising shall tell the truth, and shall reveal significant facts, the omission of which would mislead the public.

2. Substantiation
   Advertising claims shall be substantiated by evidence in possession of the advertiser and the advertising agency, prior to making such claims.

3. Comparisons
   Advertising shall refrain from making false, misleading, or unsubstantiated statements or claims about a competitor or his products or services.

4. Bait Advertising
   Advertising shall not offer products or services for sale unless such offer constitutes a bona fide effort to sell the advertised products or services and is not a device to switch consumers to other goods or services, usually higher priced.

5. Guarantees and Warranties
   Advertising of guarantees and warranties shall be explicit, with sufficient information to apprise consumers of their principal terms and limitations or, when space or time restrictions preclude such disclosures, the advertisement should clearly reveal where the full text of the guarantee or warranty can be examined before purchase.

6. Price Claims
   Advertising shall avoid price claims which are false or misleading, or savings claims which do not offer provable savings.

7. Testimonials
   Advertising containing testimonials shall be limited to those of competent witnesses who are reflecting a real and honest opinion or experience.

8. Taste and Decency
   Advertising shall be free of statements, illustrations or implications which are offensive to good taste or public decency.

(Reprinted by permission of AAF.)

NOTES

1. Public Law 93-637, effective January 4, 1975; 15 U.S.C. §2301 et seq.

2. The *NAD Case Report* of July 15, 1983 attributes 37 percent of NAD cases to NAD's own monitoring efforts and the remainder from other sources. In the *NAD Case Report* dated January 15, 1985, NAD monitoring accounted for 31 percent of cases in 1984 and, again, the remainder from these other sources.

3. *NAD Case Report*, 1/15/85.

4. *Advertising Compliance Service*, Tab #1, Bulletins #35, 59, and 84.

5. *NAD Case Report*, 7/15/83, p. 21.

6. *NAD Case Report*, 7/15/83, p. 22.

7. *NAD Case Report*, 2/15/85; see also *Advertising Compliance Service*, Tab #3, Self-Regulation, Article #58, p. 1.

8. *NAD Case Report*, 2/15/85; see also, *Advertising Compliance Service*, Tab #3, Self-Regulation, Article #58, p. 2.

9. *NAD Case Report*, 1/7/85; see also, *Advertising Compliance Service*, Tab #3, Self-Regulation, Article #56, p. 1.

10. *Advertising Compliance Service*, Tab #3, Self-Regulation, Article #50, p. 2.

11. *U-Haul International, Inc., v. Jartran, Inc.*, No. Civ 80-454, U.S. District Court for the District of Arizona (Phoenix), *final decision* filed November 27, 1984; *preliminary injunction* in 522 F. Supp. 1238, *aff'd* 681 F. 2d 1159 (9th Cir., 1982).

12. *NAD Case Report*, 1/15/85; see also, *Advertising Compliance Service* Tab #3, Self-Regulation, Article #57, p. 1.

13. *NAD Case Report*, 1/15/85; see also, *Advertising Compliance Service*, Tab #3, Self-Regulation, Article #57, p. 1.

14. *NAD Case Report*, 9/17/84; see also, *Advertising Compliance Service*, Tab #3, Self-Regulation, Article #53, p. 1.

15. *NAD Case Report*, 4/16/84; see also, *Advertising Compliance Service*, Tab #3, Self-Regulation, Article #45, p. 2.

16. *NAD Case Report*, 1/17/83; see also, *Advertising Compliance Service*, Tab #3, Self-Regulation, Article #27, p. 1.

17. *NAD Case Report*, 9/17/84; see also, *Advertising Compliance Service*, Tab #3, Self-Regulation, Article #53, p. 3.

18. *NAD Case Report*, 3/15/83; see also, *Advertising Compliance Service*, Tab #3, Self-Regulation, Article #29, p. 2.

19. *NAD Case Report*, 6/15/84; see also, *Advertising Compliance Service*, Tab #3, Self-Regulation, Article #48, p. 1.

20. *NAD Case Report*, 8/15/83; see also, *Advertising Compliance Service*, Tab #3, Self-Regulation, Article #35, p. 3.

21. *NAD Case Report*, 2/15/85; see also, *Advertising Compliance Service*, Tab #3, Self-Regulation, Article #58, p. 4.

22. *NAD Case Report*, 11/15/84; see also, *Advertising Compliance Service*, Tab #3, Self-Regulation, Article #55, p. 1.

23. *NAD Case Report*, 5/15/84; see also, *Advertising Compliance Service*, Tab #3, Self-Regulation, Article #46, p. 2.

24. *NAD Case Report*, 4/16/84; see also, *Advertising Compliance Service*, Tab #3, Self-Regulation, Article #45, p. 1.

25. *NAD Case Report*, 4/16/84; see also, *Advertising Compliance Service*, Tab #3, Self-Regulation, Article #45, p. 4.

26. *NAD Case Report*, 2/15/84; see also, *Advertising Compliance Service*, Tab #3, Self-Regulation, Article #42, p. 1.

27. *NAD Case Report*, 10/15/84; see also, *Advertising Compliance Service*, Tab #3, Self-Regulation, Article #54, p. 2.

28. *NAD Case Report*, 10/15/84; see also, *Advertising Compliance Service*, Tab #3, Self-Regulation, Article #54, p. 2.

29. *NAD Case Report*, 1/15/85; see also, *Advertising Compliance Service*, Tab #3, Self-Regulation, Article #57, p. 2.

30. *NAD Case Report*, 12/17/84; see also, *Advertising Compliance Service*, Tab #3, Self-Regulation, Article #56, p. 4.

31. *NAD Case Report*, 11/15/83; see also, *Advertising Compliance Service*, Tab #3, Self-Regulation, Article #38, p. 1.

32. *NAD Case Report*, 12/15/82; see also, *Advertising Compliance Service*, Tab #3, Self-Regulation, Article #24, p. 2.

33. *Advertising Compliance Service*, Tab #3, Self-Regulation, Article #60, pp. 1-3.

Appendix 4A

B/PAA CODE OF ETHICS

Each member of the Business/Professional Advertising Association agrees to abide by the following principles of professional conduct:

1. No form of business communications shall be prepared or knowingly accepted that contains untruthful, misleading or deceptive statements, claims or implications.

2. No claims shall be made in business communications whose truth and accuracy are incapable of substantiation through reasonable supporting documentation.

3. No form of business communications shall be prepared or knowingly accepted that unfairly disparages or attacks products, services or reputation of another company. Comparative communications which make a clear and factual product or service comparison under similar conditions shall not be considered disparaging.

4. No form of business communications shall be prepared or knowingly accepted that contains inaccurate or misleading claims or prices, comparative pricing, guarantees or warranties. Furthermore, guarantees or warranties should be fully explained or noted as to where the information could be obtained.

5. No form of business communications shall be prepared or knowingly accepted about a product or service which is unsafe and would result in harm to the user without warning.

6. No form of business communications shall be prepared or knowingly accepted that is offensive or in bad taste.

7. No form of business communications shall be prepared or knowingly accepted

that distorts or changes the meaning of quotes, statements or published material to a form other than implied by the speaker(s) or author(s).

8. No form of business communications shall be prepared or knowingly accepted that does not offer the user a fair opportunity to purchase products or services at the advertised price.

9. No form of business communications shall be prepared or knowingly accepted which in any way violates the law or government statutes.

10. No business communications shall be proposed which in any way compromises the media by using the economic power of advertising to dictate editorial content.

11. No illustrations shall be altered or used in any way which implies a material difference in appearance or performance of the product from that which is accurate.

(Copyright by B/PAA, New York, N.Y. Reprinted by permission of B/PAA).

Appendix 4B

B/PAA ETHICS REVIEW BOARD

1. All complaints should be submitted in writing to the Managing Director, B/PAA. Since experience by advertising self-regulation agencies has proven that most alleged violations are inadvertent or unintentional, the Managing Director will attempt to resolve the problem by communicating with the parties involved.

2. If the Managing Director is unsuccessful in his attempt to resolve the dispute, the case will be turned over to the B/PAA Ethics Review Board for further review. The Ethics Review Board will consist of the current Executive Committee. If the Ethics Review Board, upon reviewing the case, is of the opinion that the complaint constitutes a violation of the Code of Ethics, a formal letter will be sent to the violating member outlining the reasons the member is believed to be in violation and requesting such practice be corrected or discontinued. The violating member will be informed further that there is a possibility of his membership being revoked. A written response will be requested from the member. The member has the option to rebut if he does not agree he is in violation.

3. If the member fails to cooperate, the Ethics Review Committee will recommend to the Board of Directors that those members connected with the violation have their membership in B/PAA revoked. The Board of Directors will then act on these recommendations.

4. Complaints between members which cannot be satisfactorily resolved by the B/PAA Ethics Review Board will be referred to the National Advertising Review Board, but only upon request by the plaintiff. The complaining member will be advised that any remuneration required or expenses as a result of adjudication by the NARB will be the responsibility of the plaintiff and not B/PAA.

5. If the complaint by a member is against a non-member, who is not required to conform to B/PAA's Code of Ethics, the Ethics Review Board will advise the non-member of the reasons it is believed to be in violation of accepted ethical communi-

cations standards, if such is the opinion, and request that these practices be discontinued. If the non-member fails to cooperate, the Ethics Review Board will recommend that the member consult with his or her own company's legal counsel to determine if they should go to the NARB at their own expense or act on their own.

(Copyright by B/PAA, New York, N.Y. Reprinted by permission of B/PAA.)

Appendix 4C

SELF-REGULATORY GUIDELINES FOR CHILDREN'S ADVERTISING THIRD EDITION, 1983

The Children's Advertising Guidelines have been in existence since 1972 when they were published by the Association of National Advertisers to encourage truthful and accurate advertising sensitive to the special nature of children. Subsequently, the advertising community established the Children's Advertising Review Unit to serve as an independent manager of the industry's self-regulatory programs. The Unit edited and republished the Children's Advertising Guidelines in 1975 and revised them in 1977.

This third edition has been edited by the Children's Advertising Review Unit to be sure the Guidelines are responsive to current conditions. The assistance of children's advertisers and their agencies has been invaluable, resulting in a clarification of individual Guidelines and an improved format.

INTERPRETATION OF THE GUIDELINES

Because children's knowledge of the physical and social world is in the process of development, they are more limited than adults in the experience and skills required to evaluate advertising and to make purchase decisions. For these reasons, certain presentations and techniques which may be appropriate for adult-directed advertising may mislead children if used in child-directed advertising.

The function of the Guidelines is to delineate those areas that need particular attention to help avoid deceptive advertising messages to children. The intent is to help advertisers deal sensitively and honestly with children and is not meant to deprive them, or children, of the benefits of innovative advertising approaches.

The Guidelines have been kept general in the belief that responsible advertising comes in many forms and that diversity should be encouraged. The goal in all cases should be to fulfill the spirit as the letter of the Guidelines and the Principles on which they are based.

SCOPE OF THE GUIDELINES

The Guidelines apply to all advertising addressed to children under twelve years of age, including print, broadcast and cable television advertising. One section applies to adult-directed advertising only when a potential child safety concern exists (see [the section on] Safety).

PRINCIPLES

Five basic Principles underlie these Guidelines for advertising directed to children:

1. Advertisers should always take into account the level of knowledge, sophistication and maturity of the audience to which their message is primarily directed. Younger children have a limited capability for evaluating the credibilty of what they watch. Advertisers, therefore, have a special responsibility to protect children from their own susceptibilities.

2. Realizing that children are imaginative and that make-believe play constitutes an important part of the growing up process, advertisers should exercise care not to exploit that imaginative quality of children. Unreasonable expectations of product quality or performance should not be stimulated either directly or indirectly by advertising.

3. Recognizing that advertising may play an important part in educating the child, information should be communicated in a truthful and accurate manner with full recognition by the advertiser that the child may learn practices from advertising which can affect his or her health and well-being.

4. Advertisers are urged to capitalize on the potential of advertising to influence social behavior by developing advertising that, wherever possible, addresses itself to social standards generally regarded as positive and beneficial, such as friendship, kindness, honesty, justice, generosity and respect for others.

5. Although many influences affect a child's personal and social development, it remains the prime responsibility of the parents to provide guidance for children. Advertisers should contribute to this parent-child relationship in a constructive manner.

Product Presentations and Claims

Children look at, listen to and remember many different elements in advertising. Therefore, advertisers need to examine the total advertising message to be certain that the net communication will not mislead or misinform children.

1. Copy, sound and visual presentations should not mislead children about product or performance characteristics. Such characteristics may include, but are not limited to, size, speed, method of operation, color, sound, durability and nutritional benefits.

2. The advertising presentation should not mislead children about perceived benefits from use of the product. Such benefits may include, but are not limited to, the acquisition of strength, status, popularity, growth, proficiency and intelligence. Social stereotyping and appeals to prejudice should be avoided.

3. Care should be taken not to exploit a child's imagination. Fantasy, including animation, is appropriate for younger as well as older children. However, it should not create unattainable performance expectations nor exploit the younger child's difficulty in distinguishing between the real and the fanciful.

4. The performance and use of a product should be demonstrated in a way that can be duplicated by the child for whom the product is intended.

5. Products should be shown used in safe environments and situations.

6. What is included and excluded in the initial purchase should be clearly established.

7. The amount of product featured should be within reasonable levels for the situation depicted.

8. Representation of food products should be made so as to encourage sound usage of the product with a view toward healthy development of good nutritional practices. Advertisements representing mealtime in the home should clearly and adeqately depict the role of the product within the framework of a balanced diet.

9. Portrayals of violence and presentations that could unduly frighten or provoke anxiety in children should be avoided.

10. Objective claims about product or performance characteristics should be supported by appropriate and adequate substantiation.

Sales Pressure

Children are not as prepared as adults to make judicious, independent purchase decisions. Therefore, advertisers should avoid using extreme sales pressure in advertising presentations to children.

1. Children should not be urged to ask parents or others to buy products. Advertisements should not suggest that a parent or adult who purchases a product or service for a child is better, more intelligent or more generous than one who does not.

2. Advertisements should not convey the impression that possession of a product will result in more acceptance of a child by his or her peers. Conversely, lacking a product should not convey the impression that the child will be less accepted by his or her peers. Advertisements should not imply that purchase and use of a product will confer upon the user the prestige, skills or other special qualities of characters appearing in advertising. Benefits attributed to the product or service should be inherent in its use.

3. All price representations should be clearly and concisely set forth. Price minimizations such as "only" or "just" should not be used.

Disclosures and Disclaimers

Children have a more limited vocabulary and less developed language skills than adolescents and adults. They read less well, if at all, and rely more on information presented pictorially than verbally. Studies have shown that simplified wording, such as "You have to put it together" instead of "Assembly required," significantly increases comprehension.

1. All information which requires disclosure for legal or other reasons should be in language understandable by the child audience. Disclaimers and disclosures should be clearly worded, legible and prominent. In television advertising, both audio and video disclosures are encouraged.

2. Advertising for unassembled products should clearly indicate that they need to be put together to be used properly.

3. If any item essential to use of the product is not included, such as batteries, this fact must be disclosed clearly.

4. Information about products purchased separately, such as accessories or individual items in a collection, should be disclosed clearly to the child audience.

Comparative Claims

Advertising which compares the advertised product to another product may be difficult for young children to understand and evaluate. Comparative claims should be based on real product advantages that are understandable to the child audience.

1. Comparative advertising should provide factual information. Comparisons should not falsely represent other products or previous versions of the same product.

2. Comparative claims should be presented in ways that children understand clearly.

3. Comparative claims should be supported by appropriate and adequate substantiation.

Endorsements and Promotion by Program or Editorial Characters

Studies have shown that the mere appearance of a character with a product can significantly alter a child's perception of the product depending on the child's opinion of the presenter. Advertising presentations by program/editorial characters may hamper a young child's ability to distinguish between program/editorial content and advertising.

1. All personal endorsements should reflect the actual experiences and beliefs of the endorser.

2. An endorser represented, either directly or indirectly, as an expert must possess qualifications appropriate to the particular expertise depicted in the endorsement.

3. Program personalities, live or animated, should not promote products, premiums or services in or adjacent to programs primarily directed to children in which the same personality or character appears.

4. In print media primarily designed for children, a character or personality associated with the editorial content of a publication should not be used to promote products, premiums or services in the same publication.

Premiums

The use of premiums in advertising has the potential to enhance the appeal of a product to a child. Therefore, special attention should be paid to the advertising of premiums to guard against exploiting children's immaturity.

1. If product advertising contains a premium message, care should be taken that the child's attention is focused primarily on the product. The premium message should be clearly secondary.

2. Conditions of a premium offer should be stated simply and clearly. "Mandatory" statements and disclosures should be stated in terms that can be understood by the child audience.

Safety

Imitation, exploration and experimentation are important activities to children. They are attracted to commercials in general and may imitate product demonstrations and other actions without regard to risk. Many childhood accidents and injuries occur in the home, often involving abuse or misuse of common household products.

1. Products inappropriate for use by children should not be advertised directly to children. This is especially true for products labeled, "Keep out of the reach of children." Additionally, such products should not be promoted directly to children by premiums or other means. Medications, drugs and supplemental vitamins should not be advertised to children.

2. Advertisements for children's products should show them being used by children in the appropriate age range. For instance, young children should not be shown playing with toys safe only for older children.

3. Adults should be shown supervising children when products or activities could involve an obvious safety risk. For example, using an electrical appliance or playing in or near a swimming pool.

4. Advertisements should not portray adults or children in unsafe acts, situations or conditions or in acts harmful to others. When athletic activities (such as skateboarding) are shown, proper safety equipment should be depicted.

5. Advertisements should avoid demonstrations that encourage dangerous or inappropriate use or misuse of the product. This is particularly important when the demonstration can be easily reproduced by children and features products accessible to them.

(Reprinted with the permission of the Council of Better Business Bureaus, Inc.)

5.
BROADCASTING

FCC's ROLE

The vast majority of restrictions applicable to advertising in the print and other media apply to broadcast advertising as well. However, there's one major difference between advertising on television or radio and advertising on any other medium: broadcasters operate under a license granted by the Federal Communications Commission (FCC). Congress created FCC in 1934 with the promulgation of the Communications Act. This Act was designed to regulate "interstate and foreign commerce in communication by wire and radio so as to make available, so far as possible, to all the people of the United States a rapid, efficient, nation-wide, and world-wide wire and radio communications service . . ." (The word "radio" is also deemed to apply to television.) The Act empowers FCC to "make such regulations not inconsistent with law as it may deem necessary to prevent interference between stations and to carry out the provisions of [the] Act."[1]

Currently, there are over 10,800 licensed radio and full-service television stations in the United States. More than 9,300 of these are authorized to operate commercially and are supported by advertising, the remainder being nonprofit, noncommercial stations.[2] However, even these noncommercial stations may run paid-for ads for nonprofit organizations.

FCC's main authority lies in the fact that it has the power to grant applications to construct broadcast stations or for their licensing or license renewal. The test: Whether these grants will serve the "public interest, convenience, and necessity."[3] Accordingly, broadcasters should be keenly aware of the following concerns of FCC, as they directly affect advertising:[4]

False or Misleading Advertising—The Federal Trade Commission (FTC) has the main responsibility for protecting viewers and listeners from false, deceptive, or misleading broadcasting advertising. Nevertheless, FCC expects licensed stations to be reasonably diligent in seeing that such ads are not aired. Moreover, FCC and FTC have an agreement to exchange information on matters of common interest.

Loud Commercials—FCC has a issued policy statement advising licensees that objectionably loud commercials are contrary to the public interest. According to FCC, licensees are mainly responsible for making sure that their procedures and equipment are such that objectionably loud ads are avoided.

Sublimal Ads—FCC strongly believes that the use of subliminal techniques in advertising is contrary to the public interest since—whether they're effective or not—they're intended to be deceptive.

Tobacco Ads—Federal law forbids the advertising of cigarettes and little cigars on any electronic communications medium under FCC's jurisdiction.[5] However, broadcast advertising for other tobacco products, pipes, smoking accessories, or cigarette-making machines is not forbidden.

Sponsor Identification of Advertising—A station that broadcasts paid-for material must announce that it's paid for or sponsored, and by whom.[6]

Despite its concerns with various aspects of broadcast advertising, FCC is forbidden from censoring broadcast matter. This includes advertising. Accordingly, FCC can't require its licensees to accept or reject ads for a particular product (unless Congress has passed a law forbidding its advertisement, as in the case of cigarettes). Moreover, FCC cannot take actions against "offensive advertising" unless it's found to violate a specific law or regulation.[7]

DEMISE OF NAB CODE

The broadcast advertising world was turned upside down on March 10, 1982 when the National Association of Broadcasters (NAB) suspended enforcement of the advertising standards of its television and radio code—NAB has never reinstated its code.

NAB's action came in response to a decision on March 3 by a federal judge that one of the code standards violated the Sherman Antitrust Act.[8] Specifically, it was the NAB Television Code's multiple product standard—forbidding the advertising of more than one product in a commercial lasting under sixty seconds—that was held to violate the Sherman Antitrust Act.[9]

Ruling in a suit brought by the U.S. Justice Department in 1979, Judge Harold Greene found that: "It is apparent from the fact of this standard that it has the effect of compelling some, perhaps many, advertisers to purchase more commercial time than their economic interest might dictate. In thus artificially increasing the demand for commercial time . . . the standard raises both the price of time and the revenues of the broadcasters, to the detriment of the users of the broadcast medium and the consumers of their products."

NAB has argued that compliance with the Code is voluntary to each broadcaster and that it was not an agreement in restraint of trade. But Greene held that voluntariness is no defense to a Sherman Act charge.

Perhaps foreshadowing the NAB's reaction, Greene went on to find that the Code "is not a mere set of advisory standards which subscribers may choose to ignore, but a contractual arrangement to which they are obligated to adhere."

Following lengthy negotiations between NAB and the Justice Department, a consent decree was entered whereby NAB agreed not to issue or enforce any rules that had been challenged by the government. After this decree was entered, NAB formally dissolved its Radio and Television Code Boards and halted all Code activities.[10]

NETWORK STANDARDS

The demise of the NAB Code has placed even more importance on the network's own advertising guidelines and standards. Accordingly, it is imperative that you have a good working knowledge of these guidelines and standards. To get your copy, you should write the networks at the following addresses:

1. American Broadcasting Company, Department of Broadcast Standards & Practices, 1330 Avenue of the Americas, New York, NY 10019.

2. CBS/Broadcast Group, CBS Inc., 51 West 52 Street, New York, NY 10019.

3. National Broadcasting Company, Inc., Broadcast Standards Department, 30 Rockefeller Plaza, New York, NY 10020.

It should be stressed that each of the network standards is totally separate and unrelated to the other networks' standards. Indeed, each network strives to maintain its own individual practices so as to avoid even the appearance of working in concert with its competitive networks and face a possible accusation of a Sherman Act violation. Accordingly, a commercial acceptable to one network may be unacceptable to another network. Nevertheless, there are many areas of similarity among the three networks' standards. After all, each network is subject to the same viewer pressures, deal with the same advertisers and ad agencies, and confront the same body of ad compliance decisions, rules, and regulations. The remainder of this section examines key ad compliance areas and discusses how each of the networks' standards deals with each area. This section is not intended to be an exhaustive discussion of all of the standards and/or guidelines of the networks. That is beyond the scope of this chapter. Later, the focus of this section is on many of the key areas within the network standards/guidelines.

In particular, it should be noted that CBS's written guidelines are subject to CBS's sole interpretation and may be subject to change from time to time. Thus CBS's written guidelines may not reflect current CBS practices, interpretation, or policy. If you have any questions about any of the networks' guidelines, you should contact that network's clearance departments for clarification.

Comparative Advertising

All three networks accept comparative advertising. Their standards range from CBS's one-paragraph standard to ABC's detailed two and one-half-page guidelines. CBS notes that the applicable standards are the same ones the network applies to all of its commercials. Comparative ads are acceptable, says CBS, if its claims are "truthful, fair and adequately substantiated."[11] More detailed are NBC's comparative advertising guidelines. NBC will accept comparative ads if they meet the following guidelines:

1. Competitors shall be fairly and properly identified.

2. Advertisers shall refrain from disparaging or unfairly attacking competitors, competing products, services or other industries through the use of representations or claims, direct or implied, that are false, deceptive, misleading or have the tendency to mislead.

3. The identification must be for comparison purposes and not simply to upgrade by association.

4. The advertising should compare related or similar properties or ingredients of the product, dimension to dimension, feature to feature, or wherever possible by a side-by-side demonstration.

5. The property being compared must be significant in terms of value or usefulness of the product or service to the consumer.

6. The difference in the properties being compared must be measurable and significant.

7. Pricing comparisons may raise special problems that could mislead, rather than enlighten, viewers. For certain classifications of products, retail prices may be extremely volatile, may be fixed by the retailer rather than the product advertiser, and may not only differ from outlet to outlet but from week to week within the same outlet. Where these circumstances might apply, NBC will accept commercials containing price comparisons only on a clear showing that the comparative claims accurately, fairly and substantially reflect the actual price differentials at retail outlets throughout the broadcast area, and that these price differentials are not likely to change during the period the commercial is broadcast.

8. When a commercial claim involves market relationships, other than price, which are also subject to fluctuation (such as but not limited to sales position or exclusivity), the substantiation for the claim will be considered valid only as long as the market conditions on which the claim is based continue to prevail.

9. As with all other advertising, whenever necessary, NBC may require substantiation to be updated from time to time, and may re-examine substantiation, where the need to do so is indicated as the result of a challenge or other developments.[12]

More detailed still are ABC's comparative advertising standards. Like CBS, ABC demands that such ads be "truthful and fair."[13] And many of ABC's standards are quite similar to NBC's. For example, compare the following ABC standards with the analogous NBC standards:

- Competitive products or services must be accurately and clearly identified.[14]

- False or misleading disparagement of competitive products or services shall not be used. Falsely claiming that a competitive product or service has little or no value (i.e., 'ashcanning') is not permitted.[15]

- Identification of a competitive product or service shall be for comparison purposes. Identification may not be used solely to upgrade the advertised product or service by associating it with a competitive product or service if such association creates a deceptive or misleading impression.[16]

- Comparisons and demonstrations shall be based on specific differences between the products or services advertised, comparing similar or related properties or ingredients, dimension to dimension, feature to feature.[17]

- When aspects of products or services are compared as to performance, they must be significant and meaningful to consumers.[18]

ABC goes beyond NBC's standards in several key areas. For example, ABC's standards provide much more specific guidance about commercials using superiority claims containing such words as "better" or "best."[19] In addition, ABC discusses subjective (i.e., "puffery") claims at length and even provides examples of when such claims do and do not need to be substantiated.[20] NBC's standards to not provide such detailed guidance.

False, Misleading or Deceptive Ad Claims

All three networks, of course, agree that all advertising broadcast on their networks must conform to the definitions of false, misleading, and unfair advertising as enunciated in Federal Trade Commission cases and rulings, as well as the definitions of unfair and deceptive under the Federal Trade Commission Act. According to CBS, "False, misleading or deceptive advertising claims are unacceptable."[21] NBC will not accept in its ads: "Claims or representations, direct or implied, which are false or have the tendency to deceive, mislead or misrepresent."[22] And ABC notes that all material broadcast on it facilities has to comply with governmental laws and regulations."[23] Accordingly, a good working knowledge of all applicable advertising compliance law, including FTC "law," would serve you well in dealings with the networks.

Child-Directed Ads

Advertising to children poses additional advertising compliance problems. Because of children's reduced capacity to perceive selling messages, both governmental and ad industry self-regulatory bodies have long recognized that more stringent safeguards are required for child-directed ads.

Broadcasters also recognize that they have a special responsibility to protect children from certain kinds of child-directed advertising. Accordingly, all three networks have fairly extensive guidelines for such advertising.

Before discussing these guidelines, however, it is first essential to define just what are "child-directed ads." NBC's Children's Advertising Guidelines, for example, apply to commercials: "(a) for products primarily used by children; or, (b) which are broadcast in or adjacent to children's programs; or, (c) which are designed for or have the effect of primarily appealing to children."[24]

ABC's guidelines apply to advertising that's "designed primarily for children 12 and under,"[25] and CBS has a similar definition.[26]

All three networks have very similar concerns with child-directed ads. For example, they all consider as unacceptable: "exhortative language"; "exaggeration and distortion" of product attributes (e.g., toys); "frightening" commercials; ads that use peer pressure to sell; use of the words "only" or "just" in reference to price; commercials for nonprescription medications and/or vitamins; and commercials using celebrities or authority figures as endorsers.[27] However, there exist differences in approach among the networks in some major areas. For example, ABC flatly considers competitive and superiority claims in child-directed ads to be unacceptable.[28] Both CBS and NBC, however, will consider such claims on a case-by-case basis.[29]

In addition, all three networks have additional guidelines applicable to advertising for toys and food. Similar concerns guide all three broadcasters. For example, they all require that any view of a toy or how it works is one that a child must be "reasonably capable of reproducing."[30]

As regards food advertising directed to children, all three networks require such ads to "be in accord with the commonly accepted principles of good eating." In addition, all three networks have similar guidelines requiring at least one audio and one video showing a balanced meal in breakfast commercials. In addition, they all have guidelines for such foods that, essentially, forbid suggestions of indiscriminate or immoderate use of such foods.[31]

Both ABC and NBC have similar guidelines concerning children's premiums and offers. These guidelines, for example:

- Forbid the use of fantasy, animation, stock footage or real-life counterparts with such ads;
- Require the inclusion of such disclosures as price, offer dates and separate purchase requirements in the audio portion of the ad;
- Require simultaneous audio and video disclosure of conditions attached to "free" offers.[32]

Professional Ads

All three networks accept advertising for professional services. CBS will accept "lawful advertising for accountants, chiropractors, dentists, lawyers, physicians, psychologists and other recognized and established professionals."[33] ABC permits such ads for "members of the medical and legal professions."[34] NBC does not accept ads "for professional services which do not comply with applicable law or ethical codes," implying that those that do comply would be acceptable.[35]

What standards do the networks apply? CBS won't accept ads containing "professional advice of the kind that, under sound practice, would be given only within the context of an established practitioner-client relationship."[36] ABC's Professional Advertising Guidelines are in two sections: Medical and Legal. Both sections require that ads:

- Comply with federal, state, and local rules and ABC policy;
- Comply with stringent standards of taste and copy documentation;
- Not be aired when there's a substantial youthful audience;
- Avoid "hard-sell" techniques;
- Not play on viewers' fears or insecurities; and
- Must be approved by the network's New York Broadcast Standards and Practices department.[37]

In addition, under the medical ad guidelines, words such as "safe" or "harmless" are not acceptable. And the legal ad guidelines list the elements of permissible content of the ad (e.g., basic factual data such as name, address, and telephone number).[38]

Contests/Sweepstakes

All three networks allow the advertising of contests by advertisers and forbid the advertising of lotteries—except those conducted by the state. Reason: Federal law forbids the broadcast of ads concerning lotteries. FTC defines a lottery at 16 C.F.R. 15.57 as the combination of chance, consideration and a prize. In addition, you should also be aware that the states have their own laws concerning sweepstakes and contests. (See, generally, Chapter 8.)

Accordingly, you must research the applicable federal and state laws involving sweepstakes and contests first before you will be ready to submit your proposed commercial for network review. However, before your proposed contest can air, you must submit a host of detailed information to the network's Broadcast Standards and Practices Department for approval. (CBS won't air such spots unless they've first been approved by their Commercial Clearance and Law Departments).[39] It is highly recommended (required by ABC) that you submit all such information *before* production of the commercial.

What kind of information does the network wish to see? CBS has prepared a four-page "Contests/Sweepstakes Questionnaire" that seeks a wide variety of data about the proposed commercial. For example, CBS needs to know the final entry date, planned airdates for the spots, whether all prizes will be awarded and specific eligibility requirements. In addition to a completed contest questionnaire, CBS requires two copies each of (1) your contest's official rules, (2) the actual entry blank and/or playing piece, (3) a detailed statement of all prizes to be awarded, and (4) any applicable newspaper and magazine ads and point-of-sale displays. And, of course, don't forget to submit a copy of the commercial itself for CBS's review![40] NBC similarly requires submission of a completed questionnaire, as well as a complete copy of the rules, an entry blank, promotional material and such published information about the contest as newspaper ads.[41] ABC needs to review all details of a proposed contest, an entry blank or game card, complete rules, and list of prizes.[42]

The watchword at all three networks is complete disclosure of a wide variety of pertinent information. Each network has devised its own method, and evolved its own guidelines, to achieve that end. If you, or your client, is planning to advertise a contest or sweepstakes on a network, it is imperative that you contact the network's Broadcast Standards and Practices or Commercial Clearance Department as early in the planning stages of your ad as possible. You should obtain the latest copies of their guidelines, questionnaires, and other applicable documents. Only after reviewing these documents and discussing your proposed ad with the network, can you make a sound compliance decision. (See, generally, Chapter 8.)

Alcoholic Beverages

The advertising of beer and wine is acceptable at all three networks, subject to federal and local laws. Commercials for hard liquor (i.e., distilled spirits such as whiskey, vodka and rum) are forbidden.[43]

While wine and beer ads are acceptable, there are many network requirements of which an advertiser must be aware. For example, all three networks consider unacceptable beer and wine ads that:

- Encourage the use of such beverages by young people;
- Depict the use of such beverages in situations that may be hazardous or require a high level of alertness (e.g., driving);
- Contain statements or implications concerning increased potency or alcoholic content (e.g., "extra strength").[44]

Both NBC and ABC specifically forbid on-camera consumption of wine or beer.[45] While CBS does not, apparently, specifically forbid such on-camera representations, it does forbid even implied references to excessive consumption and only accepts ads for beer and wine that are "presented tastefully."[46] Thus, ads featuring on-camera consumption would face a rigorous review by CBS's Clearance Department.

Finally, it should be recognized that the entire area of alcoholic beverage advertising is in a state of tremendous uncertainty and flux. Groups such as Mothers Against Drunk Driving (MADD) have launched a highly effective campaign against the problem of drunken driving. There have been proposals to forbid the use of celebrities and sports figures in wine and beer ads and even suggestions to ban televised wine and beer ads altogether. Accordingly, standards that have prevailed for years may become obsolete overnight. Thus, if you, or your client, plan to advertise wine or beer on television, you should maintain regular contact with the network(s) on which your ad(s) will appear. Otherwise you might face an unwelcome— and costly—surprise when you submit a proposed commercial that was formerly acceptable but no longer is. (See Chapter 9.)

Multiple Product Announcements

Multiple product announcements are those that contain advertising for two or more products. The now-defunct NAB Code, which was followed by the networks, used to forbid the advertisement of more than one product in a commercial lasting less than sixty seconds.[47] However, it was that standard that was held to violate the Sherman Antitrust Act in the case of *U.S. v. NAB.*[48]

Current network guidelines allow multiple product announcements. CBS and NBC allow as many as two products to be advertised in a sixty-second commercial.[49] Moreover, CBS will allow ads for more than one product in a thirty-second spot so long as the announcement is "integrated." CBS considers an announcement integrated if—"the products or services are related and interwoven within the framework of the announcement, and the voice(s), setting, background and continuity are used consistently throughout so as to appear to a viewer as a single message."[50]

NBC will also allow multiple product announcements in commercials briefer than sixty seconds so long as the ad "presents the products or services of a primary and secondary advertiser."[51]

ABC allows the integrated advertising of two or more products or services in thirty-second ads. In addition, ABC allowed such ads on an experimental basis through September 1985 in "non-integrated two-product announcements."[52]

Unacceptable Products or Services

There are certain products and services that the networks refuse to be allowed to be advertised. (As we've seen, no network allows ads for hard liquor.) NBC, for example, will not allow ads for the following products or services:

1. Cigarettes.
2. Hard liquor.
3. Firearms, fireworks, ammunition and other weapons.
4. Presentations promoting a belief in the efficacy of fortune telling, astrology, phrenology, palm reading, numerology, mind reading, character reading or other occult pursuits.
5. Tip sheets and race track publications seeking to advertise for the purpose of giving odds or promoting betting. . . .
6. The sale of franchises.
7. Matrimonial, escort or dating services.
8. Contraceptives.
9. Adult or Sex Magazines.
10. X-rated Movies.
11. Abortion Services.
12. Ethical Drugs.
13. Anti-Law Enforcement Devices.[53]

ABC and CBS also do not allow ads for cigarettes (pursuant to 15 U.S.C. 1335), or astrology, fortune telling and similar services.[54]

If you are aware that one network does not allow advertisements for your product, you should not assume that the other networks also follow suit. Pregnancy test kits are one example of this. CBS doesn't accept ads for such products.[55] ABC, on the other hand, will allow ads for these products so long as, among other things, they're "restrained and inoffensive," avoid "graphic representations," and do not play on people's "fears and insecurities."[56]

Substantiation

All three networks require that you substantiate all of your material claims prior to airing. For example, CBS requires that all claims must be "fully substantiated" before approval is granted.[57] NBC requires "substantiation for all material claims and authentication of all demonstrations and testimonial statements."[58] According to ABC, "When affirmative claims are made for a product or service, the advertiser must submit substantiation or documentation providing a reasonable basis for the claims."[59] ABC's guidelines give many more specifics as to methodological questions relating to research done in substantiating claims.[60] If you are unsure as to whether a proposed television commercial contains claims that must be substantiated and what form that substantiation should take, you should contact the network's broadcast standards and practices or commercial clearance department *before* you conduct any claims research. (See, also, Chapter 2.)

Other Areas

There are many other areas discussed—often at length and in great detail —in the various networks's standards and guidelines. For example, NBC has separate guidelines (in addition to its advertising standards) concerning ads for children, health care products, personal products, alcohol products, products that control serum cholesterol, weight reduction, and gambling, betting, lotteries and games of chance. Your best compliance approach is to contact the network(s) while your commercial is still in the planning stage and obtain your own copy of their guidelines. Then you should acquire a *thorough working knowledge* of those areas that could affect your ad.

HOW TO CHALLENGE NETWORK COMMERCIALS

Any commercial aired on ABC, CBS, or NBC can be challenged.[61] The challenges are handled by each network's Broadcast Standards and Practices Department, which also reviews all commercial material before it is aired. ABC and NBC have written challenge procedures; CBS also has procedures, but they are unwritten.

Who May Challenge and Why

Most challenges are made by competing advertisers. The great majority of commercials challenged are comparative. For example, 93 percent of all commercials challenged at ABC in 1981 were comparative. The most frequent challenge, of course, is made by a competitor whose product is unfavorably compared, either explicitly or implicitly, to the advertiser's product. Challenges are also sometimes filed by public officials and organizations, trade associations, consumer groups, disgruntled customers and individual viewers.

Commercials are challenged because they are allegedly false, deceptive, or unfair; violate federal, state, or local laws or regulations; and/or violate network policies. Typically, challenges contend that a comparative ad distorts or exaggerates differences between competitive products or services, lacks adequate substantiation for the claims made, or creates a false impression. A recurring issue is whether an ad communicates an implied claim and, if so, whether that claim has been supported by the advertiser.

How to Use the Challenge Procedures

The networks require that a challenge be made in writing in a form which permits it, along with any supporting data, to be transmitted to the challenged advertiser for a response.

If the challenger reasonably considers any challenge material to be confidential, the challenger can make a specific designation of that material; the networks will honor the request that such material not be transmitted. If that request is considered unreasonable because the material doesn't appear to be truly confidential, the challenge may not be transmitted by ABC and CBS; NBC will transmit the challenge, but will take into account the disadvantage placed upon the advertiser.

All challenges are reviewed by each network's Broadcast Standards Department. If, in the opinion of the Department at ABC or CBS, the challenge appears to have merit, it will be sent to the challenged advertiser for a response; NBC will transmit the challenge under all circumstances. A challenge will be dismissed outright if it's not considered substantive or involves advertising that has completed its schedule. If a challenge is made to advertising which has not yet been approved, the substantive matters raised will generally be considered during the clearance process.

When a challenge is transmitted, ABC normally calls for the response to be due within fourteen days. However, a different deadline may be established if the circumstances warrant. CBS tries for a shorter response time. The three networks will speed up the process if a matter is urgent or relatively simple, and will grant reasonable requests for extensions of time for good cause.

Each of the networks will maintain the confidentiality of the substantiation originally submitted by the challenged advertiser to support the claims made in the advertising. Advertisers, though, are encouraged by the networks to submit a response, with supporting data, in a form which can be transmitted to the challenger.

The networks will generally permit a challenged commercial to continue to run until a response is received and the challenge is fully resolved. However, in extraordinary circumstances, approval may be withdrawn or airing may be suspended immediately after receipt of a challenge. Some commercials are accepted "subject to challenge"; this indicates borderline approval, and either withdrawal of approval upon receipt of a responsible complaint or a short deadline for response to a challenge. If approval is withdrawn or suspended, the advertiser may still proceed with the challenge and try to persuade the network to change its mind and reinstate the advertising.

Once the advertiser's response is received, the procedure at the networks varies. ABC will review it, and will only pass it on to the challenger for rebuttal if this would appear to be useful, e.g., if more information is needed, new arguments have been made, or new issues have been raised.

ABC uses the same criteria in deciding whether to transmit the challenger's rebuttal and later correspondence. NBC will ask the advertiser to respond directly to the challenger; it will make a decision on the challenge once enough information has been obtained. CBS's procedure is more formalized. Each side generally is given a chance to respond to and rebut the other side.

Each network may request a meeting with the challenger and/or advertiser. The networks may seek to encourage the parties to obtain a resolution from an acceptable third party if they believe that they do not have the expertise necessary to make a judgment.

Role of Broadcast Standards Departments

At the end of the process, the networks' Broadcast Standards Departments make independent decisions to resolve challenges. Since they act independently, they each may reach a different judgment on the same challenge. They will allow a challenged commercial to run unless: (1) it is voluntarily withdrawn by the challenged advertiser; (2) the challenged advertiser refuses to cooperate with the challenge procedures; or (3) a determination is made against the challenged advertiser by the network, by a third party to whom the matter has been referred, or by a government agency or an appropriate court, with finality. A brief letter setting forth the decision is usually sent to each side. If changes are sought in the challenged ad, network practice is to advise the challenger of that fact without detailing the requested changes.

Pros and Cons of Network Challenge

In addition to filing a network challenge against allegedly false or otherwise inappropriate advertising, a complaint can be filed with NAD (see, generally, Chapter 4) or FTC (see, generally, Chapter 1). Also, challenges can be made with individual stations or station groups which have aired a commercial; and suit can be filed against false comparative advertising under Section 43(a) of the federal Lanham Act (see, generally, Chapter 3) or under state laws. These actions can be taken separately or in any combination. Following are the pros and cons of filing a network challenge.

1. Network challenges are usually resolved more quickly than the other types of complaints (other than individual station challenges). They're less expensive to make and are more informal. Moreover, they're resolved by professionals who are highly experienced with the advertising in general and with network advertising in particular.

A Lanham Act suit can produce the fastest result if the federal district court or court of appeals is willing to grant a temporary restraining order or a preliminary injunction. However, there are drawbacks to a private civil action. There are difficult elements of proof. If a temporary restraining order or a preliminary injunction is not obtained, discovery is likely to be lengthy, time-consuming and expensive. The discovery process may give each party access to the other's marketing information and other sensitive data. Employees may be requested to give depositions. Outside experts may be required to make analyses and testify.

District court judges are not as familiar with advertising as Broadcast Standards personnel. They generally do not apply their own "expertise" to identify implied claims, for example—they rely on consumer perception surveys and expert testimony. See, e.g., *R. J. Reynolds Tobacco Co. v. Loew's Theatres, Inc.*[62] Interestingly, district court judges have taken into consideration network decisions. In *McNeilab, Inc. v. AHP Corp.*,[63] for example, the court quoted from ABC's report objecting to the contested commercial and stated that the defendant had reason to be aware of the "highly questionable" nature of its approach to advertising its product. ABC's concerns were also noted in *Vidal Sassoon, Inc. v. Bristol-Myers Co.*[64]

2. Network challenges can be based on alleged violations of company policies, such as taste standards, as well as allegations of falsity or deceptiveness. NAD will only consider complaints involving truth and accuracy. (However, its appellate arm—the National Advertising Review Board (NARB)—will consider complaints involving the taste, morality, or social responsibility of advertising in general). FTC will only consider alleged violations of the FTC Act. Lanham Act suits must contain a number of allegations necessary to state a claim upon which relief can be granted, such as, that the plaintiff has been or is likely to be injured as a result of the false advertising.

3. If a network challenge is upheld, the network advertising will be withdrawn from the entire network, including all owned-and-operated and affiliated stations. The affiliated stations—as well as independent stations—are free, however, to run locally placed commercials, even if those commercials have been successfully challenged on a network. Challenges with individual stations can be filed. While usually expeditious, they only affect the broadcast schedule of that station.

4. Filing a challenge with the networks has its limitations. The networks do not have subpoena power or other discovery procedures; they must rely on the information voluntarily submitted by the parties. This information, of course, may not tell the whole story. The judicial rules of evidence and due process do not apply. There is no hearing at which both sides appear and present arguments. Sanctions are limited. No monetary damages are permitted. The networks' ultimate sanction is to refuse to carry the challenged ad. The networks may reach different results on the same matter.

5. Successfully challenging a network commercial is generally no easy matter. If the commercial has aired, the network has already cleared it; the challenger is asking the network to revoke clearance, based on the network's own standards. The network is being asked, in essence, to change its mind.

6. The networks have as broad discretion in ruling on challenges as they do in reviewing proposed commercials. They reserve the right to accept or

reject, at any time, advertising for any product or service for broadcast over their facilities. In *CBS Inc. v. Democratic Nat'l Committee*,[65] the U.S. Supreme Court ruled that there is no "private right of access" to the broadcast media. (The issue in that case involved the network's policy of not selling advertising time to individuals or groups wishing to speak out on controversial issues of public importance, which the court resolved in favor of the networks. Nevertheless, the opinion's broad language affirming the broad discretion given to broadcast licensees to meet their "public trustee obligations" applies to commercial as well as editorial advertising.) Within each network, an appeal can be made to the corporate vice president to whom Broadcast Standards reports. Broadcast Standards can also be requested to reconsider a decision based on new information, such as new testing. In addition, a challenger can take the challenge to another forum.

Advice to Challengers

Your challenge should present arguments and facts as strongly as possible. It should be as well-written, organized, and supported as a legal brief. It doesn't have to be lengthy—Broadcast Standards Departments have no need for leisure reading matter, with over 50,000 commercials in storyboard, script or final form, and many program scripts and other material to review each year. Nevertheless, your challenge should be complete.

If comparative product testing has been conducted to disprove a claim in a commercial, the protocol and results should be substantiated.

Particular network standards and guidelines, or governmental laws or regulations, which are alleged to be violated, should be specified.

Both the challenger and the advertiser should permit as much information as feasible to be transmitted to the opposing side. The process gets bogged down considerably when the parties do not have the benefit of informed adversarial comment.

One last point is worth emphasizing: It is prudent to retain competent counsel to prosecute a challenge.

NOTES

1. Communications Act of 1934.
2. FCC Publication 8310-100, Jan. 1985.
3. Communications Act of 1934.
4. See generally FCC Publication 8310-100, Jan. 1985.
5. 15 U.S.C. §§1331-1340.
6. Communications Act of 1934, §317.
7. FCC Publication 8310-100, Jan. 1985.
8. *U.S. v. National Association of Broadcasters*, Civ. Action #79-1549, U.S. District Court for District of Columbia, Opinion of Greene, J. on cross-motion for summary judgement, March 3, 1982. See, generally, *Advertising Compliance Service*, Tab #14, Broadcasting, Article #1.

9. The Sherman Antitrust Act, c. 647, 26 Stat. 209, is now codified at 15 U.S.C. §§1-7, as amended. See, generally, Oppenheim & Weston, *Federal Antitrust Laws*, Ch. 5, "Trade Association Activities of Antitrust Significance," 3rd. ed., West, 1968.

10. *Do's and Dont's in Advertising Copy*, Section 3, Broadcasting, page 1.

11. *CBS Television Network Advertising Guidelines* (CBS Guidelines), CTN 13; excerpts from the CBS Guidelines appearing in this book are reprinted with permission of CBS Inc. © 1985 CBS Inc. All Rights Reserved.

12. *NBC Broadcast Standards for Television* (NBC Standards), p. 13; excerpts from the NBC Standards appearing in this book are reprinted courtesy of the National Broadcasting Co. Inc. © 1985 The National Broadcasting Company, Inc. All Rights Reserved.

13. *ABC Advertising Standards and Guidelines* (ABC Guidelines), §II, p. 6; excerpts from the ABC Guidelines appearing in this book are reprinted with permission of American Broadcasting Companies, Inc.

14. *ABC Guidelines*, §II, p. 7, 1(A).

15. *ABC Guidelines*, §II, p. 7, 1(C).

16. *ABC Guidelines*, §II, p. 7, 1(B).

17. *ABC Guidelines*, §II, p. 7, 2(A).

18. *ABC Guidelines*, §II, p. 7, 2(B).

19. *ABC Guidelines*, §II, p. 7, 2(E).

20. *ABC Guidelines*, §II, p. 7, 2(E), (3), and (4).

21. *CBS Guidelines*, CTN 3.

22. *NBC Standards*, p. 21.

23. *ABC Standards*, §1, p. 1.

24. *NBC Children's Advertising Guidelines*, p. 1.

25. *ABC Standards*, §I, p. 3.

26. *CBS Guidelines*, CTN 8.

27. *CBS Guidelines*, CTN 8; *NBC Children's Advertising Guidelines*, p. 1 & 2; *ABC Guidelines*, §II, pp. 2-3.

28. *ABC Guidelines*, §II, p. 3.

29. *CBS Guidelines*, CTN 9; *NBC Children's Advertising Guidelines*, p. 2.

30. *ABC Guidelines*, §II, p. 4; *CBS Guidelines*, CTN 10; *NBC Children's Advertising Guidelines*, p. 3.

31. *ABC Guidelines*, §II, p. 5; *CBS Guidelines* CTN 10; *NBC Children's Advertising Guidelines*, p. 4.

32. *ABC Guidelines*, §II, p. 5; *NBC Children's Advertising Guidelines*, p. 4.

33. *CBS Guidelines*, CTN 32.

34. *ABC Guidelines*, §I, p. 9.

35. *NBC Standards*, p. 22.

36. *CBS Guidelines*, CTN 32.

37. *ABC Guidelines*, §II, pp. 26-27.

38. *ABC Guidelines*, §II, p. 27.

39. *CBS Guidelines*, CTN 14.

40. *CBS Guidelines*, CTN 14.

41. *NBC Standards*, p. 24.

42. *ABC Guidelines*, §II, p. 9.

43. *ABC Guidelines*, §II, p. 1; *CBS Guidelines*, CTN 5; *NBC Alcohol Products Advertising Guidelines*, p. 12.

44. *ABC Guidelines,* §II, p. 1; *CBS Guidelines,* CTN 5; *NBC Alcohol Products Advertising Guidelines,* p. 12.

45. *ABC Guidelines,* §II, p. 1; *NBC Alcohol Products Advertising Guidelines,* p. 12.

46. *CBS Guidelines,* CTN 5.

47. *The National Association of Broadcasters' Television Code,* part XIV, #5, suspended March 1982.

48. See *Advertising Compliance Service,* Tab #14, Broadcasting, Article #1.

49. *CBS Guidelines,* CTN 22; *NBC Standards,* p. 20.

50. *CBS Guidelines,* CTN 22.

51. *NBC Standards,* p. 20.

52. *ABC Standards,* §I, p. 7-A.

53. *NBC Standards,* p. 22.

54. *ABC Standards,* §I, p. 6; *CBS Guidelines,* CTN 41.

55. *CBS Guidelines,* CTN 41.

56. *ABC Guidelines,* §II, p. 23.

57. *CBS Guidelines,* CTN 3.

58. *NBC Standards,* p. 12.

59. *ABC Standards,* §1, p. 2.

60. *ABC Guidelines,* §II, p. 29.

61. This section, "How to Challenge Network Commercials," is adapted from an article appearing in *Advertising Compliance Service,* Tab #14, Broadcasting Article #6, "Challenging Network Commercials," by Jeffrey S. Edelstein, an associate with Hall, Dickler, Lawler, Kent & Howley, and the former Director of Broadcast Standards and Practices of the American Broadcasting Company.

62. 511 F. Supp. 867, 876 (SDNY 1980).

63. 501 F. Supp. 517, 531 (SDNY 1980).

64. 661 F.2d 272 (2d Cir. 1981).

65. 412 U.S. 94 (1973).

6.
NEW MEDIA: NEW AD COMPLIANCE CHALLENGES

The task of the advertiser and its ad agency is not as easy as it once was. Before the communications revolution, the choice of where to place an ad was limited to the broadcast, radio, and print media. Today, that choice is expanding to include such new electronic media as cable television, satellite television, low-power television, cabletext, videotex, teletext, and videodisc merchandise catalogs.

As audiences continue their migration to these new media—often at the expense of the "old" media—advertisers and ad agencies are learning how best to use these new advertising channels. What they're discovering is the promise and pitfalls of advertising on the new media. The promise is the chance to try brand-new types of advertising, such as "informercials," to reach audiences that are deserting the old media. Among the pitfalls is the great unknown factor of how such regulatory bodies as the Federal Trade Commission (FTC) and the Federal Communications Commission (FCC) will regulate advertising on these media.

FTC'S AND FCC'S ROLES

The starting point for examining FTC's role in regulating advertising on the new media is Section 5 of the Federal Trade Commission Act. Section 5 empowers FTC to issue "cease-and-desist orders" that require any "person, partnership or corporation" from "using any unfair method of competition or unfair or deceptive act or practice in commerce."[1] In addition, other provisions of the FTC Act govern FTC's advertising compliance role. (See, generally, Chapter 1.) Over the years, many FTC and judicial decisions have defined the key terms, "unfairness" and "deception." Accordingly, if you plan to advertise on the new media, you should study the pertinent FTC cases that, so far, have largely dealt with advertising on the "old media." In determining what is "deceptive" and/or "unfair" on cable television, the cases deciding these issues in the context of broadcast television are nevertheless instructive. Reason: Both media are similar to the extent that they both offer programming, and advertising, that's intended to be viewed by audiences on their television screens. The different ways that those messages reach screens may properly form the basis for different types of regulation, (such as licensing and registration) by FCC. But the end result, and effect, on viewers of these messages is the same, whether they got there via the airwaves or through a cable.

Nevertheless, advertising regulatory differences will no doubt arise. For example, FTC is likely to confront advertising compliance issues involving cable TV that it probably will not face on broadcast television. The main reason for this is that each of the three networks have codified fairly extensive advertising guidelines that establish, to a great degree, what is appropriate in a network commercial. The guidelines are enforced by the three networks' commercial clearance departments. These departments determine the suitability of commercials broadcast on the network. For example, all three networks have laid out specific time standards for commercials. Generally, advertisers have used various commercial lengths up to sixty seconds, with thirty- and sixty-second spots being the most prevalent. (See, generally, Chapter 5.)

Cable television, on the other hand, does not have an analogous system to determine the acceptability of the commercial messages appearing in that medium. While there has been some talk in the cable industry about establishing some advertising guidelines, industry-wide standards have not yet been adopted, if they ever will be. The advertising that appears on the cable stations is pretty much left to the discretion of the cable system operators.

Nevertheless, these systems are not operating on an entirely clean slate. The vast majority of commercials of national and large regional advertisers have already been cleared by one of the three networks. This fact again points up the need to be fully conversant with the networks' advertising guidelines and clearance procedures. Moreover, FTC's position is that commercials appearing on cable television are subject to FTC authority.[2] So, a sound working knowledge of FTC's "deception" and "unfairness" jurisdiction is well advised.

While FCC plays a role in the regulation of cable television, its involvement in advertising compliance issues is a minor one. FCC rules affecting advertising include ones involving (1) cablecasts for public office (i.e., "political advertising"), (2) the Fairness Doctrine (relative to "advocacy advertising"), (3) sponsorship identification, and (4) a ban on lotteries.[3] Otherwise, FCC defers, and probably would continue to do so, to FTC's expertise in ad compliance issues involving cable television.

NEW ISSUES INVOLVING CABLE ADS

While FCC's role in the regulation of advertising on cable television is minor, its *potential* impact on future cable advertising is great. The reason can be found in the fact that FCC has placed major regulatory restraints on broadcast television but, so far, has not done so on cable television. Freed from the extensive regulatory restraints found in broadcast television, cable has attracted such innovative advertising/marketing techniques as: (1) direct-response advertising, (2) "informercials" (i.e., longer-form commercials running ninety seconds and more, (3) cable shipping programming services, and (4) interactive cable television (e.g., QUBE), videotext, teletext, and other new technologies.

Along with increased usage of these new advertising and marketing techniques will come new advertising compliance issues. The reward for those cable advertising and marketing professions who devote some time now in thinking through some of these issues will be to help avoid compliance problems later.

One of the major new forms of commercial to appear on cable is the "informercial." Essentially, these are longer-form commercials that generally run from around ninety seconds to ten minutes. The marketing motivation behind this form of commercial is the recognition that the typical thirty- or sixty-second spot appearing on broadcast television is often not the best way to sell a product or service. It's usually too difficult, for example, to show consumers in these short spots how a product works or provide information on the safe usage of a product. In addition, this short format is clearly inferior in demonstrating the virtues, or the operation, of more complicated products. The longer-form "informercial," however, fits the bill for advertisers and marketers of these products.

If you plan to advertise on cable and are instructing your ad agency (or your in-house creatives) to develop an informercial for your product or service, you should pay close attention to several potential problem areas. For example, since your commercial will contain many more facts—and thus many more "advertising claims"—you should be sure you identify all of those claims and have on hand adequate substantiation for each one *before* your informercial airs. Otherwise, your ad may run afoul of FTC's advertising substantiation program. (See, generally, Chapter 2.) Thus, failure to do this could lead to a complaint by FTC challenging your ad or to an investigation by the National Advertising Division (NAD).

If you decide to give viewers a demonstration of product usage or safety in your informercial, you should instruct your legal department to review carefully the proposed storyboards. Aside from the garden variety ad compliance problems, there may be potential products liability or personal injury problems lurking in your ad copy that they can quickly ferret out. In many cases, they should be able to recommend changes in the ad copy to avoid such problems.

Your attorneys should also scrutinize such informercials for whether the claims you make give rise to any warranties under federal and applicable state laws. If your informercial specifically offers a warranty, you should make sure that that warranty complies with the federal Magnuson-Moss Warranty Act.

Another important regulatory issue involving informercials is whether the sponsor's name should be disclosed in the commercial. Reason: A potential problem could arise if your informercial does not make it clear that it is a *commercial* and not a mini-program of some sort whose purpose is to dispense useful information about a particular product or service.

Another form of commercial that is growing in popularity on cable television is "adverprograms." An adverprogram is an ad whose content relates to, or complements, a particular program. For example, a program on cooking might include one-minute "adverprograms" interlaced throughout the show describing how a particular company's food products might be used in certain recipes featured on the show. A potential problem with such ads is the resultant blurring of the lines between programming and commercials. Nevertheless, so long as cable tv allows such commercials, they should be safe, and rewarding, to use as long as these ads are scrutinized as you would any ad for potential legal problems.

Other forms of electronic media are still in their infancy in terms of being marketed to the public. As they become more profitable and as advertising dollars help pay the way for their growth, new ad compliance issues will arise. For example, take the new media known by such names as "teletext" and "videotext." Essentially, these new media enable printed data to be received by the home tv set. One form of this media enables interaction between the viewer and the tv series. Services can range from banking at home to mail order services to shopping at home. Shopping at home may involve the use of video merchandise catalogues, whereby a viewer would browse through an electronic catalogue by punching a keyboard. A potential regulatory issue involves the availability (or disclosures to that effect) of warranty information pursuant to the Magnuson-Moss Warranty Act. In addition, the usual issues of "deception," and/or "unfairness" as well as prior substantiation of claims also arise in the context of these ads as it would for ordinary print mail-order catalogs.

NOTES

1. FTC Act, Section 5(a)(1).
2. See *Advertising Compliance Service*, Tab #15, New Media, Article #1.
3. FCC Information Bulletin, *Cable Television*, 6/84, p. 12.

7.
PROFESSIONAL ADVERTISING

If you, or one of your clients, is a professional, you should be aware of the important changes in professional advertising compliance over the past decade. Increasingly, attorneys, doctors, dentists, pharmacists and other professionals have been using advertising to attract clientele. However, these professionals are finding confusing, and often conflicting, ad compliance standards in their preadvertising research. This chapter focuses on the impact of several landmark cases on professional advertising, the role of such national licensing authorities as the American Bar Association, the role of state licensing authorities, and the Federal Trade Commission's role.

HISTORICAL BACKGROUND

Abraham Lincoln was given a nickname that pretty well summed up what his peers thought of him: "Honest" Abe. Yet when he was an attorney, Honest Abe Lincoln placed an ad in a newspaper advertising his practice and promising to attend to all legal business entrusted to him and his partner "with promptness and fidelity."[1] As the Federal Trade Commission staff noted in a recent report to the Commission, "A century later, Lincoln's advertisement might have attracted more than clients. He might have faced a bar association complaint charging him with unethical conduct. The penalty could have been quite severe, perhaps a recommendation for suspension from the practice of law."[2]

While the first state to adopt an ethical code for attorneys, Alabama, explicitly allowed newspaper ads, other states forbade the practice.[3] For example, in the late nineteenth century, a Denver, Colorado attorney was suspended for six months by the state Supreme Court for a newspaper ad that said: "Divorces legally obtained very quietly, good everywhere."[4] The court noted in this frequently cited opinion, "The ethics of the legal profession forbid that an attorney should advertise his talents or his skills as a shopkeeper advertises his wares."[5]

The American Bar Association echoed this sentiment on August 27, 1908, when it published its position on attorney advertising in its Canons of Professional Ethics: "But solicitation of business by circulars or advertisements, or by personal communications, or interviews, not warranted by personal relations, is unprofessional."[6]

While some inroads on this broad prohibition were made over the next sixty-nine years, it was not until 1977 that major change occurred in attorney advertising. The breakthrough came in the landmark decision of the United States Supreme Court in the case of *Bates v. State Bar*.[7] In that case, the High Court upheld the First Amendment right of attorneys to advertise their services. This lifted the nearly seventy-year-old ban on attorney advertising that had existed since 1908. While *Bates* only involved lawyer advertising, it paved the way for advertising by all professionals.

It should be emphasized, however, that Bates did not grant carte blanche privileges to attorneys to advertise in any place or manner they choose. The Court stressed that attorney advertising must not be false, deceptive or misleading. As the Court noted: "As with other varieties of speech, it follows as well that there may be reasonable restrictions on the time, place and manner of advertising."[8]

One of the problems with the *Bates* decision is not so much what it said, but what it left unstated. After decades of denouncing lawyer advertising as unethical or worse, state bar associations greeted *Bates* with little enthusiasm. Not used to the concept of attorney advertising, they tended to limit *Bates* to its facts, essentially allowing price advertising of certain routine legal services.

The Supreme Court again spoke on the issue in 1978. In *Ohralik v. Ohio State Bar Association*, the question involved direct solicitation, the Court noting that the truthful restrained advertising of the prices of routine legal services would not be considered unprofessional conduct. The Court also indicated that a state would have a legitimate interest in protecting the public from attorney advertising that involved such conduct as fraud, undue influence, or intimidation. As Justice Thurgood Marshall noted in his concurring opinion in *Ohralik*:

By discussing the origin and impact of the nonsolicitation rules, I do not mean to belittle those obviously substantial interests that the State has in regulating attorneys to protect the public from fraud, deceit, misrepresentation, overreaching, undue influence and invasions of privacy. But where honest, unpressed 'commercial' solicitation is involved—a situation not presented in either of these cases—I believe it is open to doubt whether the State's interests are sufficiently compelling to warrant the restriction on the free flow of information which results from a sweeping nonsolicitation rule and against which the First Amendment ordinarily protects.[9]

The Supreme Court offered further guidance in a second landmark lawyer advertising case, *In re R.M.J.*[10] The Missouri Supreme Court's Advisory Committee had brought disbarment proceedings against an attorney for violating certain attorney advertising regulations in the Missouri Code of Responsibility. The attorney was charged with among other things, violating that code by using direct mail and advertising his expertise in areas of practice (e.g., "personal injury") that deviated from the exact wording set forth in the code. The Missouri Supreme Court upheld the constitutional validity of these rules and reprimanded the lawyer. The U.S. Supreme Court, however, reversed this decision. In doing so, the Court provided its most clearly worded language yet to indicate the broad parameters of an attorney's—and by inference any professional's—right to advertise:

Truthful advertising related to lawful activities is entitled to the protection of the First Amendment. But when the particular content or method of the advertising suggests that it is inherently misleading or when experience has proved that in fact such advertising is subject to abuse, the States may impose appropriate restrictions. Misleading advertising may be prohibited entirely. But the States may not place an absolute prohibition on certain types of potentially misleading information, e.g., a listing of areas of practice, if the information also may be presented in a way that is not deceptive. Thus, the Court in *Bates* suggested that the remedy in the first instance is not necessarily a prohibition but preferably a requirement of disclaimers or explanation. . . . Although the potential for deception and confusion is particularly strong in the context of advertising professional services, restrictions upon such advertising may be no broader than reasonably necessary to prevent the deception.

Even when a communication is not misleading, the State retains some authority to regulate. But the state must assert a substantial interest and the interference with speech must be in proportion to the interest served. . . . Restrictions must be narrowly drawn, and the State lawfully may regulate only to the extent regulation furthers the State's substantial interest."[11]

The U.S. Supreme Court continues to show little patience for state restrictions on an attorney's right to advertise truthfully in its most recent landmark attorney advertising ruling of *Zauderer v. Office of Disciplinary Counsel of the Supreme Court of Ohio.*[12] Under the High Court ruling, attorneys may use accurate illustrations on their ads as well as nondeceptive advertisements that openly solicit specific types of clients. However, the decision requires some attorneys' ads to contain certain disclosures. Here are the details of this important ruling:

Philip Q. Zauderer is an attorney whose legal practice is in Columbus, Ohio. Since 1981, he placed ads in some thirty-six Ohio newspapers. One of his ads contained a line drawing of the Dalkon Shield and the question, "DID YOU USE THIS IUD?" The ad then gave the following information:

The Dalkon Shield Interuterine [*sic*] Device is alleged to have caused serious pelvic infections resulting in hospitalizations, tubal damage, infertility, and hysterectomies.

It is also alleged to have caused unplanned pregnancies ending in abortions, miscarriages, septic abortions, tubal or ectopic pregnancies and full term deliveries. If you or a friend have had a similar experience do not assume it is too late to take legal action against the Shield's manufacturer. Our law firm is presently representing women on such cases. The cases are handled on a contingent fee basis of the amount recovered. If there is no recovery, no legal fees are owed by our clients.

The ad then related Zauderer's firm name, address and a telephone number for "free information."

The ad was highly successful in attracting clients. Zauderer received over 200 inquiries concerning the ad and ultimately initiated lawsuits on behalf of 106 of the women who contacted him.

Another ad noted Zauderer's availability to represent people charged with drunken driving. That ad contained the phrase: "full legal fee refunded if convicted of drunk driving."

The Ohio Supreme Court publicly reprimanded Zauderer after ruling that the ads violated several rules in the state's Code of Professional Conduct.

On July 29, 1982, Ohio's Office of Disciplinary Counsel (ODC) charged Zauderer with several disciplinary violations arising out of both of these ads. The complaint charged that the drunken driving ad violated Ohio Disciplinary Rule 2-101 (A) in that it was "false, fraudulent, misleading, and deceptive to the public" as it offered representation on a contingent-fee basis in a criminal case, a violation under another disciplinary rule.

The complaint also charged that the line drawing in the Dalkon Shield ad violated Disciplinary Rule 2-101(B) forbidding the use of illustrations in attorney ads, and limiting the kind of information in such ads to a laundry list of 20 items. In addition, the ODC charged the ad violated another disciplinary rule forbidding a lawyer from "recommending employment, as a private practitioner, of himself, his partner, or associate to a nonlawyer who has not sought his advice regarding employment of a lawyer"; and a rule that a "lawyer who has given unsolicited advice to a layman that he should obtain counsel or take legal action shall not accept employment resulting from that advice."

Finally, the complaint charged that the ad violated another rule that requires ads mentioning contingent-fee rates must "disclose whether percentages are computed before or after deduction of court costs and expenses," and that the ad's failure to inform clients that they would be liable for *costs* (as opposed to legal *fees*) even if their claims were unsuccessful made the ad "deceptive" in violation of DR 2-101(A). Nowhere, however, was it alleged that the Dalkon Shield ad was false or deceptive. In fact, the ODC stipulated that the information and advice in the ad relative to Dalkon Shield litigation was not false, fraudulent, misleading, or deceptive and that the line drawing accurately depicted the Dalkon Shield.

The High Court ruled that the reprimand of Zauderer is not sustainable by virtue of violating state restrictions against self-recommendation and acceptance of employment resulting from unsolicited legal advice.

"Because all advertising is at least implicitly a plea for its audience's custom, a broad reading of the rules applied by the Ohio court (and particularly against self-recommendation) might suggest that they forbid all advertising by attorneys—a result obviously not in keeping with our decisions in *Bates* and *In re R.M.J.*," noted the Court. The Court added that, "Because appellant's statements regarding the Dalkon Shield were not false or deceptive, our decisions impose on the State the burden of establishing that prohibiting the use of such statements to solicit or obtain legal business directly advances a substantial governmental interest." The Court concluded that the state did not meet that burden in this case. As the Court noted, "An attorney may not be disciplined for soliciting legal business through printed advertising containing truthful and nondeceptive information and advice regarding the legal rights of potential clients."

Ohio's restrictions on the use of pictures or illustrations in attorney ads also failed for similar reasons. The Court pointed out that the state's probable purpose behind the restrictions was to insure that attorney ads are "dignified." However, the Court said it was "unsure that the State's desire that attorneys maintain their dignity in their communications with the public is an interest substantial enough to justify the abridgement of their First Amendment rights." Moreover, the State failed to cite any authority or proof for its argument that potential abuses from the use of pictures or illustrations in attorney ads could not be combatted by means other than a total ban.

Zauderer was less successful, however, on the issue of disclosure. One of the grounds for reprimand was that Zauderer failed to include in the Dalkon Shield ad "information that clients might be liable for significant litigation costs even if their lawsuits were unsuccessful." The High Court noted that Ohio's disclosure requirements do not prevent lawyers from advertising. Rather, lawyers are required by these rules to "provide somewhat more information than they might otherwise be inclined to present." Specifically, the Dalkon Shield ad said that "if there is no recovery, no legal fees are owed by our clients." And the drunken-driving ad said "full legal fee . . . refunded . . ." However, the ads didn't mention the distinction between "legal fees" and "costs." The problem with this type of ad, said the Court, was that a layman might not be aware of the distinction between "fees" and "costs." Accordingly, the U.S. Supreme Court affirmed the Ohio High Court's reprimand of Zauderer to the extent that it was based on the omission of information concerning his contingent-fee arrangements in the Dalkon Shield ads and his terms of representation in the drunken driving ads.

FTC'S ROLE

With its great expertise in the area of deceptive advertising, it's not surprising that the Federal Trade Commission has played an active role in encouraging truthful attorney advertising, specifically, and truthful professional advertising in general. FTC is authorized by federal statute[13] to prevent unfair methods of competition and unfair or deceptive acts or practices in or affecting commerce. Under this statutory mandate, FTC has tried to encourage competition among professionals to a great extent. In recent years, FTC has been looking into the competitive impact of restrictions on business arrangements that such state-licensed professionals as attorneys, doctors, and dentists can use in their practices. The Commission's goal in that effort has been to urge the removal of those restrictions that stifle competition, raise prices, and hurt consumers without offering countervailing benefits.

In November 1984, for example, FTC staff prepared a report to the Commission, "Improving Consumer Access to Legal Services: The Case for Removing Restrictions on Truthful Advertising." Before preparing that report, FTC staff surveyed some thirty-two hundred lawyers in seventeen states to find out if regulations restricting attorney advertising affect the availability of legal services and the prices that consumers pay for such services. One of its main conclusions: ". . . restrictions on the manner, content, and form of lawyer advertising have limited the flow of information to consumers about lawyers and their services."[14] In addition, the report found "convincing support for the proposition that greater flexibility to engage in nondeceptive advertising will be associated with lower prices for consumers of legal services."[15]

Another way in which FTC has played a significant role in the area of professional advertising has been to offer comments to the state licensing authorities or in *amicus curiae* briefs. For example, in 1984 two Iowa attorneys caused to be televised three commercials that contained (1) more than a single nondramatic voice, (2) background sound, (3) visual displays other than words and numbers, and (4) a list of four fields of practice which they would handle on either a percentage basis or a contingent fee basis. While not alleging or demonstrating that these ads were false, misleading, or deceptive, the Iowa State Bar Association's Committee on Professional Ethics and Conduct (henceforth "Committee") obtained a temporary injunction and sought to permanently enjoin the attorneys from using these commercials to advertise the availability of their legal services.

The committee's injunction petition charged that the three spots violated Iowa's Code of Professional Responsibility for Lawyers since they "contain more than a single non-dramatic voice, have background sound and visual displays of two or more people characterizing themselves as clients which make laudatory comment as to the defendants' services," and because they "list four areas of practice and contain no disclaimer." The Iowa Supreme Court issued a temporary injunction on September 14, 1982.

FTC entered the picture on behalf of the two attorney advertisers by filing an *amicus curiae* brief in which the Commission, among other things, urged the Iowa High Court not to take any action to restrict competition unnecessarily by limiting truthful, nondeceptive information. In its brief, the Commission listed three reasons why the challenged ads weren't deceptive:

1. The Committee didn't charge the ads made any misleading or deceptive statement or claim, nor did the Committee put any evidence in the record on which the Iowa Supreme Court could base such a finding.

2. The Committee's witness testified that according to a study he conducted, the public did not perceive the advertisements as misleading or deceptive.

3. There's no proof "in the record to support the premise generally that the technique of using dramatizations, background sounds or more than one non-dramatic voice" in a television commercial for lawyer services is inherently misleading. FTC noted that plaintiff's witness "testified that in his professional opinion, the use of such format and techniques was not inherently misleading or deceptive."

Moreover, FTC said,

The American Bar Association's Commission on Advertising found that there is no support for the belief that the use of graphic dramatizations and music in lawyer advertising is inherently misleading, or potentially more misleading than advertisements which do not contain such elements.

In addition, FTC pointed out that many state and local bar associations have used television commercials containing dramatizations, graphics, and music to advertise the availability of bar association-sponsored lawyer referral services.

The Commission strongly disagreed with the opinion that a commercial featuring clients making laudatory comments as to the attorney's services deserved an injunction. "All advertisements are, to some degree, self-laudatory," noted the Commission. FTC continued:

To the extent that defendants' advertisements may be characterized as "self-laudatory," they are no more so than if they had contained other information which is specifically allowed by DR 2-101 of the Iowa Code of Professional Responsibility for Lawyers, such as schools attended, memberships in bar associations or legal fraternities, and the names of clients regularly represented."[16]

As previously noted, FTC also offers comments to licensing authorities for other professions as well. And these comments also illustrate FTC's strong opposition, in general, to restrictions on truthful professional ads. For example, the New Jersey State Board of Dentistry proposed rules that, among other things, would forbid "any statement offering gratuitous services or the substantial equivalent thereof." In written comments sent to that board, FTC opined that "a number of provisions in the proposed advertising rules would restrain truthful communication and thereby inhibit competition."[17] In reference to the particular proposed rule quoted above, FTC noted that this provision isn't needed to protect consumers:

To the contrary, truthful advertising of the availability of free services can be of great benefit to consumers and, in addition, such offers can be a valuable professional tool for new practitioners who are trying to establish themselves. While we are aware that there is a potential for deceptive schemes in the use of such advertising we believe that a total ban on the offering of free service is overly restrictive and unnecessary."[18]

It will be interesting to see what impact FTC's comments have on the various state licensing authorities in the months and years ahead as they decide on proposals to expand advertising by professionals.

THE ABA CODE

In the years following *Bates*, the organized legal community debated several proposals involving attorney advertising. This debate culminated in August 1983 with the adoption by the American Bar Association (ABA) of its new Model Rules of Professional Conduct, including those dealing with attorney advertising. Rule 7.1, the heart of the ABA's new ad rules, is worded as follows:

A lawyer shall not make any false or misleading communication about the lawyer or the lawyer's services. A communication is false or misleading if it:

1. Contains a material misrepresentation of fact or law, or omits a fact necessary to make the statement considered as a whole not materially misleading:

2. Is likely to create an unjustified expectation about results the lawyer can achieve, or states or implies that the lawyer can achieve results by means that violate the rules of professional conduct or other law; or

3. Compares the lawyer's service with other lawyers' services, unless the comparison can be factually substantiated.[19]

Other provisions of the ABA Code affect attorney advertising in (1) the media in which an attorney can advertise, and (2) the use of trade names. In comments submitted to the ABA when this code was in the proposal stage, FTC praised this rule as containing "a clearer and more objective standard for evaluating advertising content than appeared in previous ABA codes and in many state and local bar association codes. The proposed standard would allow truthful ads and prohibit only those that are false and deceptive."

However, after FTC staff prepared its report on improving consumer access to legal services, the staff proposed its own "Model Code" that would forbid "only false or deceptive advertising and false or deceptive trade names, and explicitly recognizes the legitimacy of using any media, including electronic broadcast or direct mail, to advertise legal services."[20]

The following is the FTC staff's proposed Model Code involving attorney advertising.

COMMUNICATIONS CONCERNING A LAWYER'S SERVICES

A lawyer shall not make a false or deceptive communication about the lawyer or the lawyer's services.

Advertising

1. A lawyer may advertise services through direct mail advertising or through public media, including but not limited to telephone directories, legal directories, newspapers or other periodicals, radio or television, provided the communication is not false or deceptive.

2. A copy or recording of an advertisement or written communication shall be kept for (one year) after its dissemination along with a record of when and where it was used.*

Direct Contact with Prospective Clients

A lawyer may initiate communications with a prospective client through personal contact, through individually directed written communication, or through telephonic communication for the purpose of obtaining professional employment, unless:

1. The lawyer knows or reasonably should know that the physical, emotional or mental state of the person is such that the person could not exercise reasonable judgment in employing a lawyer;

2. The person has made known to the lawyer a desire not to receive communications from the lawyer; or

3. The lawyer knows or reasonably should know that the communication involves coercion, duress or harassment.

Communication of Fields of Practice

A lawyer may communicate the fact that the lawyer does or does not practice in particular fields of law. A lawyer shall not state or imply that the lawyer is an officially recognized or certified specialist except where the lawyer in fact has been certified in a particular field of practice.

Firm Names and Letterheads

A lawyer may use any firm name, letterhead or other professional designation provided it is not false or deceptive.[21]

While the ABA Code is clearly a key document, it is the various state bar associations—frequently acting in concert with the states' highest courts—that have direct authority over attorney conduct. Accordingly, if you are an attorney planning to advertise, you should stay apprised of the activities of your state bar association and/or highest court in considering

---

*The recordkeeping requirement of subsection (B) is optional. If any retention requirement is imposed, however, it should not exceed one year.

adoption of ABA's Model Rules. This is particularly important because following the *Bates* decision, wide variations among the various state's ethical codes relative to advertising have occurred. However, with the adoption of the ABA Model Code and the further explication of professional advertising in such cases as *In re R.M.J.*, it can be expected that greater uniformity should be seen in this area as we approach the 1990s.

It should be noted that while *Bates*, *In re R.M.J.*, and *Ohralik* involve attorney advertising, the principles involved are applicable to advertising by all professionals. Indeed, it was in the U.S. Supreme Court's ruling in *Virginia Pharmacy Board v. Virginia Consumer Council*[22]—decided prior to *Bates* and its progeny—where the High Court struck down a Virginia statute forbidding licensed pharmacists from advertising prescription drug prices. And, for example, in December 1978, the U.S. District Court for the Eastern District of Louisiana held that truthful newspaper advertising concerning the availability or cost of routine dental services was commercial speech protected by the First Amendment, and that this statute was unconstitutional to the extent that it restricted such advertising.[23]

The overall trend in professional advertising law may be towards a uniform rule that would not differ, in most respects, from the standard that already exists under Section 5 of the Federal Trade Commission Act. One advantage of such a rule is that state and federal courts have applied this rule for decades and a substantial body of case law has developed in this area.

NOTES

1. Hertz, "Abraham Lincoln: His Law Partners, Clerks and Office Boys," 44 Magazine of History with Notes and Queries (Extra Nos. 173-176) 12 (1931); "Improving Consumer Access to Legal Services: Report of the Staff to the Federal Trade Commission" (hereafter, "Improving Access"), p. 20.

2. "Improving Access," p. 20.

3. "Improving Access," p. 23.

4. "Improving Access," p. 23.

5. *People ex rel. Maupin v. MacCabe*, 18 Colo. 186, 188, 32 P. 280 (1893).

6. "Improving Access," p. 23; ABA, Canons of Professional Ethics, Canon 27 (1908).

7. 433 U.S. 350, 53 L.Ed.2d 810 (1977).

8. 53 L.Ed.2d at 836; see also *Virginia Pharmacy Board v. Virginia Consumer Council*, 425 U.S. 778, 48 L.Ed. 2d, 346 (1976).

9. 436 U.S. 447, 56 L.Ed.2d 444 (1978).

10. 455 U.S. 191 (1982).

11. 455 U.S. at 203 (1982).

12. Supreme Ct. Dkt. #83-2166, argued January 7, 1985 and decided May 18, 1985; see, generally, *Advertising Compliance Service*, Tab #19, Professional Ads, Article #11.

13. 15 U.S.C. §41 et seq.

14. "Improving Access," p. 19.

15. "Improving Access," p. 126.

16. *Advertising Compliance Service*, Tab #19, Professional Ad, Article #6; Brief of the Federal Trade Commission as *Amicus Curiae* On Behalf of the Defendants and Counterclaimants in the Case of Committee on Professional Ethics and Conduct of the Iowa State Bar Association v. Mark A. Humphrey, Fredd J. Haas, and James E. Gritzner, d/b/a Hass and Gritzner. See also: *Iowa Code of Professional Responsibility for Lawyers*, DR 2-101; American Bar Association's *Model Rules of Professional Conduct* (ABA Model Rules) Rule 7.4 (1983); and *ABA Model Rules*, Rule 7.4 comment (1983).

17. FTC Comments to Robert J. Siconolfi, Executive Secretary, New Jersey State Board of Dentistry, March 19, 1985.

18. *Advertising Compliance Service*, Tab #19, Professional Ads, Article #10; see also, Tab #19, Professional Ads, Article #8.

19. *ABA Model Rules*, Rule 7.1

20. "Improving Access," p. 151.

21. "Improving Access," Appendix F.

22. 425 U.S. 748 (1976).

23. *Dewey v. Louisiana State Board of Dentistry*, 491 F. Supp. 132 (1978), *aff'd per curiam*, 625 F.2d 499 (5th Cir. 1980).

8.
SWEEPSTAKES
AND CONTESTS

The use of sweepstakes and contests by advertisers has proliferated in recent years.[1] Many advertisers seeking to increase their market share or when introducing a new product find that these devices are an excellent attention-getter. With the increasing popularity of state-run lotteries, Americans are becoming ever more gambling conscious. Aware of this fact, many advertisers have tapped this get-rich-quick mentality in sweepstakes and contest promotions used in conjunction with advertising for their products or services.

Accordingly, successful sweepstakes or contests can spell great financial rewards for an advertiser. However, there is another side to that coin: All of the states, as well as the federal government, have laws forbidding lotteries, which these games can sometimes resemble. And these are not the typical advertising compliance laws discussed in many other parts of this book. The state antilottery laws are found in the *criminal codes* of the states. The punishment for violating these laws can be a fine—and even a *jail sentence*. William W. Rogal, Esq., an expert in the field of games-of-chance promotions, perhaps put it best in an address to an American Advertising Federation (AAF) conference when he said, "As I am sure you will agree, the threat of going to jail totally outclasses the typical penalty which an advertising mistake can produce.[2]

OVERVIEW

Rogal also noted at the AAF conference that the law in this area has become "more uniform and liberal in recent years." This trend toward liberalization and uniformity was caused "by state legislative enactments, by referendums or initiatives which produced changes in state constitutions and by regulatory authorities changing their rules or enforcement postures," he noted.

FEDERAL ENFORCEMENT AUTHORITIES

Federal Trade Commission

In 1925, the Federal Trade Commission (FTC) began issuing cease-and-desist orders against lotteries. It later issued hundreds of such orders against candy manufacturers, punch board purveyors and others. The FTC for the next 40 years was the most active anti-lottery federal regulatory agency. FTC's enforcement enthusiasm diminished in the 1970s and is now generally content to allow the Postal Service to exercise its jurisdiction when the mails are involved.

Nevertheless, FTC does have a rule governing games of chance in the food retailing and gasoline industries. Issued in the wake of complaints that games were allegedly rigged, the three Bureaus of FTC urged that the Commissioners simply declare the games in violation of Section 5 of the FTC Act. However, FTC didn't do this. Instead, FTC staff prepared a rule for Commission review. This rule was very difficult, if not impossible, to comply with and still run an effective game. Nevertheless the Commission adopted the rule, while amended somewhat—and although a rulemaking change may be in the offing—it is still almost impossible to live with (see 16 C.F.R. 419). According to Rogal, the rule requires that the game pieces must be updated frequently; this is difficult in a game that might be run by as many as 10,000 retail gas stations.

The basic purpose of the FTC rules in this area is to avoid creation of an illegal lottery. FTC defines a lottery at 16 C.F.R. 15.57 as the combination of chance, consideration, and a prize. All of the networks refuse to air lottery ads, except for state-run lotteries. It is clear that the networks would refuse to advertise a private numbers game and would almost certainly refuse a charitable lottery (even though these are often legal).

Some lottery schemes are less obvious. For instance, in *FTC v. Keppel & Bros.*[3], the U.S. Supreme Court upheld an FTC finding that a candy distribution scheme violated Section 5 of the Federal Trade Commission Act, which prohibits unfair methods of competition. There, a manufacturer sold candy from a rack. The customer took the candy, opened it up, and paid the price indicated. In some cases, the amount of candy received also differed. An extremely conservative Court had no difficulty in finding that the scheme, of the sort which violates criminal statutes, was an unfair practice subject to FTC restraint.

In the scheme that became the basis of 16 C.F.R. 15.57, a retailer sold goods to a customer who was then supposed to go to a bank to find out whether he had been awarded the merchandise as a prize. It has been ruled illegal for a soft drinks manufacturer to award prizes on the crown inside the bottle. Club plan purchase schemes also have been held illegal. In *Deere dba Savoy Mfg. Co. v. FTC*,[4] club members paid 25¢ a week into a fund. One member was given a selected piece of merchandise as a prize. The others continued to compete for the prize. Each week one member took the preselected prize. When everyone had paid in the established price of the merchandise, everyone got the prize.

FTC enforcement of lottery rules is on a case-by-case basis, except for groceries and service stations, which are governed by special rules.

U.S. Postal Service

Sending lottery materials through the mail is a criminal offense.[5] However, with most garden-variety types of advertising promotions, it's not very likely that the Postal Service will ask a United States attorney to institute criminal proceedings. The Service has a faster and more effective method of proceeding: 39 U.S.C. Section 3005. This statute authorizes the Service to issue cease-and-desist orders and orders stopping the delivery of mail to persons who are running a lottery or who are obtaining money or property by means of false representations.

In 1983, Congress added civil penalties to postal laws.[6] Under this new law, if you try to evade a stop order or violate a cease-and-desist order, you can be assessed civil penalties of $10,000 for each violation and for each day the violation continues.

Compliance with Postal Service rules, however, is going to be more difficult in the future. Effective January 2, 1985, it no longer issues "no action letters" to advertisers who wish a ruling on whether or not their proposed prize plans were lotteries and so would be challenged by the Postal Service under the Postal lottery laws.[7] Its reason: Over the years the "number and complexity" of requests for such letters increased dramatically.[8]

Definition of the term "lottery," forms the basis of Postal Service regulation of proposed prize plans. According to a Postal Service summary of the case law, a "lottery" has three essential elements: (1) distribution of prizes; (2) according to chance; (3) for a consideration.[9] Anything of value offered to induce entry can be the element of prize.[10] The element of chance exists if winning any prize at all, or one prize as opposed to another, depends on a random process beyond the entrant's control.[11] "While guessing contests have been held to involve the element of chance, the Postal Service notes, it has been held that contests in which a prize is awarded based upon a genuine exercise of skill do not."[12]

According to the Postal Service: "A requirement to purchase eligibility to be selected as a prize winner, or notification of the exact prize won, constitutes the lottery element of consideration. Requiring a purchase constitutes consideration even though a product or service is thereby obtained in addition to eligibility or notification. A prize plan having a method of entry which involves a purchase, but also providing an effectively communicated, readily practicable alternate method of entry which does not involve a purchase, lacks the element of consideration."[13]

"Until recently," Rogal noted,

lawyers in this field, including this one, were of the view that a game chance enclosed in a consumer product package violated the postal lottery law unless it was disclosed clearly in the advertising and on the package that a person could enter the contest by merely sending in a 'facsimile' in the form of a 3 × 5 card with the product's name or some other words or phrases written or printed by hand. However, in 1979 the Postal Service, by means of a 'no action' letter, approved a game promotion involving an in-pack game piece if the package itself contained a notice of 'no purchase necessary' and advised that a free game piece was available to persons who requested one by mail. In the view of the Postal Service this message offered potential entrants a genuine free entry alternative and that, therefore, persons who chose to enter by purchasing the package would be doing so voluntarily. In other words, the equivalent free entry offer eliminated the lottery element of consideration (see note 2).

Bureau of Alcohol, Tobacco and Firearms

The Bureau of Alcohol, Tobacco and Firearms (ATF) differs from the U.S. Postal Service's view as to what is a lottery. ATF believes, for example, that the element of consideration exists even if no purchase of a tobacco product is required to take part in a contest. (ATF has jurisdiction over what's contained in, attached to or printed on packages of certain tobacco products, such as cigarettes.) "The statute in question," according to Rogal, "is a section of the Internal Revenue Code of 1954, 26 U.S.C. 5723(c). This statute provides that no certificate or coupon representing a 'ticket, chance, share or interest in or dependent, the event of a lottery' shall appear in or 'on any package of tobacco products or cigarette papers or tubes,' " (see note 2).

ATF also issues advisory letters involving the lottery aspects of proposed promotions. "However, unlike the Postal Service, it has steadfastly refused to permit any kind of game promotion in which the game price is enclosed with cigarettes or cigars," according to Rogal (see note 2).

Federal Communciations Commission

A federal agency whose views closely parallel that of the Postal Service is the Federal Communications Commission (FCC). Rogal points out that in *FCC v. American Broadcasting Co., Inc. et al.,*[14] "the Commission contended that consideration in the form of money or a thing of value is not essential to a lottery finding and that a commercial benefit to the advertiser or promoter satisfied the consideration element. The Supreme Court did not agree, pointing out that the U.S. Postal Service had consistently given a 'contrary administrative interpretation' and that there could not be one lottery law interpretation for the FCC and another for other branches of the Federal government."

The broadcast lottery law, originally promulgated in 1934, forbids the broadcasting of any ad or information about a lottery or lottery results. Although violation is a criminal offense, the Commission has always proceeded administratively against violators. As it has frequently imposed fines or forfeitures on licensees, the networks scrutinize game advertising carefully before it's accepted for airing.

STATE CONTROLS

Every state in the United States defines a lottery to be a combination of chance, consideration, and a prize.

Prize—This is the stake received for winning the game. That it probably has to be something of material value does not appear to be a point of much dispute.

Chance—In the common Law of England, chance meant only and exclusively chance, such as found in a pure numbers game or raffle. Some advertising lotteries, however, fall into an intermediate category. For example, a participant may be required to send in a form naming the Super Bowl winner, and then one of the possibly thousands of correct entries will win the prize. The usual rule here is that the element of chance must predominate, but watch the exceptions. Some enterprises do not include an obvious chance factor, but have been held to be illegal lotteries because they are not likely to afford a fair chance to all participants. Pyramid sales schemes are the obvious example here, since the courts and legislators have usually banned them as lotteries on the assumption that only the initiators at the top of the pyramid would stand any chance of winning. You would be well advised to check local law if you're suspicious of any sort of pyramid sales device.

Consideration—Advertising games that run afoul of the local authorities usually do so on the basis of this criterion. Obviously, the use of money to enter a lottery constitutes an adequte consideration. But what of the need to enter a store to fill out an entry blank? What of a game that requires a purchase to enter or a purchase to win a prize after one is chosen as the winner? Under the majority rule, store purchases constitute a sufficient consideration to establish a lottery. There are a few states that perhaps might not follow the no-purchase rule, but they are few, and national advertisers usually will not accept a game that requires such a purchase. A store visit to get an entry blank usually is not considered a sufficient consideration to establish a lottery, but there are several exceptions.

Thus, if a purchase is required to enter, you have a lottery. However, the answer is usually different when the purchase is required *after* a participant has been chosen as a winner. It is not a violation of federal lottery laws to require that the winner of a game or sweepstakes must make a purchase before he claims his prize. You should be aware that an FTC staff advisory opinion[15] approved a game scheme in which the contestant had to submit a "proof of purchase" with his winning game piece to claim his prize. The advisory opinion points out that in such a situation, "the participant knows what prize he has won before he pays any consideration" and that therefore "there is no element of chance or the receipt of a prize which depends on chance."

The difference in treatment for a game which requires a purchase to enter and one which requires a purchase after the participant has entered and won stems from the definition of a lottery as found in many state statutes, constitutions or court decisions. The antilottery provision of the California Code, §319, is typical. It reads in part: "A lottery is any scheme for the disposal or distribution of property by chance, among persons who have paid or promised to pay any valuable consideration *for the chance of obtaining such property.*" (Emphasis supplied.)

Clearly, this statute is only violated when the consideration is paid "for the chance." If the "chance" to win a prize is absolutely free, the statute is not violated despite the fact that the participant must pay consideration to claim his prize. Thus, the lottery law is not violated by a game in which the prize is, for example, $100 off on an item whose regular price is more than $100 or a free item with the purchase of another item.

Games in which chances are distributed to persons who make a purchase, i.e., when the chance is enclosed in the package or given to persons in the supermarket checkout line are not lotteries if the nonpurchasing participants are offered an equal opportunity to receive a free game chance without making a purchase. Both the U.S. Postal Service and FCC have ruled that such games are not lotteries when the opportunity to get a free game chance is clearly disclosed and equal. National distributers of consumer goods comply with this stricture by disclosing on the package and in advertising that a free game piece or pieces may be obtained by writing to a listed address. While some state authorities have questioned this interpretation (e.g., Washington and Wisconsin) it appears now to be almost generally accepted.

The following is a review of the law in many key states.

California

A leading case that extensively discusses the element of consideration when some participants receive a game chance with a purchase is *California Gasoline Retailers v. Regal Petroleum Corp.*[16]

Connecticut

This state has certain mild requirements concerning the disclosure of prizes.[17]

Florida

Florida law requires that all rules and regulations for a game promotion must be filed with the Department of Legal Affairs thirty days in advance of game commencement; that rules and regulations must be posted in every retail outlet and published in all advertising copy; that the promoter must establish a trust account or obtain a bond equivalent to the total value of all prizes offered; that the promoter must provide the Department of Legal Affairs with a certified list of the names and addresses of all persons who have won a prize of more than $25 within sixty days after such winners have been determined; that a similar list of winners must either be provided to persons who request it or published in a Florida newspaper of general circulation; and that the promoter must hold all winning entries submitted for a period of ninety days after the close or completion of the game.[18]

This statute only applies to games in which the total value of the prizes exceeds $5,000 but, it applies to *all* game promotions, not only those offered by retailers. A nonrefundable filing fee of $100 must accompany the advance registration papers. Florida provides forms to aid game promoters in making the required filings.

Illinois

Ilinois has conflicting precedents on the legality of grocery store promotions, but has not enforced any lottery restrictions against game promotions.

Maine

Maine forbids gas station games.[19]

Massachusetts

Massachusetts forbids gas station games.[20]

Michigan

Michigan requires disclosure of the prizes and information concerning the number of prizes to be awarded.[21]

Missouri

On October 29, 1979, after the Missouri electorate had amended the state constitution to permit games of chance and after the legislature had enacted legislation to effect that amendment, a Missouri Court of Appeals ruled that a regulation of the Supervisor of Liquor Control, which banned games on the premises of licensees, was still valid and enforceable. *State Ex Rel Glendinning Companies, et al. v. Letz.*[22] Since most supermarkets were licensed to sell 5 percent beer, the court's ruling effectively prevented food stores from engaging in games of chance. The Missouri court assumed, but did not decide, that the games were not unlawful after the adoption of the constitutional amendment but, in effect, stated that this was immaterial and had no effect upon the "Supervisor's Statutory Power to Regulate *the sale of alcoholic beverages.*" (Emphasis in original.)

This unfortunate situation ended in December 1981 when the Division of Liquor Control amended its regulation by adding a proviso which permits promotional games if consideration is not required "for the privilege or opportunity of participating in such games or contests or for receiving the award or prize therefrom."[23]

This language tracks part of the language of the constitutional amendment approved by the voters in November 1978. Section 39 (9) appears to outlaw games in which a purchase is required after the participant had been declared a winner.

However, the constitutional amendment also contains a definition of "lottery or gift enterprize," stating that these terms: ". . . shall mean only those games or contests whereby money or something of value is exchanged directly *for the tickets or chance* to participate in the game or contest." (Emphasis supplied.)

How Missouri authorities or courts will resolve this apparent discrepancy is uncertain. However, the regulation of the Division of Liquor Control will be enforced against food stores and others which have a license to sell 5 percent beer and hence a retail game which requires a purchase "for receiving the award or prize" is probably unlawful for such licensees.

New Jersey

Insofar as gasoline station promotions are concerned it is immaterial in this state whether consideration is or is not present. Reason: New Jersey Unfair Trade Practices law, 56: 6-2 (f) flatly prohibits "games of chance, in connection with the sale of motor fuels." The courts have ruled that the definition of a lottery contained in the state's antilottery law, which makes consideration an indispensable element of a lottery, does not control interpretation or affect the application of §56: 6-2 to gasoline retailers. *United Stations of New Jersey v. Getty Oil Co.*[24]

New York

New York's General Business Law requires registration of promotional games with the Miscellaneous Records Section of the Department of State.[25] To register a game, you have to fill out an application form and enclose a

$50 fee. The application form includes requests for the names of promoters, the odds of winning, and a copy of the rules. A trust account must be established or bond posted sufficient to cover the amount of the prize to be distributed in New York State. Winners must be disclosed to the New York Department of State within ninety days after the end of the contest.

North Dakota

North Dakota is an example of a state that addresses an ambiguity in the common law of lottery. If one runs a game promotion and requires only that *some* contestants give a consideration to enter, has one established a lottery against those who do not pay? The answer in North Dakota is clearly "yes"; the fact that some patrons get free chances to enter will not permit their participation in the game if others have to pay.[26]

Ohio

Until very recently the situation in Ohio was similar to the situation which existed in Missouri prior to amendment of that state's liquor control regulations. Rule 53 of the Ohio Liquor Control Commission's regulations had been interpreted as prohibiting games in supermarkets or other establishments licensed to sell alcoholic beverages.[27] Under pressure from the courts and others the liquor authorities relaxed their enforcement posture about three years ago and permitted games if the prizes were not awarded on the premises. Thus, for the past few years, licensed food retailers could conduct a game but the winners of prizes had to mail their winning tickets to a listed address and receive their prizes by return mail. However, Ohio has now amended Rule 53 to permit games to be conducted as they are in other states. The rule change was approved by the Commission on September 5, 1984 and became effective September 20, 1984.

Rhode Island

The Rhode Island registration law differs from the laws in effect in New York and Florida in that it only applies to games conducted by retail establishments rather than to all games and in that a prize structure totaling only $500 rather than $5,000 triggers the registration requirement.

Games by retail gasoline stations are not prohibited in this state. However, state law does prohibit retail gasoline dealers from employing games of chance or awarding any prizes which "permit any purchaser to obtain motor fuel from such retail dealer at a net price lower than the posted price applicable at the time of the sale."[28] Additionally, state law prohibits coercion of retail dealers to participate in a game of chance.[29]

Washington

Article II, Section 24 of Washington's Constitution was amended in 1972 and now reads in part: "lotteries shall be prohibited except as specifically authorized upon affirmative vote of 60% of the members of each house of the legislature . . ." The holdings in *Washington v. Readers Digest Association*,[30] and several other cases were vitiated in 1974 by enactment of a new statute.[31] This statute defines the term "lottery" as meaning "a scheme for the distribution of money or property by chance, among persons who have paid or agreed to pay a valuable consideration for the chance."

Additionally, the statute provides that the term "valuable consideration" does not include listening to or watching a television or radio program, filling out and returning a coupon or entry blank received through the mail or published in a newspaper or magazine, sending in an entry blank, visiting a business establishment to obtain a game piece, expending time, thought, attention and energy in perusing game materials, or merely registering at a place of business or making or answering a telephone call.

However, the law also provides that a "drawing" conducted by a retail outlet may last for not more than seven consecutive days and only one such drawing can be conducted in a year. This "drawing" proviso effectively rules out lengthy sweepstakes type promotions for retailers but does not prevent retailers from conducting other types of games, including the popular "instant winner" ruboff games and bingo games.

Wisconsin

Wisconsin is a state with a severe bias against advertising lotteries. Wisconsin ruled during the Depression that game shows such as "Name That Tune" were illegal lotteries in Wisconsin. In 1965, Wisconsin enacted a constitutional amendment that on its face brought Wisconsin within the majority rule, but the attorney general of Wisconsin issued a decision that only skill contests were permissible. In 1982, however, Wisconsin courts upheld a bottle top game (*Coca-Cola v. LaFollette*,[32]) and in 1983 another ruling was issued stating that chance must be the *dominant* factor in a lottery (*State v. Dahik*.[33]) Thus the only remnant of the old controls on lotteries probably is *Kayden v. Murphy*,[34] which suggested in dictum that a game requiring a store visit might be void.

NETWORK STANDARDS

Contests and sweepstakes sometimes resemble illicit gambling operations and so present general issues of fairness in the manner of awarding prizes. Accordingly, all the major television networks have special rules to monitor ads of this nature.

Because of all the potential legal pitfalls, the major networks have become somewhat concerned about placing their names behind prize contests. Accordingly, each of the three major commercial networks has a specific review procedure covering such advertising.

In every case, the advertiser of a proposed game should have in order the storyboard and the game (completely worked out), along with rules, entry prizes, game pieces, etc., clearly defined. At this point, you're ready to go to the network with your idea. We'll use CBS for the first example.[35]

CBS's Procedures

At CBS, your proposed ad will be reviewed preliminarily and a questionnaire mailed out. Ad agencies will be required to complete the form and enclose a copy of the official rules just as the player will see them, an entry blank and/or playing pieces, and a detailed breakdown of all prizes awarded during the contest. Applicable point-of-sale displays and print media ads are also to be enclosed. The ad agency must, among other things, disclose on this questionnaire:

- The final date by which one can enter the contest or can claim a prize. This date must be in the commercial.
- Where entry blanks and rules will be available and how they may be obtained without a purchase.
- When the commercials will be aired and in what geographic area the contest will be promoted.
- The prizes to be awarded and the source (advertiser or prize company).
- Eligibility requirements. For example, must one be a licensed driver to enter a contest? If so, this must be clearly disclosed in the commercial.
- Limitations on the number of times one can enter a contest must be disclosed to CBS.

In addition, the ad agency must assure CBS that, if a contest is limited to "participating dealers," there will be enough outlets for contest materials so that players can be sufficiently accommodated.

CBS also wants to know what printed media will be running the contest ads. (However, it does not need to know if another network will carry the ads.)

Additionally, CBS wants to know whether the commercials will be used in children's programming. If children are the target of a game, they must be informed very clearly what the odds of winning are. The commercial must show the children the prizes that will be awarded.

CBS also wants to know whether the contest is based on skill or chance. If the contest is based on chance, CBS wants to know whether the winners will be chosen by a random drawing. If so, where, when, and who will supervise the contest? Will the winning contestant have to consent to use of his/her name to receive a prize?

If the contest is skilled in nature, the ad agency must disclose the criteria for judging, the list of judges, and their qualifications. (However, use of a firm like Reuben Donnelley would probably be sufficient in and of itself.)

CBS wants to know if duplicate prizes will be awarded. If not, how will ties be broken? Will the public be able to obtain records of the contest, the list of correct answers, and the names of winners?

After submitting this information to CBS, your proposed ad copy is ready for review by CBS's Commercial Clearance Department and by its Law Department. CBS may insist that certain visuals be added to the commercial. The visuals must disclose the words "no purchase necessary" and "void where prohibited by law." In addition, CBS may require additional disclosures on how a person can enter and win the contest as stated in the contest rules. You should also be aware that CBS's written guidelines are subject to CBS's sole interpretation and may be subject to change from time to time. Accordingly, the guidelines may not reflect current CBS practices, interpretation or policy.

NBC's Procedures

NBC provides for review of advertising of contests to assure that the proposed contest "is not a lottery, that the material terms are clearly stated, and that it is being conducted fairly, honestly and according to its rules."[36] NBC requires submission of complete details and continuity to the Broadcast Standards Department at least ten business days before the first public announcement of the contest (*not* the first NBC airing of the commercial). The network requires submission of a complete copy of the contest rules, the entry blank, a complete questionnaire similar to that just described for CBS, promotional material, and print media ads as well as the proposed broadcast copy. Required on-air contest disclosures are similar to CBS's requirements, but there is a question on the handling of station call-in or call-out quizzes. In that type of broadcast game, the contest holder must identify the criteria used to select incoming or outgoing calls.

NBC is particularly concerned about game security. There is a specific warning that game procedures must be free of tampering. A specific question in the NBC questionnaire concerns the security procedures used throughout the duration of the contest to maintain the integrity of the contest and to insure that contest rules are followed fairly.

A final NBC question asks if any aspect of the contest could be construed to alarm the public over an imaginary danger; cause crowds, traffic violations or result in damage to public or private property or divert police officers from their normal duties; or result in significant numbers of telephone calls to government agencies or private lines. (The latter question appears aimed at treasure hunts and contests requiring knowledge of particular facts). NBC's contest standards are administered by its Vice President, Broadcast Standards, East Coast. The standards specifically apply only to NBC television.

ABC's Procedures

ABC allows the advertising of contests conducted by advertisers so long as "(1) the contest offers a fair opportunity to all qualified contestants to win; (2) it complies with all pertinent laws and regulations, and (3) it is not contrary to the public interest."[37]

ABC divides contests into three categories: skill contests, lotteries, and games of chance. ABC notes that the broadcast of any advertising for a lottery is a criminal offense under federal law,[38] except for state-run lotteries.[39]

Before airing, the complete ad and details of the contest rules, prizes, and a copy of the entry blank must go to ABC's department of Broadcast Standards and Practices. A free means of entering the contest must be provided if there is an element of chance in the contest. All contestants must have an equal chance of winning a chance-based contest. ABC will refuse to broadcast any information concerning any private lottery. Methods of judging a contest must be disclosed. Sweepstakes may be aimed at children if the children in fact have a fair chance of winning and prizes are appropriate for them. The address to submit entries in children's sweepstakes must be displayed visually and given in the audio portion of the commercial as well. ABC does not have a specific questionnaire procedure.[40] (See Chapter 5, for more information about broadcast advertising standards.)

NOTES

1. This chapter is adapted from the following articles appearing in *Advertising Compliance Service*, Tab #21, Sweepstakes, Contests: (i) "Rules Governing Games of Chance: AAF Conference Highlights," Article #7, by John D. Healy, (ii) "Sweepstakes and Contests: More About State Controls," Article #6, by William W. Rogal; (iii) "Sweepstakes and Contests: State Controls," Article #5, by John D. Healy; (iv) "Sweeptakes and Contests: Network Procedures," by John D. Healy, Article #4.

2. Address by William W. Rogal, to the AAF's 8th Annual Advertising Law and Policy Conference, December 4, 1984.

3. 291 U.S. 305 (1934).

4. 152 F.2d 65 (2d Cir. 1945).

5. 18 U.S.C. §1302.

6. 39 U.S.C. §3012.

7. 18 U.S.C. §1302; 39 U.S.C. §3005.

8. Letter from George C. Davis, Assistant General Counsel, Consumer Protection Division of the U.S. Postal Service to William Rogal, 12-12-84; See also *Advertising Compliance Service*, Tab #21, Sweepstakes, Contests, Article #7.

9. *FCC v. ABC*, 347 U.S. 284 (1954).

10. *U.S. v. Rich*, 90 F. Supp. 624 (E.D. 111. 1950); *U.S. v. Purvis*, 195 F. 618 (N.D. Ga. 1912).

11. *Horner v. U.S.*, 147 U.S. 449 (1893); *Zebelman v. U.S.*, 339 F.2d 484 (10th Cir. 1964).

12. *Waite v. Press Pub. Ass'n.*, 155 F. 58 (6th Cir. 1907); *Brooklyn Daily Eagle v. Voorhies*, 181 F. 579 (C.C.E.D. N.Y. 1910).

13. *Horner v. U.S.*, 147 U.S. 449 (1893); *Garden City Chamber of Commerce v. Wagner,* 100 F. Supp. 769 (E.D. N.Y. 1951); *ABC v. U.S.,* 110 F. Supp. 374 (S.D. N.Y. 1953); *Caples Co. v. U.S.*, 243 F.2d 232 (D.C. Cir. 1957).

14. 347 U.S. 284 (1954).

15. FTC Staff Advisory Opinion, issued 6-23-77.

16. 330 P.2d 778 (1958).

17. Connecticut Statutes §53-290(a).

18. Florida Statues §849.094.

19. Maine Statutes, Title 17-2304.

20. Massachusetts Statutes 271 §6c.

21. Michigan Statutes 750.372a.

22. 591 S.W.2d 92.

23. 11 CSR 70-2. 140.

24. 246 A.2d 150 (1968).

25. §369(e).

26. Ch. 12:1-18 (North Dakota).

27. 4301:1-1-53.

28. §31-37-14 (Rhode Island).

29. 11-50-7 (Rhode Island).

30. 501 P.2d 290 (1972).

31. RCW 9.46.020.

32. 316 NW2d 129 (Wisc. 1982).

33. 330 NW2d 611 (Wisc. 1983).

34. 150 NW2d 447 (Wisc. 1967).

35. See, generally, *CBS Television Network Advertising Guidelines*, CTN 14-18.

36. See, generally, *NBC Broadcast Standards for Television*, pp. 22-24.

37. *ABC Advertising Standards*, §I, p. 4.

38. *ABC Advertising Guidelines*, §II, p. 9; 18 U.S.C. §1304.

39. *ABC Advertising Guidelines*, §II, p. 9; 18 U.S.C. §1307.

40. See generally, *ABC Advertising Guidelines*, §II, pp. 9-10.

9.
ALCOHOLIC BEVERAGE ADVERTISING

One of the hottest advertising compliance issues of the 1980s involves the acceptable limits of alcoholic beverage advertising. In recent years, there have been stepped-up efforts to restrict, or even ban, the advertising of alcoholic beverages on television, radio, and other media. These efforts are the result of a growing national concern over the serious problems of drunk driving and alcoholism. Such groups as Mothers Against Drunk Driving (MADD) have succeeded in convincing states to adopt restrictive drunk-driving legislation and laws that raise the drinking age to twenty-one.

This chapter discusses the current status of restrictions on the advertising of alcoholic beverages. It examines both federal and state regulation as well as the self-regulation of such ads.

FEDERAL REGULATION

Federal Communications Commission (FCC) rules and regulations do not forbid the advertising of alcoholic beverages in broadcasting. Two federal agencies—the Federal Trade Commission (FTC) and the Bureau of Alcohol, Tobacco and Firearms (ATF)—have concurrent jurisdiction over the advertising of alcoholic beverages.

FTC's Role

If the drive to limit the advertising of alcoholic beverages had emerged a decade sooner, it's likely that FTC would have played a key role in that movement. Headed by an activist chairman, Michael Pertschuk, FTC was at the forefront of the consumer protection movement. And the emphasis at the Commission was on regulating entire industries via the trade regulation rulemaking process. The picture is completely different, however, as we approach the second half of the 1980s. Headed by a Reagan-appointed economist, James C. Miller III (until October 1985), and chastened by a decade of Congressional attacks on its earlier alleged "overzealousness," today's FTC has reversed the earlier policy of going after whole industries. Instead, the Commission now emphasizes the case-by-case method, whereby it pursues individual violations.

How will this affect the drive to limit, or ban, the advertising of alcoholic beverages? It deprives the movement of one of the strongest weapons it could possess: the power to regulate in one decisive action (i.e., via trade regulation rulemaking) the advertising practices of the entire alcoholic beverage industry.

In fact, recent FTC actions point to the opposite situation: The Commission may become the industry's strongest ally in its fight against advertising restrictions on its products. In April 1985, FTC denied by a 4-1 vote a petition seeking industrywide proceedings to restrict the advertising of alcoholic beverages.[1] FTC told the petitioners—the Center for Science in the Public Interest (CSPI), twenty-eight other organizations and three individuals—that the Commission found "no reliable basis on which to conclude that alcohol advertising significantly affects alcohol abuse. Absent such evidence, there is no basis for concluding that rules banning or otherwise limiting alcohol advertising would offer significant protection to the public."

Prior to reaching that decision, the Commission's staff had reviewed a large amount of marketing and research data on the consumption and abuse of alcoholic beverages. Their conclusion: "the (existing) literature sheds virtually to light on the relationship between alcohol advertising and abuse." According to FTC staff, "little, if any, evidence exists indicating that alcohol advertising or marketing practices deceptively or unfairly result in alcohol abuse or even increased consumption."

Nevertheless, the Commission is not unmindful of the growing popularity of alcoholic beverage restrictions, including ones on advertising. Accordingly, the Commission took pains to tell the petitioners that it would keep on looking into "how it can best apply its advertising and marketing expertise to the important issues raised by the petition."

One final point is worthy of mention in regards to the CSPI petition. The petition cited several practices that at least one Commissioner, Patricia P. Bailey, found to be "particularly troubling." In fact, her dissent was based on her disagreement with her fellow Commissioners' "decision not even to engage in some factual inquiry with respect to certain questionable advertisements and promotions." She listed several of those "troubling promotional practices in her dissenting opinion:

1. a print advertisement depicting a beer bottle as part of a motorcycle and stating when you do it, do it with Style. [The advertised beer's] Old Style;

2. a print advertisement showing two young people waiting with a car at an inter-

section marked by a 'Beer XXing' sign and with several bottles and glasses of beer going by;

3. a print advertisement depicting four glasses next to a bottle of the product and stating, after a hard day's work pour yourself some [liquor];

4. a print advertisement depicting five brandy glasses and stating, the only thing better than [the advertised liquor] is another [of the advertised liquor];

5. various beer company promotions on college campuses involving chug-a-lug contests; and

6. various advertisements for alcoholic beverages placed in college publications in states where the drinking age is 21.

It will be interesting to observe in the months and years ahead whether these, or similar, promotions come under FTC's scrutiny as it turns its attention, using its case-by-case approach, to the issue of alcoholic beverage advertising.

ATF's ROLE, SELF-REGULATION

The other important federal regulatory agency with jurisdiction over the advertising of alcoholic beverages is the Bureau of Alcohol, Tobacco and Firearms (ATF).[2] ATF groups alcoholic beverages into three major beverage groupings—malt beverages, wine, and distilled spirits—and treats each group differently. These three groupings have been defined as follows:

Malt beverages—"A beverage made by the alcoholic fermentation of an infusion or decoction, or combination of both, in potable brewing water, of malted barley with hops, or their parts, or their products, and with or without the addition of [certain additional ingredients]." (27 CFR 7.20—Regulations under the Federal Alcohol Administration Act.) Malt beverages, it should be added, are low in alcohol content as a percentage of volume and occasionally escape regulations aimed at alcoholic beverages in general promulgated by the states.[3]

Wine—includes grape wine, sparkling grape wine, citrus wine, apertif wine, raisin wine, and sake.[4]

Distilled spirits—includes vodka, whisky, gin, brandy, rum, tequila, cordials and liqueurs, flavored spirits as well as imitations of any of these beverages.[5]

In order to comply with ATF requirements, every ad must include the name and city of the manufacturer of the product and the designation of the type of product involved. Your ad may not make any false statements or a statement misleading in any material respect or one that disparages a competitor's product, or any statement that the involved beverage has intoxicating properties. Producers may not make any representation that the product has curative or therapeutic effects.

You may not advertise any alcoholic beverage using any statement, design or representation concerning analyses, standards, or tests that may be considered misleading. You may not make a statement in your advertising that's inconsistent with your product's label. In addition, you may not make any guaranty in your ad that is misleading. Nor can you use official flags, government insignia, or statements that can be construed as relating to the armed services.

There are other specific requirements that pertain to each type of alcoholic beverage, as follows:

Malt Beverages

ATF forbids advertising the alcoholic content of a malt beverage and forbids designating any product containing less than one-half of one percent alcohol by volume as "beer," "lager beer," "lager," "ale," "porter," or "stout."

The voluntary code governing beer advertising is that of the United States Brewers Association, Inc., 1750 K Street, N.W., Washington, D.C. 20006. The USBA guidelines add to the ATF standards in several significant respects:

- Beer ads should neither suggest nor encourage overindulgence;
- Beer advertising should not suggest or portray drinking by individuals below the legal drinking age nor the purchase of those products by those below the legal age;
- No beer ad should encourage or condone drunk driving;
- Your ad should not contain "scenes of inebriation, revelry, comical drunks, or any other depiction of beer drinkers who have in any way lost control of themselves";
- Beer ads should not "associate or portray beer drinking before or during activities in situations which require a high degree of alertness";
- Religious themes should not be used in beer ads;
- Beer ads should never showing littering;
- Beer advertising shouldn't associate beer with crime or illegal activity.

(For the full text of the *Brewing Industry Advertising Guidelines*, see Appendix 9A at the end of this chapter.)

Wines

ATF forbids ad statements that tend to create the impression that a wine contains distilled spirits, or is comparable with a distilled spirit or has intoxicating qualities. The use of vintage and bottling dates and of the word, "old," is strictly controlled. So is the use of appellation of origin, and domestic products cannot be described as imported.

The only voluntary code governing wine producers is that of the Wine Institute, 165 Post Street, San Francisco, California 94108. Since all the members of the Wine Institute are in California, the Code only governs wines produced in that state. The most distinctive feature of this code provides:

A distinguishing and unique feature of wine is that it is traditionally served with meals or immediately before or following a meal. Therefore, when subscribers to this Code use wine advertising which visually depicts a scene or setting where wine is to be served, such advertising shall include foods and show that they are available and are being used or are intended to be used.

Additional guidelines include provisions that an ad should not suggest that wine is crucial for successful entertaining. Ads should not use models who appear to be under twenty-five years of age. Your wine advertising, says the code, should not use cartoon characters directed at those below the legal drinking age. Wine should not be presented in ads in association with "rites of passage" to adulthood. In addition, your wine ads should not exploit the human form or show provocative or enticing poses.

The Wine Institute's *Code of Advertising Standards* applies to all advertising media. (For the full text of this code, see Appendix 9B at the end of this chapter).

Distilled Spirits

Under ATF rules alcoholic content by proof must be stated for all distilled spirits, except that it may be stated in terms of percentage by volume for cordials and liqueurs, cocktails, highballs, bitters and other specialities as approved by the Director of the BATF. The words "bond", "bonded," "bottled in bond," "aged in bond" or synonymous terms cannot be used unless they appear on the label pursuant to BATF regulations. "Pure" can be used only if part of the bona fide name of the permit holder or retailer for whom the distilled spirits are bonded. The words "double distilled" and "triple distilled" are forbidden.

The Distilled Spirits Council of the United States (DISCUS), 1250 I St., N.W., Washington, D.C. 20005 is the voluntary code authority governing distilled spirits advertising. The Code forbids the advertising of distilled spirits by radio or television, including closed circuit TV. Ads may not appear on the comic pages, on theater screens, nor in publications devoted primarily to religious topics. Ads may not be "in any manner directed or primarily intended to appeal to persons below the legal drinking age." DISCUS members may not seek plugs on television. They cannot use advertising including Santa Claus or any biblical character. No ad should depict a child or suggest the presence of a child. Code subscribers may accept the public acknowledgment of charitable contributions. DISCUS members may accept the acknowledgment of public broadcasting support, but only when the "audience in the principle broadcast area is likely to be composed

primarily of persons above the legal drinking age." There is a Code Review
Board to consider complaints lodged by DISCUS members or other interested parties.

(For the full text of the *Code of Good Practice of the Distilled Spirits
Council of the United States, Inc.*, see Appendix 9C at the end of this
chapter).

NETWORK GUIDELINES

Wine and beer ads—but not those for distilled spirits—may appear on the
national networks. NBC forbids the advertisement of alcoholic beverages as
"necessary to maintain social status, obtain personal achievements, relieve
stress or as a solution to personal problems." On-camera consumption is
forbidden. Ads for liquor outlets are acceptable to NBC provided there is
no reference to unacceptable wine or distilled spirits. Ads on NBC or its
owned and operated stations for airlines and restaurants may make incidental reference to cocktails, but advertising of mixed drinks is not acceptable, nor is the use of terms like "Martini" or "Bloody Mary." Glassware
associated with distilled spirits is not an acceptable prop to NBC except in
connection with a permitted incidental reference. NBC will review advertisements alerting the public to the dangers of alcohol abuse on a "case-by-
case" basis. ABC has a very similar set of guidelines; one minor difference
is that ABC prohibits even the incidental display of cocktail props. CBS has
a policy against direct or implied references to excessive consumption of
beer and wine.

RECENT STEPS BY ATF

A comprehensive review of alcoholic beverage advertising by ATF began
on November 21, 1978, when that agency issued an advance notice of proposed rulemaking. Following an extended comment period, ATF issued
draft regulations on December 9, 1980.

On August 8, 1984, ATF published final regulations affecting the advertising and labeling of alcoholic beverages. The agency delayed decision,
however, on such controversial issues as the use of the terms, "natural" and
"light."

One of the most significant portions of these final regs deals with the
comparative advertising of alcoholic beverages. The final regs require that
comparative ads shall "not be disparaging of a competitive product."
Additionally, the regs require advertisers to follow "any scientifically
accepted procedure" in so-called taste tests. Advertisers must also include
the name and address of the testing administrator in taste-test ads. Both
broadcast and print ads must comply with these rules.

Some people profess to see the letters "S," "E," and "X" and other subliminal messages and shapes on ice cubes and elsewhere in certain alcoholic beverage ads. No hard proof, however, exists that such subliminal techniques have been used in alcoholic beverage or, for that matter, any other print or broadcast ads. Nevertheless, ATF tackled the controversial subliminal advertising issue in its final regs. The regs say simply that "subliminal or similar techniques are prohibited." The regs go on to define subliminals as the:

use of any device or technique that is used to convey or attempts to convey a message to a person by means of images or sounds of a very brief nature that cannot be perceived at a normal level of awareness.

ATF also left undecided at that time the issue of athlete endorsement of alcoholic beverages, as well as the issue of what attitude ATF might take towards the industry's voluntary codes.

Ads by currently active athletes have long been precluded by Rev. Rul. 54-513, which states, "References to the illustrations of prominent athletes consuming or preparing to consume the advertised malt beverages are considered likely to mislead the public and therefore are subject to provisions (concerning misleading alcohol advertising.)" Likewise, Rev. Rul. 54-326 forbids the use of illustrations of athletic activities in connection with distilled spirits. It is expected that ATF will consider proposals to ban all ads featuring celebrities and present or past athletes.

STATE CONTROLS

Of course, the most extensive control of liquor advertising comes from the states. They have restricted advertising on billboards, in circulars, and on radio and television. Displays on retail premises, newspaper and magazine advertising, retailer novelties, consumer novelties, premium offers, cents-off offers, samples, contests, and refunds have not escaped their attention. Neither has the placement and use of signs. While this extensive scheme of regulation is too detailed for discussion in this chapter, it is worth looking at the constitutional dimensions of the problem.

First, it is argued that the Twenty-first Amendment to the Constitution gives the states some special powers beyond the usual exercise of the police power. This argument was accepted by the Circuit Court of Appeals in *Capital Cities Cable, Inc. v. Crisp*;[6] the Supreme Court in that case ultimately sidestepped the issue and decided against the state regulation on the basis of federal preemption. In a landmark 9-0 decision, the U.S. Supreme Court ruled against Oklahoma's advertising ban requiring cable television operators to screen out alcoholic beverage advertising contained in the out-of-state signals they retransmit by cable to their subscribers. The main rationale behind the High Court's ruling: Since cable television operates under Federal Communications Commission (FCC) regulations, Oklahoma's ban is preempted by federal law. In addition, Oklahoma's ban conflicts with specific FCC regulations and is at odds with FCC's regulatory goal of making the benefits of cable television available nationally.

Since the High Court reached its decision in *Crisp* on the basis that Oklahoma's ban was preempted by federal law, the Court did not address the broader First Amendment question involved.

Two other widely noticed cases have upheld state control of liquor ads. In *Queensgate Inv. Co. v. Liquor Control Comm'n*, the United States Supreme court dismissed per curiam an appeal from an Ohio state court's ruling upholding an Ohio regulation prohibiting retail liquor permittees from advertising the price of alcoholic beverages off their premises.[7] The Fifth Federal Circuit then followed that precedent and upheld Mississippi statutes and regulations that effectively ban liquor advertising on billboards, in print, and over the air within the state (*Dunagin v. City of Oxford, Mississippi*).[8]

NOTES

1. Denial of the CSPI Petition to Regulate Unfair and Deceptive Alcoholic Beverage Advertising and Marketing Practices, 4-15-85.

2. See, generally, *Advertising Compliance Service*, Tab #18, Alcoholic Beverages, Article #8, Healy, "Controls on Alcoholic Beverage Advertising: Existing and Proposed."

3. Cf. *Capital Cities Cable, Inc. v. Crisp*, 81 L.Ed 2d 580 (1984) at 587 n.3.

4. 27 CFR 4.21.

5. 27 CFR 5.22.

6. 81 L.Ed 2d 580 (1984), reversing *Oklahoma Telecasters v. Crisp*, 699 F.2d. 490 (10th Cir. 1983).

7. 103 S. Ct. 31 dismissing appeal from 69 Ohio St. 2d 361, 433 N.E. 2d. 138 (1982) (per curiam).

8. 718 F.2d. 738 (5th Cir., 1983) (en banc). For a more complete discussion, see Mandel, "Note—Liquor Advertising: Resolving the Clash between the First and Twenty First Amendment," 59 NYU L.Rev. 157 (April 1984).

Appendix 9A

BREWING INDUSTRY ADVERTISING GUIDELINES
DECEMBER 1984

INTRODUCTION

These Brewing Industry Advertising Guidelines have been developed as a service to those responsible for the advertising of beer. They are intended to provide guidance which will assist brewers in maintaining the highest ethical standards in their advertising. The brewing industry first developed voluntary Guidelines on advertising in the 1940s. Over the years, the industry has periodically revised and updated these Guidelines.

BASIC GUIDELINES FOR BEER ADVERTISING

Beer is a refreshing, wholesome beverage meant to be consumed in moderation. Its origins are ancient, and it has held a respected position in nearly every culture and society since the dawn of recorded history. Advertising is a legitimate effort by brewers to make consumers aware of the particular types, brands and prices of malt beverages that are available.

Three basic principles which have long been reflected in the policies of the brewing industry continue to underlie these Guidelines. First, beer advertising should not suggest directly or indirectly that any of the laws applicable to the sale and consumption of beer should not be scrupulously complied with. Second, brewers should adhere to standards of candor and good taste applicable to all commercial advertising. Third, brewers are responsible corporate citizens, sensitive to the problems of the society in which they exist, and their advertising should reflect that fact.

These Guidelines consist of more specific provisions describing the advertising policies of the brewing industry.

1. Beer advertisements should neither suggest nor encourage overindulgence.

Because beer is a beverage of moderation, advertising should not portray or suggest its abuse, even in a comical vein.

2. Beer advertising should neither portray nor encourage drinking by individuals below the legal age of purchase.

3. No beer advertisements should in any way suggest noncompliance with legal age of purchase limitations.

4. No beer advertisements should encourage or condone drunk driving.

5. Advertisements should not include scenes of inebriation, revelry, comical drunks, or any other depiction of beer drinkers who have in any way lost control of themselves.

Beer advertisements should never directly or indirectly suggest misuse or abuse of the product.

6. Beer advertisements should make no scientifically unsubstantiated health claims.

If there exists significant controversy in the medical or scientific community regarding the accuracy of a claim, the making of that claim without simultaneously revealing the existence of the controversy should be avoided.

7. Beer advertisements should not associate or portray beer drinking before or during activities in situations which require a high degree of alertness.

Beer is for relaxation and is not compatible with driving or performing hazardous jobs.

8. Advertising should neither state nor carry any implication of alcohol strength.

Advertisements should not refer to the "strength" of a beer or boast subtly of "kick," or otherwise promote its relative alcohol content. Nor should advertisements include other subtle references to alcohol, such as puns on words like "spirit" or "proof," or any overt or implicit association with distilled spirits. Any claim of alcohol content permitted by applicable law or regulation shall be deemed to be in compliance with this Guideline.

9. Beer advertising should not portray sexual passion, promiscuity, or any other amorous activity as a consequence of drinking beer.

Beer is not related to sexual stimulation, and should not be portrayed in any fashion implying or suggesting that it is.

10. Advertisements should not contain suggestive double entendres or any other material that might be considered lewd or obscene.

11. Advertisements should not associate beer with crime, criminals, or any illegal activity.

Advertisements should not associate beer with any illegal activity or disreputable circumstances. Men and women portrayed in beer advertisements should be law abiding and mannerly.

12. Taverns or other places portrayed in beer advertisements should always be depicted as well-kept and respectable gathering places.

13. Religion and religious themes should never be employed in the advertising of beer.

14. Advertisers of malt beverages should not improperly disparage competing beers. Comparisons in advertising should be objective, truthful, and significant.

Advertising should address the merits of the products being offered. It should not characterize competing products falsely or inaccurately or in a misleading fashion. Comparisons in advertising should be objective and truthful. Consistent with Federal regulatory policies, comparisons must be adequately substantiated. Moreover, such advertising should provide useful and significant information to the consumer.

15. Advertising should never suggest that competing beers contain objectionable additives or ingredients.

These include representations or implications that other beers contain "synthetic additives" or other "artificial ingredients." Because these words often have pejorative meanings, their use is inappropriate. No beer may contain ingredients not permitted or approved by the Food and Drug Administration and authorized by the Bureau of Alcohol, Tobacco, and Firearms.

16. Beer advertisements should not make exaggerated product representations.

Beer advertisements should restrict themselves to an honest and accurate statement of facts. This is desirable in all advertising. Unfulfilled and false claims about a product do not benefit consumers.

17. Advertising should not use scientific or pseudo-scientific terms to convey to convey the impression that a beer has special or unique qualities if in fact it does not.

18. No beer advertisements in college, campus, or other media should portray beer drinking as being important to education, nor should beer advertising directly or indirectly degrade study.

19. Beer advertising on television should make no representation of on-camera drinking, including sound effects of drinking.

20. Beer advertising should never show littering.

(Reprinted by permission of the United States Brewer's Association, Inc.)

Appendix 9B
CODE OF ADVERTISING STANDARDS:
WINE INSTITUTE

PREAMBLE

Informal principles of good advertising practice for the winegrowing industry were first adopted in 1949. In recent years, it has become evident that more specific and significantly stronger standards are desired by wine advertisers to reflect the industry's concern with maximum social responsibility. This code is designed to encourage continued high standards so that wine advertising may increasingly be viewed as a positive contribution to society.

April 1978

GUIDELINES

These guidelines shall apply only to the voluntary subscribers to this Code of Advertising Standards.

1. A distinguishing and unique feature of wine is that it is traditionally served with meals or immediately before or following a meal. Therefore, when subscribers to this code use wine advertising which visually depicts a scene or setting where wine is to be served, such advertising shall include foods and show that they are available and are being used or are intended to be used.

   This guideline shall not apply to the depiction of a bottle of wine, vineyard, winery, label, professional tasting, etc., where emphasis is on the product.

2. Wine advertising should encourage the proper use of wine. Therefore, subscribers to this code shall not depict or describe in their advertising:

   a. The consumption of wine for the effects its alcohol content may produce.

   b. Direct or indirect reference to alcoholic content or extra strength, except as otherwise required by law or regulation.

   c. Excessive drinking or persons who appear to have lost control or to be inappropriately uninhibited.

   d. Any suggestion that excessive drinking or loss of control is amusing or a proper subject for amusement.

   e. Any persons engaged in activities not normally associated with the moderate use of wine and a responsibile life-style. Association of wine use in conjunction with feats of daring or activities requiring unusual skill is specifically prohibited.

  f. Wine in quantities inappropriate to the situation or inappropriate for moderate and responsible use.

3. Advertising of wine has traditionally depicted wholesome persons enjoying their lives and illustrating the role of wine in a mature life-style. Any attempt to suggest that wine directly contributes to success or achievement is unacceptable. Therefore, the following restrictions shall apply to subscribers to this code:

  a. Wine shall not be presented as being essential to personal performance, social attainment, achievement, success or wealth.

  b. The use of wine shall not be directly associated with social, physical or personal problem solving.

  c. Wine shall not be presented as vital to social acceptability and popularity or as the key factor in such popularity.

  d. It shall not be suggested that wine is crucial for successful entertaining.

4. Any advertisement which has particular appeal to persons below the legal drinking age is unacceptable. Therefore, wine advertising by code subscribers shall not:

  a. Show models and personalities in advertisements who appear to be under 25 years of age.

  b. Use music, language, gestures or cartoon characters specifically associated with or directed toward those below the legal drinking age.

  c. Appear in children's or juveniles' magazines, newspapers, television programs, radio programs or other media specifically oriented to persons below the legal drinking age.

  d. Be presented as being related to the attainment of adulthood or associated with "rites of passage" to adulthood.

  e. Suggest that a wine product resembles or is similar to another type of beverage or product (milk, soda, candy) having particular appeal to persons below the legal drinking age.

  f. Use traditional heroes of the young such as those engaged in pastimes and occupations having a particular appeal to persons below the legal drinking age. (For example, cowboys, race car drivers, rock stars, etc.)

  g. Use amateur or professional sports celebrities, past or present.

5. Code subscribers shall not show motor vehicles in such a way as to suggest that they are to be operated in conjunction with wine use. Advertising should in no way suggest that wine be used in connection with driving.

6. Wine advertising by code subscribers shall not appear in or directly adjacent to television or radio programs or print media which dramatize or glamorize overconsumption or inappropriate use of alcoholic beverages.

7. Wine advertising by code subscribers shall make no reference to wine's medicinal values.

8. Wine advertising by code subscribers shall not degrade the image or status of any ethnic, minority or other group.

9. Wine advertising by code subscribers shall not exploit the human form, feature provocative or enticing poses nor be demeaning to any individual.

All advertising—including, but not limited to direct mail, point-of-sale, outdoor, displays, radio, television and print media—should adhere to both the letter and the spirit of the above code.

Wine Institute
The Trade Association of
California Winegrowers
165 Post Street
San Francisco, California 94018
(415) 986-0878

(Reproduced by permission of the Wine Institute, The Trade Association of Califonia Winegrowers).

Appendix 9C

CODE OF GOOD PRACTICE OF THE DISTILLED SPIRITS COUNCIL OF THE UNITED STATES, INC.
Approved November 15, 1983

PREAMBLE

The members of the Distilled Spirits Council of the United States, Inc. (DISCUS), the trade association representing the distilled spirits industry, adopt this Code of Good Practice to restrict advertising of distilled spirits to responsible adult consumers, to avoid advertising and promotion of sale of distilled spirits to minors, and to provide guidelines to ensure that such advertising is presented in a tasteful and dignified manner.

Since repeal of the Eighteenth Amendment to the United States Constitution, which prohibited sale of beverage alcohol, the distilled spirits industry has openly acknowledged the problems inherent in abusive consumption of beverage alcohol and has joined with government and civic groups in efforts to encourage moderate and responsible use. The industry has both initiated and actively supported undertakings of many different kinds, i.e., informational, educational, research, and rehabilitative, in an effort to better understand, prevent, and combat misuse of its products. Included among such efforts is the adoption and voluntary adherence to this Code of Good Practice by the members of DISCUS.

The members of DISCUS voluntarily adopt the provisions of this Code as guidelines to achieve the foregoing objectives. Since it is recognized that opinions may differ as to the interpretation of such guidelines, such questions will be addressed by the CODE REVIEW BOARD.

Therefore, the members of DISCUS voluntarily pledge to establish and maintain exemplary standards and practices by adhering to the following:

I. ADVERTISING

A. Distilled Spirits should not be advertised:

1. By means of radio or television, including both public and private closed circuit TV;

2. On the comic pages of newspapers, magazines, or other publications;

3. In publications devoted primarily to religious topics;

4. In any manner directed or primarily intended to appeal to persons below the legal drinking age;

5. On the screen of motion picture theaters or similar assemblies.

B. No advertisement of distilled spirits should contain advertising copy or an illustration unless it is dignified, modest, and in good taste. In addition, no advertisement should claim sexual or physical prowess as a result of the consumption of distilled spirits.

C. Members should not, directly or indirectly, provide any compensation for advertising "plugs" on radio or television.

D. No advertisement of distilled spirits should contain the name of or depict Santa Claus or any Biblical character.

E. No advertisement of distilled spirits should depict a child or immature person, portray objects (such as toys) suggestive of the presence of a child, or in any manner be designed to be especially appealing to children or immature persons.

F. All advertisements of distilled spirits should be modest, dignified, and in good taste.

II. GOOD FAITH COMPLIANCE

The provisions of this Code should not be violated or evaded through subterfuge or indirection, such as through institutional advertising and/or program sponsorship.

Financial support of or contributions to charitable organizations or events and to public broadcasting and public telecommunications entities as defined in Title 47 of the United States Code are approved where the contribution is publicly acknowledged by the recipient by reference only to the name of the grantor making the contribution. The name of the grantor may include a brand name but should not include a class or type or other product description (e.g. The XYZ Whiskey Distilling Company or XYZ Whiskey). In the case of contributions to public broadcasting and public telecommunications entities the contributor should specify that the acknowledgement is to be made when the audience in the principal broadcast area is likely to be composed primarily of persons above the legal drinking age.

III. MEMBERS SUBSCRIBE

The members of DISCUS voluntarily subscribe to this Code.

IV. JURISDICTION

This Code is applicable to the states of the United States only.

V. CODE REVIEW BOARD

There shall be established and maintained a CODE REVIEW BOARD, which shall meet when necessary to consider complaints lodged by DISCUS members or other interested parties.

The CODE REVIEW BOARD shall be comprised of no less than five (5) members in good standing of the Board of Directors of DISCUS. Each member shall serve for a term of not more than three (3) years and shall, upon the vote of a majority of the members of the Board of Directors, be succeeded by another member of the Board of Directors who has not served as a member of the CODE REVIEW BOARD for a period of at least two (2) years.

Findings of the majority of the members of the CODE REVIEW BOARD shall be communicated promptly to the responsible advertiser and in appropriate circumstances to all members of the Board of Directors of DISCUS.

(Reproduced by permission of the Distilled Spirits Council of the United States, Inc.)

10.
COMMERCIAL SPEECH

The indisputably enormous, and growing, role that advertising plays in American society is evident to even the casual observer. For good or ill, advertising has transformed the United States into a nation of advertising-driven consumer-citizens, whose actions and beliefs may well be shaped more by advertising than by even the news media.[1]

Yet advertising itself has undergone a remarkable transformation over the past decade. Advertising on virtually every medium has become far more visually and/or aurally compelling than ever before for a variety of technological and creative reasons. But perhaps advertising's greatest triumph is its increased level of acceptability throughout American society. A major reason for that societal acceptance today is the United States Supreme Court's acceptance of advertising as a form of expression worthy of protection under the First Amendment to the U.S. Constitution.

However, the protection of advertising, or "commercial speech" as the courts have called it, was not always the case. Indeed, until relatively recently, commercial speech was not protected by the First Amendment. In the landmark advertising case of *Valentine v. Chrestensen*,[2] the U.S. High Court upheld a New York statute forbidding the distribution of handbills, reasoning that "purely commercial advertising" was not protected. The ruling was widely criticized, not least of all by Justice William O. Douglas, who called it "casual, almost offhand" in his concurrence in a later decision, *Cammarano v. United States*.[3]

Nevertheless, the doctrine remained. Even Justice Douglas's fellow defender of First Amendment rights, Justice Hugo Black, believed that a city ordinance forbidding door-to-door solicitation of magazine subscriptions "could constitutionally be applied to a 'merchant' who goes from door to door 'selling pots' " (See, *Breard v. Alexandria*.)[4]

A CRITICAL YEAR: 1975

Nineteen seventy-five was a critical year in the history of the protection of commercial speech. In that year, the Supreme Court was confronted with an attempt by Virginia to prevent advertising in a local newspaper announcing the legality of abortions in New York along with a referral service. The High Court found that the ad "did more than simply propose a commercial transaction. It contained factual material of clear 'public interest,' " (i.e., the legality of abortions in New York). (See, *Bigelow v. Virginia*.)[5]

Before 1975, cases involving purely commercial speech generally fell into two categories, both of which allowed the Court to avoid creation of a new First Amendment right: (1) laws limiting advertising but not banning it altogether, and (2) rules or actions against false or deceptive ads.

Members of regulated professions faced total bans on advertising. So they found themselves in the strongest position to establish a First Amendment right to advertise. They were, however, reluctant to do so, and the seminal case in this field was brought by Virginia *consumers* asserting a First Amendment right to receive the competitive benefits of price advertising of prescription drugs by Virginia's pharmacists, who were prohibited by law from engaging in such advertising.

While the pharmacists themselves sat on the sidelines, and despite the strenuous objections of Justice William Rehnquist, the Court granted standing to the consumers: "If there is a right to advertise, there is a reciprocal right to receive the advertising, and it may be asserted by these appellees." (See, *Virginia Pharmacy Board v. Virginia Consumer Council*.)[6]

Rejecting what it called Virginia's "highly paternalistic approach," (i.e., a ban on advertising), the High Court said a better alternative "is to assume that this information is not in itself harmful, that people will perceive their own best interests if only they are well enough informed, and that the best means to that end is to open the channels of communication rather than to close them . . . It is precisely this kind of choice, between the dangers of its misuse if it is freely available, that the First Amendment makes for us."[7]

But the Court made clear that First Amendment *protection* would *not* be absolute. "Mere time, place, and manner" restrictions would survive, the Court said, if they

1. Are justified without reference to the content of the regulated speech,
2. Serve a significant governmental interest, and
3. Leave open alternative means of expression.

These caveats apply equally to noncommercial speech.

But in a significant footnote, the Supreme Court went even further, and cautioned that First Amendment protections envisioned for purely commercial speech would be narrower than those accorded other speech:

> In concluding that commercial speech enjoys First Amendment protection, we have not held that it is wholly undifferentiable from other forms. There are commonsense differences between speech that does 'no more than propose a commercial transaction,' [citation omitted] and other varieties.
>
> Even if the differences do not justify the conclusion that commercial speech is valueless, and thus subject to complete suppression by the State, they nonetheless suggest that a different degree of protection is necessary to insure that the flow of truthful and legitimate commercial information be unimpaired.
>
> The truth of commercial speech, for example, may be more easily verifiable by its disseminator than, let us say, news reporting or political commentary, in that ordinarily the advertiser seeks to disseminate information about a specific product or service that he himself provides and presumably knows more about than anyone else. Also, commercial speech may be more durable than other kinds. Since advertising is the *sine qua non* of commercial profits, there is little likelihood of its being chilled by proper regulation and foregone entirely.
>
> Attributes such as these, the greater objectivity and hardiness of commercial speech, may make it less necessary to tolerate inaccurate statements for fear of silencing the speaker [citation omitted]. They may also make it appropriate to require that a commercial message appear in such a form, or include such additional information, warnings, and disclaimers, as are necessary to prevent its being deceptive. [citations omitted]. They may also make inapplicable the prohibition against prior restraints.[8]

In *Virginia Pharmacy*, the Court emphasized that pharmacists' prescription drug advertising would be mostly for prepackaged drugs. In his concurring opinion, Chief Justice Burger said that "quite different factors would govern were we faced with a law regulating or even prohibiting advertising by the traditional learned professions of medicine or law."

Justice Rehnquist disagreed: "I cannot distinguish between the public's right to know the price of drugs and its right to know the price of title searches or physical examinations or other professional services for which standardized fees are charged." As it turned out, neither could the Court.

GROWING FIRST AMENDMENT PROTECTION

In a later decision, the Court considered a disciplinary action taken against a legal clinic for running newspaper ads listing prices of standard services. (See *Bates v. State Bar of Arizona*.)[9] The claims did not relate to the *quality* of services provided.

The Court rejected the various justifications offered for the suppression of price advertising, and held that states cannot "prevent the publication in a newspaper of appellants' truthful advertisement concerning the availability and terms of routine legal service."

It had now become clear that purely commercial speech promoting goods and services would enjoy at least *some* First Amendment protection. Nevertheless, two Supreme Court decisions raised questions concerning *how far* those constitutional rights would extend.

In 1976, the Court struck down an antiblockbusting ordinance enacted by Willingboro, N.J. to stem "white flight"—and preserve an integrated community—by prohibiting the placement of "for sale" signs on lawns. *Linmark Associates, Inc. v. Willingboro.*[10] The Court refused to characterize this as a "time, place, or manner" restriction, and went on to question whether the ordinance was really motivated by—or necessary to prevent—white flight in Willingboro. The Court contrasted the facts with those in *Barrick Realty, Inc. v. City of Gary*,[11] in which a similar law was upheld, upon a clear demonstration of panic selling by whites, and refused to say whether the *Virginia Pharmacy* decision would have made the Gary statute equally as unconstitutional as Willingboro's.

In the second case, the High Court refused to extend First Amendment protection to the use of trade names by optometrists, and upheld a Texas statute forbidding the practice. The Court distinguished trade names from other forms of advertising by finding that trade names have "no intrinsic meaning."

It found that Texas's concerns about "the deceptive and misleading uses of optometrical trade names were not speculative or hypothetical," and that the ban had "only the most incidental effect on the content of the comercial speech of Texas optometrists." (See *Friedman v. Rogers*)[12]

Justices Blackmun and Marshall dissented, citing the usefulness of trade names to consumers in locating "the goods, services, and prices they prefer on a continuing basis with substantially lower search costs than would otherwise be the case"[13]

THE FOUR-PART ANALYSIS: CENTRAL HUDSON

In 1980, the Court reviewed a total prohibition on advertising to promote the use of electricity imposed on the Central Hudson Gas & Electric Corp. by New York's Public Service Commission (*Central Hudson Gas v. Public Service Commission*).[14]

The utility argued that its First Amendment rights had been violated, but the Commission said the ban was justified by the urgent need for energy conservation. To balance these claims, the Court looked at the series of cases beginning with *Virginia Pharmacy* and developed the following four-part analysis to determine whether a statement came within the purview of the commercial speech doctrine:

1. Is the activity lawful and the commercial speech free of misleading claims?

2. Is the governmental interest in the suppression of the commercial speech substantial?

3. If so, does the regulation directly advance the governmental interest asserted?

4. Is the governmental regulation no more extensive than necessary to further the interest asserted?

The Court found the advertising in question to concern lawful activity, and found the utility's monopoly status no bar to the usefulness of its advertising to consumers. It also found the state's interest in energy conservation substantial. But it struck down the ban primarily because it was not the least restrictive alternative.

ATTORNEY ADVERTISING

Ever since the *Central Hudson* case, its "least restrictive alternative" test has indeed proved the most fertile area of attack for challengers of bans or prescriptive restraints on advertising. One of the most important Supreme Court decisions in this area involves attorney advertising: *In re R.M.J.*[15] However, the importance of this case extends to *product* advertising as well.

Here are the facts: A lawyer's ad had listed areas of specialty beyond those exclusively approved for ads by the state bar. In addition, the ad included a list of states in which the lawyer was licensed to practice. (The Missouri bar had prohibited such listings).

The Court held the First Amendment protected the attorney's alternative approaches. His choice of words to describe his specialties were "more informative" than those prescribed, and posed "no apparent danger of deception."

The Court also protected his list of jurisdictions, caling the information "factual and highly relevant."[16]

An attorney's right to advertise truthfully his or her services continued its steady expansion with the 1985 decision of *Zauderer v. Office of Disciplinary Counsel of the Supreme Court of Ohio.*[17] In that ruling, the High Court reversed a public reprimand of an Ohio attorney, Philip Q. Zauderer, to the extent that it was based on his use of an illustration in his ad in violation of a state disciplinary rule, and his offer of legal advice in violation of another rule.

COMMERCIAL, BUT NOT PURELY

The Supreme Court has let stand an appeals court decision enjoining enforcement against a free newspaper called *Piggy Back* of an ordinance forbidding door-to-door distribution advertising. In *Ad World, Inc. v. Township of Doylestown,*[18] Ad World distributed *Piggy Back* by leaving it on doorknobs.

The township enacted an ordinance forbidding this method of distributing advertising. Its reason: The accumulation of such material was an invitation to burglary. Ad World contended that enforcement of the ordinance against it was unconstitutional.

While conceding that *Piggy Back* "includes a few pages of consumer and community information," the district court characterized the material as purely commercial speech. Perhaps the court's observation that "all costs are paid by the bulletin's advertisers, and there is no charge to the recipients" led to this conclusion. The court then applied the *Central Hudson* test and, satisfied on all counts, upheld the ban.

But the Third Circuit reversed, characterizing *Piggy Back* as noncommercial speech:

Piggy Back performs functions that larger metropolitan or regional newspapers undertake: spreading information generally, and providing a medium for advertising. . . .

The fact that a publication carries advertisements or that it is for profit does not render its speech commercial for first amendment purposes. . . .

The important question is whether the publication as a whole relates solely to the economic interest of the speaker and its audience (citing *Central Hudson*). Even if a publication such as *Piggy Back* had contained only advertisements, it might be possible to view the publication as qualitatively different from an advertising leaflet put forth by an individual merchant to tout only its own products, because the publication would create a forum in which advertisers compete for consumers' attention.[19]

CONSUMERS, ADVERTISERS, AND THE PUBLIC INTEREST

Traditional first amendment battles pit a speaker's rights against various state interests. But *advertisers* asserting their first amendment rights find an important twist in constitutional protection for purely commercial speech: The first amendment interests protected by the courts are primarily those of the *recipients* of the ads.

Since most restrictions on advertising are also alleged to be in the interest of the potential recipient, the result is that both parties in these cases—the government agency and the advertiser—vie to convince the court that they best represent the public interest.

IMPORTANT FTC CASES

In two recent decisions enforcing broad FTC orders against Sears, Roebuck & Co. and Litton Industries, Inc., the Ninth Circuit gave short shrift to First Amendment claims.

Although Sears' alleged misrepresentations were only in connection with its Lady Kenmore dishwasher, FTC ordered Sears to substantiate future claims for fourteen major appliances. Sears objected, arguing that its constitutional right to truthful speech was infringed. The court was unimpressed:

The Commission may require prior reasonable substantiation of product performance claims after finding violations of the Act, without offending the first amendment.[20]

Nor does the order offend the vagueness doctrine of the first amendment . . . [It] forbids false and unsubstantiated performance claims as to certain specific products.[21]

BALANCING: METROMEDIA AND BOLGER

In *Metromedia v. City of San Diego*,[22] the U.S. Supreme Court had an early chance to apply its balancing test. There was no majority opinion in this case, but it is clear that a majority of the Court believed: (1) that San Diego could validly forbid all commercial billboards located within that municipality, and (2) San Diego could also constitutionally ban billboards, while enacting no prohibition of on-site signs. What split the Court was the treatment of noncommercial billboards, as the disputed ordinance permitted some noncommercial structures, but it did not permit others. The plurality reached its conclusion in *Metromedia* quite readily. While the justices affirmed their support of the four-part *Central Hudson* test, they noted that the city's aesthetic interest in controlling billboard ugliness and in traffic control outweighed the commercial interests asserted. Justices Brennan and Blackmun found the ordinance unconstitutional due to overbreadth, as the city prohibited any billboards at all regardless of where located. The Chief Justice and Justice Rhenquist stressed the power of local governments over distractions within the community (echoing obscenity cases), while Justice Stevens stressed the ugly billboards' effect on property values.

In *Bolger v. Youngs Drug Products Corp.*,[23] the Supreme Court found that the interest in commercial speech outweighed the governmental interests. In this case, a manufacturer and distributor of contraceptives brought a declaratory judgment in the U.S. District Court for the District of Columbia. The drug concern proposed to mail to the public unsolicited advertisements including informational pamphlets promoting its products, but also discussing venereal disease and family planning. The Postmaster General notified the drug concern that the proposed mailing would violate Sec. 30001(e) of the Postal Code—the so-called Comstock Act. The district court ordered that multi-item drugstore flyers containing promotion of contraceptives could be mailed to the same extent such flyers could be mailed if they did not contain such promotion.

With respect to flyers and pamphlets devoted to promoting the desirability or availability of contraceptives, the district court attached four conditions to unsolicited mailings: (1) flyers must be mailed in a completely opaque envelope; (2) the envelope must state that the material has not been solicited by the addressee; (3) the envelope must contain a prominent warning that the contents promote contraceptive products; and (4) the envelope must note that federal law permits the recipient to have his name removed from the mailer's mailing list.

On direct appeal to the Supreme Court, the ruling was affirmed unanimously. Speaking through Justice Marshall, the Court characterized Young's informational booklets as commercial speech. Citing *Times v. Sullivan*, Marshall noted that the fact that a given form of expression is an ad does not make it commercial speech, but that an advertisement disseminated with a commercial motivation for mailing the pamphlets and making reference to a specific product is sufficient to render the expression commercial speech. The mere fact that an ad links a product to a current public debate does not entitle the statement to First Amendment protection. Nor are false and misleading commercial statements entitled to constitutional protection merely because the ads make reference to public issues.

Marshall conceded that the involved statute originated in 1873 as part of the Comstock Act "for the suppression of trade in [the] circulation of obscene literature and articles of immoral use." The government did not defend that statute as an obscenity regulation, however, and, of course, it would be difficult for the government to do so in light of *Griswold v. Connecticut*,[24] which held that statutes prohibiting the sale of contraceptives violated the right of privacy. Instead, the Postal Service tried a line of argument closer to part two of *Central Hudson* and to *Metromedia*. It argued that the statute shielded the privacy of mail recipients and helped ensure parental control of children's receipt of information concerning sexual relations. The Court found, however, that anyone offended by Young's mailing had merely to throw the offending material in the trash can. If really offended, the recipient may take advantage of the postal regulation that allows addresses to give notice to a mailer that they wish no further mailings which, in their sole discretion, they believe to be erotically arousing or sexually provocative. As for parental control over children's sexual information, it is up to the parents to remove offending material from the mailbox. The Court will not deprive adults of reading matter merely because it might not be suitable for minors. Finally, there is an interest in truthful matter relating to birth control for adolescents. Thus, the Postmaster General's position was rejected.

NOTES

1. This chapter is adapted from the following articles appearing in *Advertising Compliance Service*: (1) "Commercial Speech and the First Amendment," by

William H. Feldman, Tab #10, Commercial Speech, Articles #1 & 2; and (ii) "Commercial Speech: An Update," by John D. Healy, Tab #10, Commercial Speech, Article #3.

2. 316 U.S. 52 (1942).

3. 358 U.S. 498, 514 (1959).

4. 341 U.S. 622, 650 (1951).

5. 421 U.S. 809, 822 (1975).

6. 425 U.S. 748, 757 (1975).

7. 425 U.S. at 770.

8. 425 U.S. at 771-772, n.24.

9. 433 U.S. 350 (1977).

10. 431 U.S. 85 (1977).

11. 491 F.2d 161 (7th Cir. 1974).

12. 440 U.S. 1, 12, 16 (1979).

13. 440 U.S. at 22.

14. 447 U.S. 557 (1980).

15. 455 U.S. 191 (1982).

16. See also, *Advertising Compliance Service*, Tab #19, Professional Ads, Article #2.

17. U.S. Sup. Ct. Dkt. #83-2166, argued January 7, 1985 and decided May 28, 1985.

18. 510 F. Supp. 851 (E.D. PA 1981).

19. *Ad World, Inc. v. Township of Doylestown*, U.S. Ct. Appls., 3rd Cir., Dkt. #81-1497, 2-5-82; U.S. Sup. Ct., Dkt. #81-1765, *cert. denied*, May 1982.

20. 598 F.2d at 1252.

21. *Sears, Roebuck & Co. v. FTC*, U.S. Court of Appeals for the 9th Cir. (San Francisco), Dkt. #80-7368, 5-6-82, Slip Op. at 22-23. See also *Litton Industries, Inc. v. FTC*, U.S. Court of Appeals for the 9th Cir. (San Francisco), Dkt. #81-7148, May 3, 1982, Slip Op. at 16.

22. 453 U.S. 490 (1981).

23. 103 S. Ct. 2875 (1983).

24. 381 U.S. 479 (1965).

11.
RIGHTS OF PUBLICITY, PRIVACY

Good name in man and woman, dear my lord,
Is the immediate jewel of their souls:
Who steals my purse steals trash; 'tis something, nothing;
'Twas mine 'tis his, and has been slave to thousands;
But he that filches from me my good name
Robs me of that which not enriches him.
And makes me poor indeed.[1]

William Shakespeare, who penned these words in his famous play *Othello*, perhaps did not envision the phenomenon of mass media advertising of the twentieth century. For not a few advertisers have "filched" many a good name and have been enriched (at least monetarily) for their efforts.

A growing trend in advertising is for advertisers to exploit the likenesses of celebrities commercially in selling their products or services. These advertisers are using the likenesses of celebrities who are living, as well as those that are dead, who owe their fame to show business as well as those who achieved fame from other walks of life, and with these celebrities' (or their heirs') permission as well as without it.

The advent of modern video technology and the resultant new advertising sophistication this techology has spawned, have caused the courts to face new issues of privacy and publicity rights. Where does a celebrity's right of privacy end and an advertiser's right of freedom of speech begin? Does a celebrity have a right of publicity that only he or she alone can exploit? Does this right of publicity survive the celebrity's death and, if so, who is entitled to exploit that right? When can an advertiser use the name, likeness, physical attributes, or public image of a famous person, living or dead? The answer to this question for the use of likenesses of deceased personalities is bound up in the issue over whether there is a "descendible" right of publicity for the heirs or estate of the deceased entertainer or public figure.

If the right to that person's image survives his death, then an advertiser would have to pay the heirs for use of the person's likeness. If there is no such right, advertisers would be free to use likenesses without payment or permission.

This chapter briefly examines the historical background of both the right of privacy and the right of publicity as it relates to the use of a person's likeness in commercial advertisements. It also examines the growing trend tending towards greater judicial protection of these rights.

RIGHT OF PRIVACY

Both the right of privacy and the right of publicity have common roots. The right of privacy can be traced directly to a major article on the subject, entitled, appropriately enough, "The Right to Privacy." Written by Samuel Warren and Louis Brandeis and published in the Harvard Law Review in 1890, this seminal statement on the privacy right focused on the right of an individual to be left alone under the protection of a "principle which protects personal writings and all other personal productions, not against theft and physical appropriation, but against publication in any form, [and which] is in reality not the principle of private property, but that of inviolate personality."[2] While the first courts to consider this new "right" had difficulty with this concept—and at least in one instance explicitly rejecting it[3]—later courts came to recognize the right of privacy "as an independent, common law right." Indeed, this right "was eventually accepted by most American courts."[4] As further evidence of judicial acceptance of this new right is the fact that the U.S. Supreme Court has recognized the existence of a marital right of privacy (in the context of a state criminal statute involving the use of contraceptive drugs or devices).[5]

RIGHT OF PUBLICITY

The right of publicity, on the other hand, is a much newer theory. Along with the increasing popularity of "movies" and, later, radio and television, arose a new and growing class of persons whose success depended, in large measure, on giving up their privacy. Paralleling these developments was the growing interest in sports, and particularly professional baseball and football. These "entertainers" and sports figures thrived on publicity yet saw others enriching themselves by commercially exploiting the public personas that they had created. However, the right of privacy proved inadequate to redress this group's legitimate concerns. Its inadequacy stems from the concept of "waiver." By making their lives public, it was reasoned, these entertainers and sports figures had waived their right to privacy.[6]

While the first courts to grapple with protecting this group took this approach,[7] the important Second Circuit Court of Appeals saw things differently in its landmark decision of *Haelan Laboratories v. Topps Chewing Gum, Inc.*[8] That decision involved a contract dispute over the use of a baseball player's likeness in connection with the sale of gum. In that decision, the right of publicity was expressly recognized for the first time. As the Appeals Court noted in *Haelan Laboratories*:

We think that, in addition to and independent of that right of privacy (which in New York derives from statute), a man has a right in the publicity value of his photograph, i.e., the right to grant the exclusive privilege of publishing his picture, and that such a grant may validly be made 'in gross,' i.e., without an accompanying transfer of a business or of anything else. Whether it be labelled a ''property' right is immaterial; for here, as often elsewhere, the tag 'property' simply symbolizes the fact that courts enforce a claim which has pecuniary worth. This right might be called a 'right of publicity.'

POST-DEATH RIGHT OF PUBLICITY

While the U.S. Supreme Court has recognized the existence of the right of publicity,[9] the main battles over this right have been on its scope.[10] One of the most intriguing questions in this regard is whether the right to publicity survives the celebrity's death.

The first case to hold that the right of publicity could be inherited was *Lugosi v. Universal Pictures Co.*[11] The action was brought by heirs of Bela Lugosi, who had played the title role in the film "Dracula."

Lugosi's heirs sought to enjoin licensing agreements authorizing the use of the Count Dracula character as popularized by Lugosi during his lifetime. Mrs. Lugosi enjoyed brief success at the trial level, at which judgment was entered for damages and an injunction against the defendant.

But the trial court's decision was reversed by an appellate court and the reversal was upheld by the Supreme Court of California. That court ruled that regardless of whether a right of publicity could be exploited during one's lifetime, it could *not* be inherited.[12]

Ironically, the short-lived inheritable right of publicity found by the *Lugosi* trial court gave rise to a line of cases in New York which has survived *even* after the reversal of the trial court's decision by the California Supreme Court. Thus between 1972, when the first Lugosi decision was rendered, and 1977, when it was first reversed, a federal district court sitting in New York decided *Price v. Hal Roach Studios, Inc.*[13]

There, the successors of comedians Laurel and Hardy maintained a successful claim for a descendible right of publicity. The court, hard-pressed to find any decisions in New York which recognized such a descendible right of publicity, looked for guidance to the *Haelan* case and the first *Lugosi* decision. Although the *Lugosi* decision was to be short-lived, the *Price* decision established, at least in New York, that the right of publicity can be asserted by a celebrity's heirs.

MOST SIGNIFICANT JURISDICTIONS

Unlike the law of copyright, which is a matter of federal statute, the right of publicity is a matter of the common law or legislation of each of the fifty states. Thus an advertiser or producer might face an almost prohibitive task in approaching a project with nationwide distribution.

The most significant jurisdictions, due to their size and influence on other state legislatures and courts, are New York and California. In the case of California, the issue is, for the time being, settled. The highest court of the state has ruled that the right of publicity cannot be inherited.

In New York, the matter is unsettled because the issue of "descendibility" has been squarely addressed only by federal courts sitting in New York. These courts are bound to make a decision based on their expectation of what the courts of the state of New York will eventually hold if the issue arises before them.

Potentially, in New York the right could be erased by a single decision of the court of appeals, the highest state court. Pending such an unpredictable event, however, there is some guidance for advertisers in this area.

THE PRESLEY CASE

By far the largest influence on the development of the right of publicity in recent years has been generated by Factors Etc., Inc., the company that was assigned whatever right of publicity the late Elvis Presley had. Factors, a vigorous defender of those rights, obtained a successful decision upholding the descendibility of Presley's right of publicity in New York in 1978, *Factors Etc., Inc. v. Pro Arts, Inc.*[14]

There, the Second Circuit Court of Appeals upheld the granting of a preliminary injunction against the use of Presley's photograph on a poster. The court held that in recognizing this postdeath right, it was relying on the fact that Presley had sought to exploit the right during his lifetime and had also taken steps to preserve it after his death by vesting it in an entity charged with exploiting such rights.

More recently, a federal district court sitting in New Jersey also upheld the right of Presley's successors to enforce the right of publicity in a case decided in 1981, *Estate of Presley v. Russen.*[15]

However, in contrast to the favorable treatment which the successors of

Presley had received in New York and New Jersey, a federal appellate court located in his home state of Tennessee decided that the right of publicity ended at Presley's death. In *Memphis Development Foundation v. Factors Etc., Inc.*,[16] the court said:

We are called upon in this diversity case to determine whether, under Tennessee law, the exclusive right to publicity survives a celebrity's death. We hold that the right is not inheritable. After death the opportunity for gain shifts to the public domain, where it is equally open to all.[17]

After the ruling in *Memphis Development*, Factors returned to its New York litigation and sought summary judgment in *Factors Etc., Inc. v. Pro Arts*, in which it had earlier obtained an injunction against the sale of Presley memorial posters.

In a surprising decision, the Court of Appeals for the Second Circuit, which had affirmed the descendibility of the right of publicity by affirming the injunction previously obtained by Factors, refused to sustain summary judgment in favor of Factors. *Factors Etc., Inc. v. Pro Arts.*[18]

Instead, it deferred to the decision of the Sixth Circuit in its perception of the common law of Tennessee, as set out in the *Memphis Development* case. Even though the Second Circuit maintained that it still believed that the law of New York recognized a descendible right of publicity, it was persuaded that the law of the state where the entertainer made his home should govern.

This legal square dance was not, however, to be so quickly ended. The Court of Appeals in the Tennessee case had attempted to predict Tennessee law, which had been unsettled. The Court of Appeals of New York (while making its own assessment of the unsettled law of the State of New York) was inclined to defer to the federal court located in Tennessee.

Finally, in 1981 a state court in Tennessee decided the issue according to state law. It expressly held that a descendible right of publicity exists in that state. *The Estate of Lester Flat v. Coors of the Cumberland Inc.*[19] Predictably, this new statement of the law of Tennessee may affect the outcome of the *Factors* case in New York yet again, although it is not likely to change the Court of Appeals perception of what the law in New York should be.

THE GROUCHO MARX CASE

The existence of a descendible right of publicity in New York was further affirmed by another decision of the U.S. District Court for the Southern District of New York in *Groucho Marx Productions Inc. v. Day and Night Company, Inc.*[20] In the *Groucho Marx* case, assignees and heirs of the Marx Brothers brought an action to enforce a right of publicity against the producers and authors of a Broadway play entitled, "A Day in Hollywood/A Night in the Ukraine."

A portion of the play contained a skit in which actors, apparently portraying the Marx Brothers, enact their own version of Chekhov's work, "The Bear." The literary material used by the actors was written for the play; however, the characters employ the mannerisms, speech patterns, and many of the gimmicks associated with the Marx Brothers. In addition, they dressed to resemble the Marx Brothers.

The plaintiffs in the action moved for a partial summary judgment on the issue of liability. On October 2, 1981, Judge Conner granted the motion, upholding the descendibility of the right of publicity in New York.

Judge Conner broadened the availability of the right to heirs of the celebrity by holding—unlike the court in the *Factor's* case—that it was not necessary for the celebrity to make any disposition of his rights while still alive or in a will in order to preserve them.

Moreover, he held that the right was descendible even if the celebrity did not exploit the right of publicity by means of endorsements or commercial tie-ups when the celebrity exploited self-created characters in his occupation.

In addition to raising questions regarding the existence and the descendibility of the right of publicity in New York, the defendants in the Marx Brothers case also argued that the play in question was protected from the claims of the plaintiffs by virtue of the First Amendment to the U.S. Constitution. The Court rejected this contention as well as the others.

RIGHT OF PUBLICITY V. FIRST AMENDMENT

The primary counterbalances, as a matter of social policy, to the exercise of the right of publicity and the required permission of heirs for use of likenesses are the First Amendment guarantees of free speech and press. Although the guarantees of the First Amendment are primarily associated with insuring the integrity of the political process, the courts have clearly held that the First Amendment also insures the freedom to communicate cultural experiences and expressions whether for informational purposes or purely for entertainment. See *Joseph Burstyn v. Wilson.*[21]

The consciousness of the social purposes served by the First Amendment does not, however, serve as a very reliable indicator of whether a particular type of media portrayal is a form of protected speech. Although there are no certain guidelines, the courts have frequently focused on the *purpose* of the portrayal as a significant factor.

The role of the purpose of a media portrayal is carefully analysed in an article entitled "Privacy, Publicity and the Portrayal of Real People by the Media," by Felcher and Rubin.[22] In the article, which has been widely relied upon by courts, the authors have described a hierarchy of uses, from the most protected to the least protected.

Those works that get the fullest First Amendment protection are portrayals which are primarily informative and considered *news*. A second category consists of works designed for artistic or entertainment purposes, which includes fictionalized history; stage, motion picture, or television works set against a background of real people. This category includes, of course, *parody* and is considered by Felcher and Rubin worthy of a high degree of First Amendment protection.

The final category described by Felcher and Rubin includes "media portrayals . . . that neither inform nor entertain, but merely sell a specific product." This category immediately recalls the distribution of posters of Elvis Presley enjoined in the *Factors* case and would seem to make *advertisement* use of celebrities names, likenesses, or other characteristics the *least likely* enterprises to use successfully the First Amendment as a shield.

This "media-purpose test" undoubtedly gives the least First Amendment comfort to commercial advertisers and merchandisers. However, this test has not, in all cases, given comfort to purely cultural or entertainment ventures either. As mentioned above, the Court in the *Marx Brothers* case rejected the argument that the play in question was protected. The Court, providing its own artistic judgment on the play, observed as follows:

Defendants contend that the play is a parody of the Marx Brothers' performance and cite reviews of the play terming it a 'spoof,' 'compendium' and 'parody.' . . . Applying the principles discussed above to the present case, I find as a matter of law that the defendants' production of the play is not protected expression. At the request of the parties, I reviewed the play in connection with an aborted motion for preliminary injunction. Although entertainment can merit first amendment protection, entertainment that merely imitates 'even if skillfully and accurately carried out, does not really have its own creative component and does not have a significant value as pure entertainment.'[23]

By the foregoing holding, the Court in *Marx Brothers* attempted to follow the decision of the New Jersey District Court in *Presley v. Russen*. In the *Russen* case, the plaintiffs successfully enjoined a performance of a Presley look-a-like singing songs popularized by Presley in the Presley manner.

The issue seized upon by both courts was the imitative quality to the two productions.

However, there is an important distinction between imitation which is the recreation or reenactment of a work or character accomplished by the talent of a *new* artist, and imitation which is merely the product of mechanical reproduction such as a photograph or duplication or a sound recording.

THE USE OF "LOOK-ALIKES"

Let the word go forth—there is no free ride. The commercial hitchhiker seeking to travel on the fame of another will have to learn to pay the fare or stand on his own two feet.

So said New York Supreme Court Justice Edward Greenfield in the recent case *Onassis v. Christian Dior-New York, Inc.*[24] The issue in the case: Whether the use for commercial purposes of a "look-alike" of a well-known personality violates the right of privacy legislatively granted in New York.[25]

The plaintiff in this action was Jacqueline Kennedy Onassis, former First Lady of the United States, widow of President John F. Kennedy and Aristotle Onassis, and a well-known personality in her own right. She sought a preliminary injunction under New York's Civil Rights Law to restrain defendants—all of whom were associated with an ad campaign to promote the products and the image of Christian Dior-New York, Inc.— from using or distributing a certain ad and for other relief.

The essence of her complaint: that defendants prepared and/or published an ad for Dior products that included her likeness in the form of a photograph of look-alike Barbara Reynolds; that Reynolds' picture caused her to be identified with the ad to which she has not given her consent; that this was a violation of her rights of privacy; and that it caused her irreparable injury.

The applicable statutes were Sections 50 and 51 of the New York Civil Rights Law. Section 50 provides:

A person, firm or corporation that uses for advertising purposes, or for the purposes of trade, the name, portrait or picture of any living person without having first obtained the written consent of such person . . . is guilty of a misdemeanor.

Section 51 goes on to provide civil remedies for violation as well, including injunction and damages:

Any person whose name, portrait or picture is used within the state for advertising purposes or for the purposes of trade, without his written consent first being obtained as above provided, may maintain an equitable action in the supreme court to prevent the use thereof, and may also recover damages for any injuries by reason of such use and if the defendant shall have knowingly used such person's name, portrait or picture in such manner as is forbidden or declared to be unlawful by the last section, the jury in its discretion may award exemplary damages . . .

The case arose out of one of a series of advertisements sponsored by Christian Dior-New York Inc. to advertise and promote Dior products. The series featured a trio of one woman and two men, known collectively as the

Diors. This trio, which attained a certain notoriety, has been characterized as "idle rich, suggestively decadent, and aggressively chic." The advertisements were designed to present the Diors and, by association, the Dior products as "chic, sophisticated, elite, unconventional, quirky, audacious, elegant and unorthodox."

The particular advertisement at issue in the litigation depicted the wedding of two of the Diors, with the trio surrounded by their apparently intimate friends, including television personality Gene Shalit, model Shari Belafonte, actress Ruth Gordon, and a woman who bore a striking resemblance to Jacqueline Kennedy Onassis. Actually, it was Barbara Reynolds, a secretary who pursues a side career based on her resemblance to Mrs. Onassis. The advertisement was entitled, "Christian Dior: Sportswear for Women and Clothing for Men." The copy read: "The wedding of the Diors was everything a wedding should be: no tears, no rice, no in-laws, no smarmy toasts, for once no Mendelssohn. Just a legendary private affair." As the court observed, the most legendary guest at this affair would clearly have been Jacqueline Onassis. The court found that Mrs. Onassis has never permitted her name or picture to be used in connection with the promotion of commercial products and allows it to be used only sparingly in connection with certain specific public services and civic, art, and educational projects. Knowing that Mrs. Onassis would undoubtedly not consent to appear in the ad, the defendants contacted the Ron Smith Celebrity Look-Alikes agency and specifically requested a Jacqueline Onassis look-alike. Barbara Reynolds was chosen for the role.

The novel issue raised by this case was whether the use of a look-alike falls within the purview of Section 51, which prohibits the use of an individual's "name, portrait or picture." Justice Greenfield held that it does.

The court's rationale for the decision was that it filled a gap:

Is the illusionist to be free to step aside, having reaped the benefits of his creation, and permitted to disclaim the very impression he sought to create? If we were to permit it, we would be sanctioning an obvious loophole to evade the statute. If a person is willing to give his or her endorsement to help sell a product, either at an offered price or at any price, no matter—hire a double and the same effect is achieved. The essential purpose of the statute must be carried out by giving it a common sense reading which bars easy evasion.

When enacted in 1903, Section 50 and 51 altered the common law of New York, which did not recognize any cause of action for invasion of privacy. Section 51 provided civil relief for infringement; Section 50 created a penal sanction for violations. Under fundamental principles of statutory interpretation, a statute that derogates from the common law—and particularly one that carries potential penal sanctions—is to be strictly construed. This canon of interpretation has been applied, for example, to prevent recovery for the imitation of a bandleader's idiosyncratic style of performance.[26] Yet the restrictive wording of the statute, and the possibility of circumventing it, has prompted other courts to decline a strict interpretation and apply the statute according to its spirit rather than its literal meaning.

The lack of a consistent judicial approach has resulted in a curious set of distinctions. The use of a vocal impersonator to imitate a well-known voice of a celebrity on voice-over ads has been held not to infringe the Act.[27] However, the reproduction of a costume that's identified only with one person, even though someone else is depicted wearing the costume, does infringe the Act.[28]

In adopting "a common sense reading which bars easy evasion," the Court in *Onassis* relied heavily on the Court of Appeals decision in *Binns v. Vitagraph Co. of America*,[29] which held, "A picture within the meaning of the statute is not necessarily a photograph of the living person, but includes any representation of such person." That court was faced with the use, as in *Onassis*, of an actor hired to portray an individual who had attained a degree of notoriety in the public eye. Unfortunately, the *Onassis* decision fails to reconcile its reliance on *Binns* with later decisions that restricted *Binns* to its facts, including the use of John Binns' name in the offending film, see, e.g., *Toscani v. Hersey*.[30]

Instead, Justice Greenfield supported his decision with an analysis of the statute itself. In particular, he examined dictionary definitions of the statutory terms, "picture" and "portrait," noting that "picture" is defined to include "anything closely resembling or strikingly typifying something else," and "portrait" includes "any close likeness of one thing to another."

He concluded his analysis with the finding that the use of the disjunctive phrase, " 'portrait or picture' gives wider scope to encompass a representation which conveys the essence and likeness of an individual, not only [in] actuality, but the close and purposeful resemblance to reality."[31]

The decision continues:

The principle to be distilled from a study of the statute and of the cases construing it is that all persons, of whatever station in life, from the relatively unknown to the world famous, are to be secured against rapacious commercial exploitation. While the statute may not, by its terms, cover voice or movement, characteristics or style, it is intended to protect the essence of the person, his or her identity or *persona* from being unwillingly or unknowingly misappropriated for the profit of another.[32]

Notwithstanding the decision in *Onassis*, not all advertisements that are evocative of a particular person are actionable under Section 51. First, the *Onassis* case addresses only intentional misappropriations of identity. The defendants, well aware that Jacqueline Onassis would not only refuse to appear in the ad, but was opposed on principle to any commercial associations with her name and identity, deliberately sought out a woman who closely resembled Mrs. Onassis, used make-up, hairstyle and accessories to enhance the resemblance, and carefully constructed the picture and the copy to suggest that Mrs. Onassis was present. As the court observed, the suggestion of her actual appearance was supported by the actual appearance of other well-known personalities.

Second, the court carefully limited the scope of its holding as follows:

There are many aspects of identity. A person may be known not only by objective indicia—name, face, and social security number, but by other characteristics as well—voice, movement, style, coiffure, typical phrases, as well as by his or her history or accomplishments. Thus far, the legislature has accorded protection only to those aspects of identity embodied in name and face. Imitators are free to simulate voice or hair-do, or characteristic clothing or accessories, and writers to comment on and actors to re-enact events. No one is free to trade on another's name or appearance and claim immunity because what he is using is similar to but not identical with the original.[33]

Finally, Section 51 only applies where the use is "for advertising purposes, or for the purpose of trade." The *Onassis* case addressed the use of impersonators in a purely commercial context, where Jacqueline Onassis was intentionally misrepresented as endorsing and advertising Christian Dior sportswear. As such, it presented an easy set of facts that dramatically demonstrated the potential improper uses of look-alikes. It is important, however, that clear lines of demarcation be drawn between uses that are purely commercial and those that enter the sphere of artistic expression, protected by the First Amendment.

The impersonation of well-known personalities on the stage and in motion pictures has emerged in recent years as a theatrical genre. Such presentations have included a one-man depiction of Samuel Pepys, containing excerpts from his seventeenth-century diaries; Hal Holbrook's famous impersonation of Mark Twain; impersonations of Elvis Presley; and the parody of the Marx Brothers, entitled "A Day in Hollywood/A Night in the Ukraine."

A consideration of the limitations of the right to impersonate celebrities in the context of entertainment, as opposed to direct commercial exploitation, has recently been undertaken in two important cases dealing with Elvis Presley and the Marx Brothers. Neither of these cases was brought under a civil rights statute such as New York's Section 51. Instead, claims were asserted based on the "right of publicity," a common-law extension and expansion of the "right of privacy." Briefly stated, the right of publicity seeks to protect not merely unauthorized uses of one's portrait, picture, or name, but also other attributes of various famous persons. Such a right has, in some jurisdictions, been held to survive death, unlike the right of privacy.

Both the *Russen* and *Groucho Marx* cases[34] indicate the potential danger that impersonations, albeit in entertainment productions, might be held as violative of a right whether known as the right of publicity or the right of privacy. The court in *Russen* held that the impersonation of the performance and likeness of Elvis Presley was without First Amendment protection, though the court noted no facts had been supplied to it that would have permitted a contrary finding. The district court in the *Groucho Marx* case reached the same conclusion, although in that case arguments had been raised that the impersonation and evocation of the Marx Brothers' comedic performances were protected by the First Amendment.

The Court of Appeals for the Second Circuit reversed the holding of the district court in the *Groucho Marx* case that the right of publicity of the heirs of the Marx Brothers had been violated. Although the holding of the case was not based upon an evaluation of the First Amendment issue (a constitutional question that could not be reached because the case was decided on a conflict-of-law basis), it is significant that in a footnote to the decision Judge Newman stated as follows:

We note, however, that any consideration of such questions would have to examine closely defendants' substantial argument that their play is protected expression as a literary work, especially in light of the broad scope permitted parody in First Amendment law.''[35]

The footnote acknowledging the significance of the First Amendment issue in this area may be viewed as an indication that, notwithstanding the decision below and the decision in the *Russen* case, impersonation of celebrities for entertainment purposes, as opposed to impersonation made directly for the purpose of selling products, will be protected by the First Amendment. This section is consistent with the decision of Judge Greenfield in *Onassis* and marks a reasonable limitation upon the ability of celebrities asserting a right, by whatever name, to prevent impersonations.

The distinction between protected impersonations and those that infringe the right of privacy was stated by Justice Greenfield in *Onassis* as follows:

Some of the contentions raised by the defendant are palpably feeble, for example that there is a recognized exception for artistic as distinguished from commercial endeavors, and that defendant Barbara Reynolds is somehow going to be impeded in her artistic career. While some imitators may employ artistry in the use of voice, gesture and facial expression, a mere similarity of features is no more artistry than the mimicry of the Monarch butterfly by its look-alike, the Viceroy butterfly. To paint a portrait of Jacqueline Kennedy Onassis is to create a work of art; to look like Jacqueline Kennedy Onassis is not.[36]

The court continued:

Miss Reynolds may capitalize on the striking resemblance of facial features at parties, TV appearances, and dramatic works, but not in commercial advertisements. Similarly, defendant Ron Smith Celebrity Look-Alikes can market its clients for fun and profit in various areas, but may not capitalize on natural resemblance to a well-known person for trade or advertising. No one has an inherent or constitutional right to pass himself off for what he is not.[37]

The crucial distinction to be made is whether the work involved possesses cultural or entertainment value, or is simply a disguised commercial advertisement for the sale of goods and services. The *Onassis* decision properly prevents the use of a look-alike to advertise products. Impersonation of cultural or entertainment value, however, falls within the protection of the First Amendment and should not be restrained.

NOTES

1. Speech by Iago, in *Othello, The Moor of Venice*, by William Shakespeare, Act III, Scene III.
2. Warren and Brandeis, "The Right to Privacy," 4 Harv. L. Rev. 193, (1890).
3. See, *Roberson v. Rochester Folding Box Co.*, 171 NY 538, 64 N.E. 442 (1902).
4. Fikes, "The Right of Publicity: A Descendible and Inheritable Property Right," 14 The Cumberland L. Rev. 347, 349.
5. *Griswold v. Connecticut*, U.S. Supreme Court, 381 U.S. 479 (1965).
6. Nimmer, "The Right of Publicity," 19 Law & Contemporary Problems 203, 204, n.1 (1954). (See, also, 14 The Cumberland L. Rev. 349.)
7. See, e.g., *O'Brien v. Pabst Sales Co.*, 124 F.2d 167 (5th Cir. 1941).
8. 202 F. 2d 866 (2d Cir. 1953).
9. *Zacchini v. Scripps-Howard Broadcasting Co.*, U.S. Supreme Court, 433 U.S. 562 (1977).
10. This section is adapted from the article appearing in *Advertising Compliance Service*, "The Right of Publicity," by James A. Janowitz, Tab #13, Rights of Publicity, Privacy, Articles #1-3.
11. 172 US.P.Q. 541 (Super. Ct. L.A. Co. 1972).
12. 25 Cal. 3d 813, 603 P.2d 425, 160 Cal. Rptr. 323 (1979).
13. 400 F. Supp. 836 (S.D.N.Y. 1975).
14. 579 F.2d 215 (2d Cir. 1978), *cert. denied*, 440 U.S. 908 (1979).
15. 513 F. Supp. 1339 (D.N.J. 1981).
16. 616 F.2d 956 (6th Cir.) *cert. denied*, 101 S. Ct. 358 (1980).
17. *Memphis Development*, supra at 957.
18. 652 F.2d 278 (2nd Cir. 1980) *cert. denied*, April 19, 1982.
19. Case No. 81-1252-III (Chanc. Ct. Davidson Co., Tenn. 1981).
20. 523 F. Supp. 485 (S.D.N.Y. 1981).
21. 343 U.S. 495, 72 S. Ct. 777 (1952).
22. Felcher and Rubin, Privacy, Publicity and the Portrayal of Real People by the Media, Yale Law Journal (1979).
23. *Elvis Presley v. Russen*, 513 F.Supp. at 1359. *Marx Brothers*, supra at 492.
24. N.Y. Supreme Court (County of New York), Special Term, part I, Index #27662/83.

25. This section is adapted from the article appearing in *Advertising Compliance Service*, "N.Y. Judge: Use of 'Look Alike' in Ad Violates Privacy Right," by James A. Janowitz & Barbara L. Kagedan, Tab #13, Rights of Publicity, Privacy, Article #7.

26. *Lombardo v. Doyle, Dane & Bernbach, Inc.*, 58 A.D.2d 620, 396 N.Y.S.2d 661 (2nd Dept. 1977).

27. *Lahr v. Adell Chemical Co..*, 300 F.2d 256 (1st Cir. 1962).

28. *Loftus v. Greenwich Lithographing Co.*, 192 App. Div. 251, 182 N.Y.S. 428 (1st Dept. 1920).

29. *Binns v. Vitagraph Co. of America*, 210 N.Y. 51 (1913).

30. 271 App. Div. 445, 65 N.Y.S. 2d 814, 817 (1st Dept. 1946).

31. *Onassis, supra* at p. 7, col. 2.

32. *Id.* at p. 7, col. 2.

33. *Id.* at p. 7, col. 3.

34. *Estate of Presley v. Russen*, 513 F. Supp. 1339 (D.N.J. 1981); *Groucho Marx Productions, Inc. v. Day and Night Company, Inc.* 523 F. Supp. 485 (S.D.N.Y. 1981), *rev'd* 689 F. 2d 317 (2d Cir. 1982).

35. See *Elsmere Music, Inc. v. National Broadcasting Co.*, 623 F.2d 252, 253, n.1 (2d Cir. 1980); 689 F.2d at 319.

36. *Onassis, supra* at p. 7, col. 3.

37. *Id.*

12.
CORRECTIVE
ADVERTISING

Its advocates touted "corrective advertising" as an important enforcement weapon in FTC's arsenal. Recent events, however, indicate a limited role for this remedy over the course of the next several years and, perhaps, the remainder of this decade.

The use of corrective advertising by FTC during the past seven or eight years has diminished to nearly the vanishing point for several reasons. First, there was the assault by Congress during the 1970s on FTC for overreaching its authority. Next came the advent of the "Reaganauts" at FTC led for most of the first half of the 1980s by Chairman James C. Miller III, with a view to allowing the marketplace to cure most advertising ills. Both of these historical trends have left FTC with far less of its former zeal in rooting out deception. The result is that today's FTC is far less likely to use such creative enforcement techniques as corrective advertising. As Richard S. Cornfeld noted in a law review article on the subject: "If Victor Hugo were alive today, he might well label corrective advertising 'an idea whose time has gone'—if, indeed, it could be said the idea had a 'time' at all."[1]

Nevertheless, corrective advertising remains a powerful potential remedy in FTC's enforcement scheme: A shift in political tides, and in the makeup of Commissioners, is not outside the realm of possibility in the years to come. Moreover, some advertisers have sought corrective advertising remedies in their Lanham Act lawsuits against competitor's comparative advertising campaigns. In the famous "Battle of the Burgers" litigation for example, Wendy's International, the giant fast food chain, sought, among other things, a corrective advertising remedy. Specifically, Wendy's asked for $25 million so it could prepare and publicize any corrective ads ordered by the judge, or, alternatively, to require Burger King to spend $25 million for corrective ads.[2] While the case was eventually settled quietly out of court, it illustrates that advertisers are well aware of this advertising remedy, and are prepared to use it themselves, in an appropriate case. Accordingly, this chapter examines this potentially important remedy, its recent history, and many of the key corrective advertising cases, including the highly important "Listerine" case.

THEORETICAL UNDERPINNINGS

Before launching into a discussion of the history of corrective advertising and many of the major cases, it is first appropriate to examine the theoretical underpinnings of this remedy. Essentially, corrective advertising is a requirement that an alleged deceptive advertiser take steps in the future to dispel from the minds of consumers deception that was present in past advertising. FTC's standard for imposing corrective advertising has been stated as follows:

If a deceptive advertisement has played a substantial role in creating or reinforcing in the public's mind a false and material belief which lives on after the false advertising ceases, there is clear and continuing injury to competition and to the consuming public as consumers who continue to make purchasing decisions based on the false belief. Since this injury cannot be averted by merely requiring respondent to cease disseminating the advertisement, we may appropriately order respondent to take affirmative action designed to terminate the otherwise continuing ill effects of the advertisement.

This standard takes on added significance because it was quoted with approval by the U.S. Court of Appeals, District of Columbia Circuit, in the landmark "Listerine" case.[3]

The logic justifying corrective advertising is as follows: Advertisers spend tens of billions of advertising dollars each year to implant their advertising message in the public psyche. Once a particular message is so implanted, it persists for many years, even decades in many consumer's minds. If that message is deceptive and the advertiser stops the deceptive advertising campaign, that will often not be enough to dispel lingering deception from their minds. This is particularly true, it is argued, if the suspect ad campaign has gone on for a long period of time. There will be residual deception that cannot be alleviated through the use of such traditional remedies as the cease-and-desist order which, basically, says nothing more than "go forth and sin no more." The argument is that the deceptive advertiser will continue to reap profits from the deception since many consumers will continue to purchase the product or service on the basis of the past deceptive advertising. The role of corrective advertising is to have the advertiser spend its own advertising dollars to reach these misinformed consumers, hence dispelling this residual deception.

HISTORY

FTC has traditionally proceeded against companies allegedly engaged in deceptive advertising by using the cease-and-desist order. A major problem with this approach, historically, has been that it generally takes a long period of time to halt a deceptive advertising campaign. Moreover, FTC's order does nothing about the increased profits generated to the benefit of the advertiser by the offending ad campaign. Indeed, by the time the order is issued, the ad campaign is generally over and the advertiser has launched a new one.

In the early 1970s, FTC responded to this perceived gap in its enforcement effectiveness with the corrective advertising remedy. The idea of this remedy was first presented to FTC by a group of law students called, Students Opposing Unfair Practices, Inc. (SOUP). SOUP had filed a petition to intervene in an action involving Campbell Soup Company.[4] While FTC did not order a corrective advertising remedy in this case, it stated in its opinion that it did have the power to do so where the facts warranted.

In the early 1970s, FTC began several corrective advertising proceedings. It brought complaints against Standard Oil of California,[5] Coca Cola Company,[6] American Home Products Corporation,[7] Amster Corporation,[8] and Warner-Lambert Pharmaceutical Company.[9]

FTC's first use of the corrective advertising remedy came in 1971 in an order involving ITT Continental Baking Company.[10] In that case, the company had advertised its bread as a diet aid since it had fewer calories per slice. It had not noted in its ads, however, that the bread was sliced thinner than competitor's breads. Pursuant to the FTC order, the company agreed to devote at least 25 percent of its ad budget for one year to disclose that its bread was "not effective for weight reduction."

THE "LISTERINE" CASE

However, the most successful use of the corrective remedy came in the landmark "Listerine" decision, *Warner-Lambert Co. v. FTC.*[11] At issue in that case, were advertisements touting Listerine mouthwash as a cold preventative. Ever since its introduction in 1879, Listerine had been represented as being beneficial for colds and sore throats. Direct ads to consumers, which included the cold claims, started in 1921.

Following lengthy hearings before an FTC administrative law judge, the Commission ordered Warner-Lambert to cease and desist from representing that its Listerine mouthwash product:

(1) Will cure colds or sore throats, prevent colds or sore throats, or that users of Listerine will have fewer colds than non-users, and

(2) is a treatment for, or will lessen the severity of, colds or sore throats; that it will have any significant beneficial effect on the symptoms of sore throats or any

beneficial effect on symptoms of colds; or that the ability of Listerine to kill germs is of medical significance in the treatment of colds or sore throats or their symptoms.[12]

But the most interesting—and most innovative—portion of FTC's order was the corrective advertising remedy. Specifically, FTC's order required ads for Listerine to clearly and conspicuously disclose the following language:

Contrary to prior advertising, Listerine will not help prevent colds or sore throats or lessen their severity.[13]

Moreover, FTC ordered this requirement to apply to the next ten million dollars of Listerine advertising.

On appeal to the U.S. Court of Appeals for the District of Columbia, Warner-Lambert argued that FTC's ruling was unsupported by substantial evidence and that FTC had exceeded its statutory authority by ordering corrective advertising. The company also argued that this remedy was unconstitutional or violative of its First Amendment rights.

The Appeals Court rejected the argument that FTC's order wasn't supported by substantial evidence. It had been revealed that FTC had refused to reopen the proceedings after a Food and Drug Administration (FDA) study came out purporting to contradict FTC's findings. However, the Appeals Court noted the report was in "draft" form and hadn't been adopted by the FDA Commissioner.[14]

The Appeals Court also rejected the company's argument that FTC lacked the statutory authority to order corrective advertising. The Court noted that even though Section 5 of the Federal Trade Commission Act does not expressly give FTC authority to go beyond cease-and-desist orders, many U.S. Supreme Court decisions have held that regulatory agencies do have the power to go beyond the core statutes involved.[15] The Court concluded that FTC does have the authority to use the "corrective advertising" remedy even though the Federal Trade Commission Act doesn't specifically mention this power.

Moreover, on petition for rehearing, the Court ruled that FTC's use of corrective advertising here was not unconstitutional under the First Amendment in light of the then-recent Supreme Court decision in *Virginia State Board of Pharmacy v. Virginia Citizens Council, Inc.*[16] In that case, the Supreme Court had rejected prior rulings that held commercial speech to be outside the First Amendment's protection. Noting that the Supreme Court had stressed that only "truthful claims" are protected by the First Amendment, the Appeals Court said, "there can be no question of the legitimacy of the FTC's role in regulating and preventing false and deceptive advertising."[17] The Appeals Court noted that in this case, Warner Lambert had "over a long period of time, worked a substantial deception upon the public; it has advertised Listerine as a cure for colds and consumers have purchased its product with that in mind."[18]

Viewed in a backdrop of over 50 years of allegedly deceptive advertising, the Court opined that "continued advertising continues the deception."[19] Citing language in *Virginia State Board* that in some cases it may be "appropriate to require that a commercial message appear in such a form, or include such additional information, warnings, and disclaimers, as are necessary to prevent its being deceptive."[20] The Appeals Court concluded that this was such a case. Nevertheless, the Court did agree to delete the phrase, "Contrary to prior advertising" from FTC's order. The Court's reasoning: The phrase wasn't needed to attract attention to the remainder of the corrective advertising message. It noted the requirements for large type size in printed ads, the simultaneous presentation of the disclosure in both audio and visual portions of televised ads, and the fact that no other sounds, including music, may occur during the disclosure or tv and radio spots. These requirements assured the Court that the message would reach the public without subjecting the company to the humiliation of broadcasting the "contrary to prior advertising" portion.

FUTURE OF CORRECTIVE ADVERTISING

An indication of the future of corrective advertising—at least for the next several years—may have been illustrated by the Commission's modification of a 1980 consent agreement with AHC Pharmacal, Inc., so that the company needn't have to run corrective ads for its acne treatment products.

In 1980, AHC Pharmacal had entered a consent agreement with FTC whereby the company agreed not to make certain claims unless they were backed by "competent and reliable scientific or medical evidence." Specifically, FTC had charged that ads placed by AHC and its president claimed their acne preparations could "cure" acne and were superior to other acne products. After this 1980 order was issued, an expert panel advising the Food and Drug Administration (FDA) concluded that benzoyl peroxide (the active ingredient in AHC's products) is generally recognized as safe and effective in treating acne.

The 1980 FTC order required AHC to run corrective ads disclosing that "no product can cure acne" before it could further advertise its "AHC Gel," "Acne Control Regime," or any other acne product. AHC later petitioned FTC to modify the scheduling of these corrective ads, citing financial woes. The Commission went even further than asked by AHC. It eliminated entirely the corrective advertising remedy by a 3-2 vote of the Commission.[21]

In this, and other recent FTC cases, it is evident that the Commission will not vigorously pursue corrective advertising as a remedy in the near future.

Nevertheless, FTC's statutory authority to order it still exists. This fact, coupled with the apparent trend of advertisers seeking corrective advertising in the context of comparative advertising and the Lanham Act, demonstrate that corrective advertising is still a force to be reckoned with.

NOTES

1. Cornfeld, "A New Approach to an Old Remedy: Corrective Advertising and the Federal Trade Commission," 61 Iowa L.R. 693 (1976).

2. *Wendy's International, Inc. v. Burger King Corporation*, U.S. District Ct. (So. Dist. of Ohio, Eastern Div.), *Complaint*, Civil Action No. C-2-82-1175, filed 9-27-82; see also *Advertising Compliance Service*, Tab #8, Remedies (Private) Article #4.

3. *Warner-Lambert Co. v. FTC*, 562 F.2d 749, 762 (D.C. Cir. 1977) *cert. denied*, Dkt. #77-855, 98 S.Ct. 1575, 435 U.S. 950, 55 L. Ed. 2d 800 (1978).

4. *Campbell Soup Co.*, 3 CCH Trade Reg. Reptr. ¶¶19,539, 19,681, 19,780. See also, Johnston, Comment: "Corrective Advertising: Panacea or Punishment," 17 Duquesne L.R. 169, '78-'79.

5. 3 CCH Trade Reg. Rptr. ¶19,352 and ¶19,428.

6. 3 CCH Trade Reg. Rptr. ¶19,351.

7. 3 CCH Trade Reg. Rptr. ¶19,673.

8. 3 CCH Trade Reg. Rptr. ¶19,696.

9. 3 CCH Trade Reg. Rptr. ¶19,838.

10. *ITT Continental Baking Co.*, CCH Trade Reg. Rptr. (1970-73 Transfer Binder) ¶19,681.

11. 562 F.2d 749 (D.C. Cir 1977), *cert. denied*, Dkt. #77-055, 98 S.Ct. 1575, 435 U.S. 950, 55 L.Ed.2d 800 (1978). For further analyses of the *Warner-Lambert* case, see: (i) Haas, Comment, "*Warner-Lambert Co. v. FTC*: The Possibilities and Limitations of Corrective Advertising," 13 New England L.R. 348 (1977); (ii) Wenthe, Note, "*Warner-Lambert Co. v. FTC*: Corrective Advertising Gives Listerine a Taste of Its Own Medicine," 73 Northwestern Univ. L. R. 957 (1978); (iii) Note, (untitled), 47 University of Cincinnati L.R. 129 (1978); (iv) Wattwood, Case Comments, "Corrective Advertising: An Advertiser's Atonement," 30 University of Florida L.R. 490 (1978); (v) Mercer, Note, (untitled), 1978 Wisconsin L.R. 605.

12. 562 F.2d at 753.

13. 562 F.2d at 763.

14. 562 F.2d at 755.

15. See, e.g., *Pan American World Airways Inc. v. U.S.*, 371 U.S. 296, 83 S.Ct. 476, 9 L.Ed.2d 325 (1963).

16. 425 U.S. 748, 96 S.Ct. 1817, 48 L.Ed. 2d 346 (1976).

17. 562 F.2d at 769.

18. 562 F.2d at 769.

19. 562 F.2d at 769.

20. 562 F.2d at 769.

21. In the matter of *AHC Pharmacal, Inc.*, a corporation and James E. Fulton, M.D., individually and as corporate president, FTC Dkt. #C-3017, February 8, 1983.

13.
ADVERTISING
OF WARRANTIES

You have to do your homework long before you reach the point of deciding whether to advertise your warranty in the print or broadcast media, in brochures or point-of-sale materials, or otherwise. In particular, you should scrutinize the law of the state(s) where your proposed warranty advertising should appear, including a review of those personal injury cases where the theory of recovery was express warranty. You should also gain a sound working of the ten-year-old Magnuson-Moss Warranty-Federal Trade Commission Improvement Act[1] as well as applicable provisions of the Uniform Commercial Code. It would also be helpful to study the applicable sections of such self-regulatory guidelines as the Better Business Bureaus' "Code of Advertising,"[2] and—if you plan to advertise your warranty on television—the applicable network standards.[3] The purpose of this chapter is to examine many of the key issues you should consider before advertising a warranty.

MAGNUSON-MOSS WARRANTY ACT

When Congress enacted the Magnuson-Moss Warranty Act a decade ago, it gave the federal government a potentially dominant role in warranty law. While the Act still hasn't lived up to initial expectations, it is, nonetheless, a major force to be reckoned with. If you offer a warranty or guarantee on a product or service, one of the first things you need to know is whether the Magnuson-Moss Warranty Act applies to your warranty. It may apply *if* your warranty is in writing as Magnuson-Moss is applicable to written warranties.

Essentially, there are two types of written warranties under the Act: "full" and "limited." If you decide to offer your customers a "full" warranty, it means, among other things, that:

- You will fix or replace a defective product for free within a reasonable time;
- You won't require your customer to do anything unreasonable to get warranty service;
- Your warranty is good for anyone owning the product during the warranty period;
- You will give your customer the choice of a new product or his or her money back if the product can't be fixed or hasn't been fixed after a reasonable number of attempts.

If you offer a "limited" warranty, it means you're offering less than what a full warranty provides. For example, a limited warranty may cover only parts and not labor, cover only the first buyer, or charge for handling.[4]

In addition, there are a wide variety of important provisions in both the Warranty Act and its implementing regulations that are applicable to a wide range of situations that you should explore before you decide to offer a written warranty. If you're a manufacturer or retailer offering a written warranty, the Magnuson-Moss Act demands substantial analysis and compliance effort on your part. Nevertheelees, a good warranty can be a major selling point. So it's well worth the effort required to gain a sound working knowledge of this important Act.[5]

GUIDES AGAINST DECEPTIVE ADVERTISING

Once you have made certain that your warranty complies with Magnuson-Moss, the next step is making your warranty known and understood by consumers. An excellent way to accomplish that purpose is through advertising. At this point, you should familiarize yourself with the FTC's *Guides Against Deceptive Advertising of Guarantees*.[6] These Guides are extremely important to you if you advertise, or plan to advertise, your warranties. In May 1985, FTC revised these Guides, which had been originally issued in 1960.[7] The newly revised Guides are based on FTC case law and reflect the Commission's interpretations of cases in light of the Magnuson-Moss Warranty Act and FTC's Pre-Sale Availability Rule.

In issuing the revised Guides, FTC stressed that the Federal Trade Commission Act is still the "ultimate legal standard governing warranty advertising." The Commission's intent is for the Guides to aid advertisers in avoiding law violations. Based on FTC case law, the Guides "also reflect the changes in the legal landscape effected by the Magnuson-Moss Warranty Act."

Disclosures

Originally, the Guides required disclosures of virtually all warranty terms in ads mentioning warranties. However, FTC decided that to require disclosure of all warranty terms in ads may deter advertisers from mentioning warranty coverage at all. Since the Pre-Sale Availability Rule assures that warranty terms are available to consumers at the store, FTC also concluded such detailed disclosures in ads are not needed. Instead of such detailed disclosures, the revised Guides recommend disclosure in warranty ads promoting a product covered by the Pre-Sale Availability Rule[8] of the fact that the warranty document is available for examination before purchase of the warranted product.

The revised Guides contain a similar approach for mail order and catalogue sales. One provision calls for ads for mail order or catalogue sales to disclose "information sufficient to convey to consumers that they can obtain complete details on the written warranty free upon specific written request, or from the catalogue or solicitation (whichever is applicable).

In a footnote to one of the new Guide provisions (concerning disclosures), FTC spelled out how advertisers can insure that disclosure of warranty information (i.e., "that warranties are available for inspection prior to sale") will be clear and prominent. This footnote says that TV ads will comply with the Guides if the ads "make the necessary disclosure simultaneously with or immediately following the warranty claim. The disclosure can be presented either in the audio portion or in the video portion as a printed disclosure, provided that a video disclosure appears on the screen for at least five seconds."

However, disclosures called for by other Guide provisions may require advertisers to use other methods. "For example," notes FTC, "it may be necessary for multiple disclosures of the material limitations on a satisfaction guarantee to be disclosed in the audio portion of an advertisement, or to be disclosed for a longer period of time than five seconds in order for the disclosures to be clear and prominent."

Conspicuous by its absence in the new Guides is specific guidance as to such factors as "the size of the letters in a video disclosure" or "the degree of contrast between the letters and the background against which they appear."

Satisfaction Guarantees

Satisfaction guarantees are very popular in advertising, particularly on television and in mail order ads. The revised Guides suggest that if you're an advertiser, you should use satisfaction guaranteed representations only if you plan to refund the full purchase price at the buyer's request. The Guides also suggest that if this type of representation is subject to material limitations or conditions (e.g., "an express limitation of duration, or a limitation to products returned in their original packaging"), then your ad should disclose that limitation or condition.

"Lifetime" Representations

The original Guides suggested that use of the term, "lifetime," in describing the duration of a guarantee or warranty can mislead consumers unless clarified as to what "life" is being referred to. The new Guides retain this basic concept, but provide for clarification of the life to which the representation refers whether or not it refers to the buyer's life.

Warranty Performance

The new Guides keep the principle embodied in the old Guides "that a warrantor or guarantor should ensure performance on advertised warranties or guarantees."

Other Areas

The new Guides made other changes as well. For example, FTC deleted the section that dealt with claims such as "guaranteed lowest price in town," and will deal with this problem in the future on a case-by-case basis. The Commission also deleted the old Guide provision that said a guarantee can be used in a manner that is "a representation of material fact about a product, and that a guarantor must not only perform the warranty, but also take care that such representations are true." FTC stressed, however, that the now-deleted provision "is an accurate statement of Commission law about which there is no question or controversy." Nevertheless, FTC thought some advertisers might be deterred from advertising warranties because of a possible inference from that provision "that a violation of Section 5 may occur simply because a substantial number of warranted products fail in use—notwithstanding the fact that the warrantor fully performs all warranty obligations." Thus, FTC deleted the provision.[9]

SELF-REGULATORY ASPECTS

If you're planning to advertise your warranty, you should also be aware of the various self-regulatory bodies that may have concerns with your ads. The most important ad industry self-regulatory mechanism is the Better Business Bureaus' (BBB) National Advertising Division/National Advertising Review Board (NAD/NARB).[10] An important pamphlet to obtain is the BBB's "Code of Advertising." This pamphlet contains basic advertising standards issued for the guidance of advertisers, ad agencies, and the advertising media. In particular, Section 8 of that Code provides:

8. Warranties (or Guarantees)

a. When the term "warranty" (or "guarantee") is used in product advertising, the following disclosure should be made clearly and prominently:

a statement that the complete details of the warranty can be seen at the advertiser's store prior to sale, or in the case of mail or telephone order sales, are available free on written request.

b. (1) "satisfaction guarantee," "money back guarantee," "free trial offer," or similar representations should be used in advertising only if the seller or manufacturer refunds the full purchase price of the advertised product at the purchaser's request.

  (2) When "satisfaction guarantee" or similar representations are used in advertising, any material limitations or conditions that apply to the guarantee should be clearly and prominently disclosed.

c. When the term "lifetime," "life" or similar representations are used in advertising to describe the duration of the warranty or guarantee, the advertisement should clearly and prominently disclose the life to which the representation refers.

d. Sellers or manufacturers should advertise that a product is warranted or guaranteed only if the seller or manufacturer promptly and fully performs its obligations under the warranty or guarantee.

e. Advertisers should make certain that any advertising of warranties complies with the Consumer Products Warranty Act, effective July 4, 1975, relevant Federal Trade Commission requirements and any applicable state and local laws.[11]

NETWORK GUIDELINES AND WARRANTY ADS

If you plan to advertise your warranty on one of the major networks, you should consult the network's clearance department long before the production phase of your commercial. Both ABC and NBC have extensive guidelines pertaining to the advertising of warranties or guarantees. Both of these networks will require you to clearly and conspicuously disclose in your commercial that refers to a warranty or guarantee whether your warranty is full or limited. In addition, both of these networks will require you to make additional disclosures in the audio or video portions of your commercial, or in both. ABC will require that you disclose: "specific duration, major limitations (e.g., parts excluded or costs or responsibilities the customer must undertake), and see dealer for details or a similar statement."[12] Under NBC's Broadcast Standards, you will have to disclose: "the nature and extent of the guarantee; the identity of the guarantor; the manner in which the guarantor intends to perform; information concerning what a purchaser wishing to claim under the guarantee need do before the guarantor will perform pursuant to its obligations under the guarantee."[13]

In addition, ABC has guidelines for "satisfaction or your money back" representations, "savings guarantees," "guarantees as a representative," "lifetime guarantees," and "prorated adjustment of guarantees."[14]

EXPRESS WARRANTY AND PERSONAL INJURY

We've seen some of the promise, and many of the pitfalls that can occur to advertisers that plan to offer warranties on their products or services.[15]

But what about those advertisers that do not plan to offer a warranty? Should they be at all concerned with the warranty area? The answer is an unqualified, "Yes." Reason: You may unintentionally create an express warranty by language in your ads. And you may then be found liable for personal injuries, or other harm, caused by the express warranty you created.

Probably the most widely available theory of recovery in the United States today is express warranty. Through statements or pictures appearing in advertising on television, radio, in newspapers, magazines, catalogs, on labels, through direct mail, etc., you may make a statement of fact or describe the attributes of a product. If the statement of fact creates a false impression about the product, the user relies upon this statement in utilizing a product, and a personal injury results, you can be held liable for breach of an express warranty.

An easier method of recovery for a plaintiff, and consequently *a more dangerous one to the advertiser*, is innocent misrepresentation, which has been recognized in a number (but by no means a majority) of states throughout the United States. Under innocent misrepresentation, an advertiser may be held strictly liable for physical harm to a consumer that results from a misrepresentation in advertising of the character or quality of the product sold, even though the misrepresentation in question is an innocent one. Under this theory of recovery, a plaintiff need only establish a false material representation which he or she relied upon in using the product. If the plaintiff under these circumstances sustains an injury, the advertiser may be liable for any personal injuries suffered by the plaintiff.

The remainder of this chapter discusses the defenses available to an advertiser if you have been sued as a result of a misrepresentation that appeared in your ad.

An excellent defense in a misrepresentation case is for you to assert that whatever statement or picture appeared in your ad has been complied with—in other words, the product performs as depicted in your ad.

General Motors successfully used this argument in a case arising out of an accident involving a 1967 Chevrolet C-10 pickup truck.[16] GM advertised the truck as possessing a host of safety features, among them, a telescoping steering column. The plaintiff sustained injuries when during a collision his body struck the steering column. The court ruled that the auto in fact had a telescopic steering column and therefore the advertising had been complied with by General Motors.

To recover for personal injuries, the injured party must be able to establish the existence of a material misrepresentation upon which he or she relied. The statement must be one which would be of importance to a normal buyer, one which the seller would expect to influence this normal buyer in deciding whether to purchase a product.

The main defense to misrepresentation suits is that the statement in question was just a statement of opinion or loose general praise—otherwise known as puffing. A good example of puffing might be the statement, "You will be happy with this product." This is the seller's opinion. A buyer may not rely upon such a statement in deciding whether to purchase a product. If the buyer purchases the product and is *not* happy with it, there is nothing he or she can do. The buyer should have examined the product and decided for himself or herself the likelihood of satisfaction with the product.

The danger is that a seller may make generalized statements of praise thinking they are harmless, but a court may not view the statement in question as harmless. Over the years, the courts have grown less receptive to the defense that generalized statements of praise are harmless, and an advertiser cannot rely upon this defense with 100% certainty.[17]

It is entirely possible that an advertising statement might be construed as a statement of fact, not opinion. Today, the possibility that a representation will be construed by a court as a statement of fact, rather than mere puffing, is greater than ever.

An excellent test for determining when a statement if puffing, enunciated by a court in an express warranty case, is:

The decisive test for whether a given representation is a warranty or merely an expression of the seller's opinion is whether the seller asserts a fact of which the buyer may be expected also to have an opinion and exercise his judgment. . . . General statements to the effect that goods are 'the best . . .' 'of good quality . . .' or will 'last a lifetime . . .' are generally regarded as expressions of the seller's opinion or 'the puffing of his wares' and do not create an express warranty.[18]

However, clear as this test may seem, predicting how a court will classify a given statement is difficult. The trend has been to limit the number of statements classified as puffing.[19]

Several important cases dealing with innocent misrepresentation have rejected the defense of puffing. In one case,[20] the plaintiff claimed the product in question, the Golfing Gizmo, had been misrepresented by the advertiser. This product was used as a training device by unskilled golfers to improve their games. The manufacturer made the following statement: "Completely Safe Ball Will Not Hit Player." While the court could have construed this as mere puffery, it did not. In another case,[21] the plaintiff relied on promotional literature involving a mace gun made by the defendant. The defendant made the following claim: "Rapidly vaporizes on face of assailant effecting *instantaneous incapacitation.* . . . It will *instantly stop and subdue* entire groups . . . *instantly stops assailants in their tracks* . . ."

Unfortunately for Mr. Klages, it did not instantly stop all assailants in their tracks. While on duty as a desk clerk in a motel, he sprayed the mace point blank in the face of a robber. The robber rushed around the desk and shot Klages several times in the head. Quite clearly, this statement was material to Klages in deciding to buy the gun. And he relied on the statement when he sprayed the product in the criminal's face. The court, quite properly, did not characterize this ad as mere puffery.

The representation need not, of course, be oral or written.[22] In one case, the plaintiff relied on a picture on the carton in which his helmet was delivered. Although the helmet was originally bought by the Denver Police Department for use in riot control, the picture on the box depicted a motorcyclist wearing the helmet. Plaintiff wore the helmet while riding his motorcycle and sustained serious head injuries when he took a spill. He won a judgment based on innocent misrepresentation. The court ruled the seller must assume the economic consequences for the physical harm resulting from inadvertent misrepresentations it has made about its product. Because this misrepresentation (the depiction of a motorcyclist wearing the helmet) had been made to the public through advertising literature as well as on the packing box, the court ruled that any user who justifiably relied on the misrepresentation and suffered physical harm as a result may recover.

Not every statement impresses every court as a material misrepresentation. Accordingly, in *Berkebile v. Brantly Helicopter Corp.*,[23] the court found the statements concerning a helicopter (i.e., "safe, dependable," "not tricky to operate" and "beginners and professional pilots alike agree . . . [it] . . . is easy to fly") to be mere puffing. Other courts have found similar statements to be mere puffing. However, predicting the outcome of a case is not easy. For this reason, it is prudent not to assume that a court will characterize a given statement as puffery.

Many persons fail to recover because, although the seller stated a fact in the ad, the buyer never relied on the statement in deciding to buy or use the product. All misrepresentation theories of recovery—with the exception of the implied warranty of merchantability—require proof of reliance, or something very similar to reliance, for the plaintiff to recover damages. The Uniform Commercial Code technically requires the statement to have been "part of the basis of the bargain," which is akin to reliance. In the absence of proof of such reliance, the plaintiff will be unable to recover. (See U.C.C. §2-314). An implied warranty of merchantability arises automatically by operation of law, and not as a result of a specific statement made by the seller. Actually the Code requires, for all types of warranties, proof that the warranty was part of the "basis of the bargain" as opposed to reliance. Most commentators agree this is very much like reliance.[24]

Suppose that in an ad, the seller claims its permanent wave for hair won't damage the hair. Ms. Smith uses the product and her hair falls out. She never saw or heard the ad before using the product. May she bring suit based on a misrepresentation by the seller? No.

Consider the case of *Frank v. National Dairy Products Corp.*[25] The plaintiff bought shortening manufactured by the National Dairy Products

Corporation. The seller asserted in a brochure furnished to users that the shortening could be used safely. While draining a pan of shortening, the plaintiff was sprayed with hot grease. The court refused to allow recovery in this case based on an innocent misrepresentation contained in the brochure because the plaintiff had testified unequivocally that he did not rely on the brochure in using the product.

The lesson is clear: Even if an advertiser misrepresents some attribute concerning its product, that fact alone will not permit a recovery by the plaintiff. The plaintiff must establish that he or she was aware of the ad in question, took it into consideration in deciding to buy or use the product, and was injured as a result of the reliance on the false statement. It should be reemphasized, however, that the reliance may be supplied by someone other than the injured party. And technically only proof that the statement was part of the basis of the bargain between the parties—as opposed to reliance—is required to establish breach of an express warranty.

An innocent misrepresentation can give rise to a products liability suit. The injured party need not point to a defect in the product which injured him or her. In fact, the product may be safely designed and constructed. The advertising, in such cases, is what makes the product defective. Statements in the advertising which misrepresent product attributes mislead the public. Telling consumers a product can do something it cannot do can make an otherwise safe product unsafe.

Your problem as an advertiser, of course, is how to lawfully advertise your product without falling into the trap of making a material misrepresentation which can lead to a personal injury suit. By examining those cases which construe statements as puffing as a defense, the line between the two seems very unclear.

What is the difference, for instance, between the statement, "Completely Safe Ball . . . " and "safe, dependable, not tricky to operate"? Yet the California Supreme Court found the former statement to be a material misstatement of fact while the Pennsylvania Court found the latter statement to be mere puffing. What can you do as an advertising professional to avoid problems arising in your ads?

You should carefully examine every piece of promotional literature, every advertisement, catalog, brochure, and label to make certain that it fairly and correctly portrays the actual attributes of your product. If you have any doubt, it is best for you to strike the questionable material. Those advertisers who wish to live dangerously by using more questionable statements should realize that the ad may, at a later date, be used by an injured party in a personal injury case. This is true whether the advertiser sincerely believed the statement was true or not.

The best strategy is to tailor carefully the advertising. Include only those statements which you can fully and completely substantiate and which accurately portray your product's attributes. If you intend to use "puffing" in your ad, be sure the language that you use is just that—preferably statements which no buyer could take too seriously in making a buying decision. Nevertheless, there is still a chance that some court may find that such a statement is a statement of fact and preclude the use of puffing as a defense.

NOTES

1. Public Law 93-637, 93rd Congress, S. 356, approved January 4, 1975, effective July 4, 1975; 15 U.S.C. 2301 et seq.

2. Section 8, Warranties (or Guarantees), p. 9.

3. See, e.g., *NBC Broadcast Standards for Television*, p. 16 and *ABC Advertising Standards*, §I, p. 6 and *Guidelines*, §II, p. 19.

4. See 15 U.S.C. §2303.

5. To obtain a copy of the Magnuson-Moss Act, implementing regulations, and explanatory pamphlets on the law, you should write to the Federal Trade Commission, Washington, D.C. 20580.

6. 16 CFR Part 239.

7. 50 Fed. Reg. 18462 et seq., May 1, 1985.

8. 16 CFR Part 702.

9. See, generally, *Advertising Compliance Service*, Tab #22, Warranties, Article #5.

10. See Chapter 4, Self-Regulation of Advertising.

11. BBB *Code of Advertising*, §8, p. 9; issued May 1985; reprinted with permission of the Council of Better Business Bureaus, Inc.

12. ABC *Guidelines* §II, p. 19.

13. NBC *Broadcast Standards for Television*, p. 16.

14. ABC *Guidelines* §II, p. 20.

15. This section is adapted from the *Advertising Compliance Service* article, "Structuring Your Ads to Avoid Personal Injury Claims," by Douglas Whitman, Tab #9, State Law, Article #9.

16. *General Motors Corp. v. Howard*, 244 So. 2d 726 (Miss. 1971).

17. G. Rosden and P. Rosden, The Law of Advertising, Section 14.03[1].

18. *Royal Business Machines, Inc. v. Lorraine Corp.*, 633 F.2d 34, 41-42 (7th Cir. 1980).

19. J. White and R. Summers, *Uniform Commercial Code*, Section 9-3 (1980).

20. *Hauter v. Zogarts*, 120 Cal. Rptr. 681, 534 P.2d 377 (Cal. Sp. Ct. 1975).

21. *Klages v. General Ordnance*, 367 A.2d 304 (Pa. Superior Ct., 1976).

22. *Winkler v. American Equipment Corp.*, 604 P.2d 693 (Colo. Ct. Appls., 1979).

23. 462 Pa. 83, 337 A.2d 893 (Sp. Ct. Pa. 1975).

24. 3 R. Dusenberg and L. King, Bender's Uniform Commercial Code Service, Section 6.01 (1980).

25. 282 F. Supp. 528 (W. D. Tex 1968), *aff'd*, 414 F.2d 682 (5th Cir 1969). See, generally, D. Whitman, "Reliance as an Element in Product Misrepresentation Suits: A Reconsideration," 35 Southwestern Law Journal 741-773 (1981).

14.
LABELING

One area that advertisers often neglect is their compliance duties involving labeling requirements for their products. Perhaps the main reason for this is the fact that there are a number of labeling laws that affect a wide variety of products. For example, various provisions of the federal Food, Drug, and Cosmetic Act regulate labeling claims for food, drugs, and cosmetics. These provisions are administered by the Food and Drug Administration (FDA). Other examples include wool products (regulated under the Wool Products Labeling Act of 1939), fur products (Fur Products Labeling Act), and textile products (Textile Fiber Products Identification Act). These Acts forbid mislabeling (referred to as "misbranding" under the various Acts) and are regulated by the Federal Trade Commission (FTC).

In addition, there are a host of other statutes, rules, and regulations that in some way affect labeling, too numerous to be discussed here. Moreover, the focus of this volume is advertising compliance; accordingly, the thrust of this chapter is on those issues dealing with the ad compliance aspects of labeling.

INTERPLAY BETWEEN FDA AND FTC

As a general rule, FDA maintains labeling jurisdiction over food, drug and cosmetic products while FTC has jurisdiction over the truth or falsity of advertising relating to these products. A memorandum of understanding between FTC and FDA clarifies this difference in jurisdiction:

With the exception of prescription drugs, the Federal Trade Commission has primary responsibility with respect to the regulation of the truth or falsity of all advertising (other than labeling) of foods, drugs, devices and cosmetics. In the absence of express agreement between the two agencies to the contrary, the Commission will exercise primary jurisdiction over all matters regulating the truth or falsity of advertising of food, drugs (with the exception of prescription drugs) devices and cosmetics.[1]

FDA's LABELING JURISDICTION

FDA enforces such laws affecting labeling as the Federal Food, Drug, and Cosmetic Act (FDC Act)[2] and the Fair Packaging and Labeling Act (FPL Act).[3] These Acts apply to foods and drugs for humans or animals, as well as cosmetics and medical devices. The FDC Act is the United States' basic law regulating food, drugs, and cosmetics. Moreover, many states have similar laws, often patterned after the FDC Act. Among other things, this Act is designed to insure that labeling and packaging is truthful, non-deceptive and informative. The FPL Act affects the placement and contents of information on packages and labels.

Essentially, the FDC Act forbids distribution in the United States, or importation, of products that are adulterated or "misbranded." "Misbranding" includes statements, designs, or pictures on labels that are false or misleading, as well as failure to show required information in labeling.[4] In addition, the FDC Act contains detailed definitions of "misbranding" and numerous court decisions have interpreted these definitions.

For example, the FDC Act says that a food is "misbranded" if "its labeling is false or misleading in any particular."[5] Drugs are also deemed to be misbranded if their labels are false or misleading in any particular.[6] For example, testimonials of users is misbranding if the impression given is that the drug is effective for a certain condition and it really isn't or hasn't been proven effective. The FDC Act defines "labeling" as all labels and other written, printed, or graphic matter accompanying the product. You should be aware that FDA, and the courts, interpret "accompanying" very broadly. Accordingly, "labeling" may include material not physically accompanying the product so long as it helps identify the article, tell its uses, and give directions.[7] Thus, FDA can even proceed against a false or misleading food or drug ad under this expansive view of its jurisdiction. If FDA sees a threat to the public health in such ads, they can attempt to link the ad with the product to give the agency the legal authority to act. Several years ago, former FDA Commissioner, Dr. Arthur Hull Hayes, Jr., in a speech before an American Advertising Federation (AAF) conference, noted that:

The line between advertising and labeling sometimes is very thin. In certain cases, advertising may become labeling when it accompanies a product. For example, tear sheets from newspapers or magazines, when they are placed on the counter next to the product, are labeling. Catalogues may be labeling, as may brochures used to promote a product. Courts have held that written, printed or graphic promotional material accompanying a product is labeling, regardless of the nature of the material, or the manner in which it became associated with or accompanies the article."[8]

At that same conference, Dr. Hayes provided three examples of when FDA might take action against an ad:

1. A drug or medical device product is legally misbranded if its advertising contains conditions, purposes or uses for which the labeling does not bear adequate directions for use;
2. A drug or device product may not be promoted, in either its labeling or advertising, with any representation or suggestion that approval by FDA is in effect; and
3. A drug or medical device product is legally misbranded if its advertising is false or misleading in any particular.

PRESCRIPTION DRUG ADS

It should be noted that the regulation of prescription drug ads is treated differently than ads for over-the-counter (OTC) drugs. OTC drug advertising is regulated by FTC. However, ads for prescription drugs are regulated by FDA. Reason: These ads are usually directed to doctors and the medical community. Prescription drug ads have to show the drug's established name in type at least half as large as that used for the trade name, the drug's quantitative formula to the same extent required on the drug label, and a true and nonmisleading brief summary of information as to adverse side effects, contraindications, and effectiveness of the drug. Regulations define the requirements in greater detail and also provide for so-called "reminder ads" to the health profession[9] and ads to provide price information to consumers.[10] Dissemination of prescription drug ads that do not comply with the regulations is misbranding under the FDC Act.[11]

LABELING AND THE LANHAM ACT

In recent years, competitors have increasingly been bringing each other into court in advertising cases. A federal statute of central importance in that trend is Section 43(a) of the Lanham Trademark Act. While most of the cases to date have been brought against advertising, this statute applies to labeling as well. The statute provides:

Any person who shall affix, apply, or annex, or use in connection with any goods or services, or any container or containers for goods, a false designation of origin, or any false description or representation, including words or symbols tending falsely to describe or represent the same, and shall cause such goods or services to enter into commerce, and any person who shall with knowledge of the falsity of such designation of origin or description or representation cause or procure the same to be transported or used in commerce or deliver the same to any carrier to be transported or used, shall be liable to a civil action by any person doing business in the locality falsely indicated as that of origin or in the region in which said locality is situated, or by any person who believes that he is or is likely to be damaged by the use of any such false decription or representation.[12]

In light of this statute, let's say you wanted to refer to your competitor's trademark—pursuing your comparative ad campaign—right on your product label! Can you do it and stay on the right side of the Lanham Trademark Act? One important court, the Third Circuit Court of Appeals, has answered "yes" to this question, so long as your label reference is truthful.[13]

This case arose under Section 43(a) of the Lanham Trademark Act and involved a vegetable laxative marketed and sold by two competitive pharmaceutical firms. Since 1934, Searle marketed this highly profitable laxative product (i.e., psyllium hydrophilic mucilloid) under the registered trademark METAMUCIL. A competitor, Hudson Pharmaceutical Corp., began marketing the same laxative (i.e., psyllium hydrophilic mucilloid) in 1964 under the registered trademark name REGACILUM.

Hudson tried to get a larger market share by using a comparative advertising strategy. Hudson pursued this tactic for many years, not only in trade catalogs but also in point-of-purchase ads, which bring product names and their prices to the consumer's attention at the retail display counter. Since 1972, Hudson has included in its comparative ads the recital that REGACILIUM is "Equivalent to METAMUCIL."

Until 1980, both of these companies' competitive products were packaged very differently. In that year, however, Hudson changed its product's packaging to resemble its competitor's packaging. Moreover, Hudson's new package label now contained the statement Hudson had long used in trade catalogs and point-of-purchase advertising: "Equivalent to METAMUCIL."

The new packaging with its comparative statement brought on this lawsuit. Searle sued Hudson to enjoin any mention of METAMUCIL on the REGACILIUM container. On May 29, 1981, Judge Meanor issued a temporary restraining order precluding further reference to METAMUCIL on the REGACILIUM container,

unless the defendant's container is changed such that 'METAMUCIL' appears in type no larger than the word 'Equivalent' and in green letters on the white background. Defendant shall place an ® next to the METAMUCIL mark and shall state adjacent to said mark the statement 'a product of G.D. Searle, not a Hudson product.'

On March 26, 1982, Judge Meanor ruled that a permanent injunction should issue. Both pharmaceutical companies appealed the permanent injunction. However, the Third Circuit affirmed the permanent injunction. Citing *Société Comptoir de L'Industrie v. Alexander's Department Stores, Inc.,*[14] as support, the court concluded that it was "proper for Hudson, on its REGACILIUM container, truthfully to characterize REGACILIUM as 'Equivalent to METAMUCIL.' "

Perhaps more importantly, the Third Circuit enunciated this test, which is instructive on a key labeling/advertising issue raised by the Lanham Act: "Whether one is entitled to refer to a competitor's trademark depends not on where the reference appears but on whether the reference is truthful."

FDA LABEL REGULATION AND FREE SPEECH

Since 1975, commercial speech has been a protected form of speech under the First Amendment.[15] U.S. Supreme Court case law since that time has expanded and clarified that principle. An emerging issue is how far FDA can go, in light of this line of cases, in regulating truthful and nondeceptive labels. For example, FDA panels issue "monographs" whereby OTC drugs may be generally recognized as safe and effective and not misbranded. Among other things, these monographs prescribe specific wording for the labeling of these drugs that often excludes certain claims desired by the manufacturer (called the "exclusivity policy"). An interesting issue that may well be litigated in the years ahead is whether FDA can exclude such claims—even if they're truthful and nondeceptive—consistent with the First Amendment.[16]

However, FDA recently proposed a modification that, if adopted could go a long way in moderating this stringent rule. On April 22, 1985, FDA proposed to modify the exclusivity policy.[17] A major problem with FDA's present exclusivity policy is this: It requires that final monograph language is the exclusive language allowed in labeling for indications for use. (FDA defines indications for use as "terms that describe the physiological conditions for which the product is intended as safe and effective therapy.")[18]

What is FDA's justification for such a severe limitation? FDA feared that if manufacturers could use alternative language, this would cause "consumer confusion and deception."

FDA's proposed modification would be a significant liberalization of this policy. Under the proposal, the labels of OTC drugs would still have to contain—in a prominent and conspicuous location—a section describing the product's indications for use. However, the language used to express the "indications for use" can be given in any one of the three following forms:

1. Within a boxed area designated 'APPROVED USES' (or other similar expressions using only the specific wording on indications for use established under a final OTC drug monograph;
2. Within a nonboxed area using other terminology that is not false or misleading; or
3. Using both option one's boxed area containing approved terminology and, elsewhere in the labeling, option two's truthful and nonmisleading alternative terminology.[19]

The proposal would enable FDA to use the final OTC drug monograph as its "standard in determining whether alternative statements are accurate or require regulatory action.''[20] The result: greater flexibility for manufacturers in their choice of permissible language.

What are the prospects that this proposal will ultimately be adopted? At this writing, its chances look good. On July 22, 1985, the Federal Trade Commission's (FTC) Bureaus of Consumer Protection, Competition and Economics submitted to FDA comments backing this proposal. Main reason: The current approach may inhibit manufacturers from giving consumers useful information "about effective uses for OTC drugs that would otherwise be available to them."

As the FTC comments point out, the U.S. Supreme Court has ruled that "governmental restrictions on truthful, nonmisleading commercial speech are permissible only when they serve some substantial governmental interest.''[21] Accordingly, the comments note that these restrictions can't be more extensive than needed to advance that interest directly. The proposed FDA modification, the comments conclude, "strike a more appropriate balance between the needs for free expression and for consumer protection, and advances adequately FDA's interests in a far less restrictive manner than the existing exclusivity policy.''[22]

NOTES

1. 36 Fed. Reg. 18539.
2. U.S.C. §§301-392.
3. 15 U.S.C. §§1451-1461.
4. FDC Act, §§403, 502 and 602; see, also, HHS Publication No. (FDA) 85-1115, p. 1.
5. 21 U.S.C. §343(a) (1).
6. FDC Act §502.
7. HHS Publication No. (FDA) 85-1115, p. 44.
8. Speech by Dr. Arthur Hull Hayes, American Advertising Federation Conference, 12-8-81.
9. 21 CFR 202.
10. 21 CFR 200.200.
11. HHS Publication No. (FDA) 85-1115, p. 46.
12. 15 U.S.C. §1125(a).
13. *G. D. Searle & Co. v. Hudson Pharmaceutical Corp.*, U.S. Court of Appeals (3d Cir.), Nos. 82-5600 & 5621, 8-29-83; see, generally, *Advertising Compliance Service*, Tab #11, Labeling, Article #5.
14. 299 F.2d 33 (2d Cir. 1962).
15. *Bigelow v. Virginia*, 421 U.S. at 826 (1975); see, generally, Chapter 10 of this book.
16. For an enlightening commentary on this area, see McNamera, *FDA Regulation of Labeling and the Developing Law of Commercial Free Speech*, 37 Food, Drug, Cosmetic LJ 394 et seq. (1982).
17. 50 Fed. Reg. 15810, April 22, 1985; see, generally, *Advertising Compliance Service*, Tab #11, Labeling, Article #7.
18. Memorandum from William E. Gilbertson, Pharm. D., Director, Division of

OTC Drug Evaluation, to All OTC Advisory Panel Members, "OTC Drug Labeling Policy: 'Indications for Use' are Limited to the Terms Provided for in the Applicable OTC Drug Monograph," dated May 16, 1977, at p. 1.

19. See 50 Fed. Reg. 15810, 15814; proposed 21 CFR §§330. 1(c)(2)(i)-(iii).

20. See 50 Fed. Reg. 15812.

21. *Central Hudson Gas & Elec. Corp. v. Public Service Comm'n of New York*, 447 U.S. 557, 564 (1980).

22. In the Matter Of Labeling Of Drug Products For Over-The-Counter Human Use—Proposed Rule, Comments of The Bureaus Of Consumer Protection, Competition and Economics Of The Federal Trade Commission, Docket 82N-0154, 21 CFR Parts 330, 331, 332 and 352 before the Food and Drug Administration Department of Health And Human Services, Rockville, Maryland, July 22, 1985.

15.
STATE LAW

In making your advertising compliance plans you should not overlook state statutes and regulations. In particular, you should have a good working knowledge of those state unfair and deceptive acts and practices ("UDAP") statutes extant in the states where you advertise.

Over the past twenty years or so, nearly every state has put some type of consumer protection law on the books.[1] Many of these statutes paralleled the Federal Trade Commission Act and are called "Little FTC Acts" or "Mini FTC Acts." However, unlike the FTC Act many of these statutes afford consumers the right to bring civil actions for damages and other kinds of relief.[2]

FOUR BASIC TYPES

There are four basic types of UDAP statutes:[3]

Unfair Trade Practice and Consumer Protection Laws

The model for this type of UDAP statute was drafted by the Federal Trade Commission along with the Committee on Suggested State Legislation of the Council of State Governments. There are three versions of this model: (1) pure "Little FTC Acts," that forbid "unfair methods of competition and unfair or deceptive acts or practices." This version has been adopted in fourteen states (i.e., Connecticut, Florida, Hawaii, Illinois, Louisiana, Maine, Massachusetts, Montana, Nebraska, North Carolina, South Carolina, Vermont, Washington, and West Virginia); (2) prohibition of false, misleading, or deceptive practices. This type of statute can be found in Kentucky and Texas; (3) prohibition of various specific practices, plus "any other practice that is unfair or deceptive." This version can be found in

Alabama, Alaska, Georgia, Idaho, Maryland, Mississippi, New Hampshire, Pennsylvania, Rhode Island, and Tennessee.

Uniform Consumer Sales Practices Act

This act was developed by the American Bar Association and the National Conference on Uniform State Laws. It applies only to consumer transactions and forbids deceptive and unconscionable practices. This version has been adopted by Kansas, Ohio and Utah.

Uniform Deceptive Trade Practices Act

This act gives businesses a remedy against competitors that use deceptive techniques to gain customers. However, this Act has been applied to consumer cases. Twelve states have adopted different forms of this model (i.e., Colorado, Delaware, Georgia, Hawaii, Illinois, Maine, Minnesota, Nebraska, New Mexico, Ohio, Oklahoma, and Oregon).

Consumer Fraud Acts

These statutes forbid such practices as misrepresentation, fraud, deception, and unfair or unconscionable acts. States that have such acts include: Arizona, Arkansas, Delaware, Indiana, Iowa, Michigan, Missouri, Nevada, New Jersey, New York, North Dakota, South Dakota, Virginia, Wyoming, as well as the District of Columbia.

ENFORCEMENT POWERS

UDAP statutes offer a wide range of remedies, including actual damages, multiple damages, injunctive relief, rescission of contract, and attorney's fees.[4] Accordingly, it's important for you to be aware of the remedies available in your state as well as in those states where you advertise.

Many ad compliance planners are familiar with the way the FTC Act is enforced by FTC. However, the enforcement scheme under the UDAP statutes is not as simple. While these statutes are frequently enforced by the state's attorney general or another governmental authority, that's generally not the only source of enforcement. Consumers and businesses in most states also can "enforce" these statutes, through private actions, as well. Most states allow such private actions except Arkansas, Iowa, Nevada, and North Dakota. Private litigants have been defined to include both consumers and competitors.

Another important enforcement power is injunctive relief. Some UDAP statutes explicitly authorize injunctions, whereas others allow "appropriate" or "other" relief.

Class actions are still another important enforcement power. In certain states, special UDAP provisions expand on the state's basic class action statute. An important case involving class action is *Miner v. Gillette.*[5] In that case, the Illinois Supreme Court said an Illinois consumer could bring a class action under Illinois's UDAP statute on behalf of both resident and nonresident class members. The writ of certiorari was dismissed by the U.S. Supreme Court in this case. Reason: The Illinois High Court had ruled only that the plaintiff could proceed with the class action. Accordingly, there was no "final judgment" for the U.S. Supreme Court to Review.

NOTES

1. J. Sheldon & G. Zweible, *Survey of Consumer Fraud Law* 13 (1978). See also: *Advertising Compliance Service*, Tab #9, State Law, Article #5, and Leaffer & Lipson, "Consumer Actions Against Unfair or Deceptive Acts of Practices; The Private Uses of Federal Trade Commission Jurisprudence," 48 Geo. Washington LR 521, May 1980.

2. 48 Geo. Washington LR 522; *Advertising Compliance Service*, Tab #9, State Law, Article #5.

3. These sections are based on an article appearing in *Advertising Compliance Service*, Tab #9, State Law, Article #5, which reported on a speech made by Bruce P. Keller, of the New York City law firm of Debevoise & Plimpton, at an Advertising Compliance Service-sponsored conference on May 12, 1983.

4. Id.

5. 87 Ill. 2d 7, 428 N.E.2d 478 (1981), *cert. dismissed*, 51 USLW 5013 (12-6-82).

16.
POLITICAL ADVERTISING

Since the earliest days of our two-party system, politicans have used some form of political advertising. And no other form of speech enjoys more protection under the First Amendment to the Constitution than does political advertising. Such political advertising methods as campaign posters, leaflets, and buttons have long been staples of our political system. Beginning with the campaign of John F. Kennedy, televised campaign advertising has come into its own as the dominant form of political advertising. Today, political candidates spend tremendous sums of money on television ads. The power of television advertising raises a variety of questions involving the content of political ads, the role of ad agencies and the media, the applicable standards for political ads, and the relation of such standards to the First Amendment.

If you are involved in some way with the compliance aspects of political advertising, you should be aware of an important federal statute—the Federal Election Campaign Act (FECA) of 1971—that affects political advertising. Sections of this Act, for example, discuss the disclosures a candidate should make in his or her ads, the time availability of the media, the contribution of services by an ad agency to a candidate, and many other areas.

According to the FECA, ads advocating the election of a candidate or seeking contributions must clearly name the candidate, authorized political committee, agent, or other person who paid for the ad. Campaign ads and other literature published by a political committee or person that isn't authorized by a candidate to publish the material must also carry notice of the nonauthorization.

The FECA also requires broadcasters to allow reasonable access or allow candidates to buy reasonable amounts of time for federal elective office. However, newspapers and magazines aren't required to make space available to candidates.

The Federal Election Commission (FEC) was created by 1974 amendments to the FECA. FEC regs define "contribution" or "expenditure" as including any "direct or indirect payment distribution, loan, advance, deposit or gift of money, or any services . . ." This includes any materials or services that ad agencies offer to a candidate without requesting payment.

In addition, ad agencies should be aware of this pitfall for the unwary: If a candidate fails to pay an advertising agency, it must try to collect the debt, or else it will be considered a contribution.

All three groups—the candidate, the candidate's ad agency, and the media—should be aware of the American Association of Advertising Agencies' (4A's) guidelines for political advertising. These guidelines are as follows:

POLITICAL ADVERTISING—A SHARED RESPONSIBILITY

The Candidate

1. We regard the candidate as the advertiser. The candidate bears the same responsibility as any other advertiser for the content of any ad or commercial run in his behalf. This responsibility cannot be delegated to support groups.

2. We believe every candidate should sign and comply with the Code of Fair Campaign Practices administered by the Fair Campaign Practices Committee.

The Advertising Agency

1. We believe the advertising agency bears the same responsibility for the truth and accuracy of political advertising it prepares as it would for product advertising.

2. We believe the agency has a professional obligation to maintain standards of good taste and to avoid personal vilification and disparagement in the advertising it prepares for a candidate.

3. We see it as the agency's duty to use its communication skills to acquaint the electorate with the candidate, his character, programs and stands on issues. Techniques of communication should be used to inform, not to distract from the real issues.

4. Should the agency find that it no longer exercises sufficient control over the content or execution of the messages, we think it is the duty of the agency to make a public statement to that effect and to cease activity on that campaign. The 4 A's will make its public relations resources available to any member or nonmember agency for such a statement.

The Media

1. We believe that all media should exercise the appropriate clearance standards and controls over the taste, content, truth and accuracy of political advertising as it would for product advertising. Media have the professional responsibility to reject any political messages which do not meet their standards of fairness and good taste.

2. We suggest that in addition to selling conventional time segments for political messages, broadcasters offer segments of at least five minutes for political announcements.[1]

(Reprinted by permission of the American Association of Advertising Agencies).

In addition, the 4As' Board of Directors has reapproved the following "Code of Ethics for Political Campaign Advertising":

CODE OF ETHICS
FOR POLITICAL CAMPAIGN ADVERTISING

The advertising agency has become an increasingly important factor in the conduct of American political campaigns. Just as the political candidate must observe the highest standards of fairness and morality in his campaign, so must the advertising agency operate under a code that reflects the finest values of our political system rather than any unethical temptations that arise in the heat of the battle.

The advertising agency should not represent any candidate who has not signed or who does not observe the Code of Fair Campaign Practices of the Fair Campaign Practices Committee, endorsed by A.A.A.A.

The agency should not knowingly misrepresent the views or state record of any candidates nor quote them out of proper context.

The agency should not prepare any material which unfairly or prejudicially exploits the race, creed or national origin of any candidate.

The agency should take care to avoid unsubstantiated charges and accusations, especially those deliberately made too late in the campaign for opposing candidates to answer.

The agency should stand as an independent judge of fair campaign practices, rather than automatically yield to the wishes of the candidate or his authorized representatives.

The agency should not indulge in any practices which might be deceptive or misleading in word, photograph, film or sound.[2]

(Reprinted by permission of the American Association of Advertising Agencies).

The 4A's *Code of Fair Campaign Practices* condemns the use of personal vilification, character defamation, whispering campaigns, libel, or misleading or falsified campaign material. Candidates that endorse the Code agree to the following practices and constraints, reproduced here in full text:

CODE OF FAIR CAMPAIGN PRACTICES

I SHALL CONDUCT my campaign in the best American tradition, discussing the issues as I see them, presenting my record and policies with sincerity and frankness, and criticizing without fear or favor the record and policies of my opponent and his party which merit such criticism.

I SHALL DEFEND AND UPHOLD the right of every qualified American voter to full and equal participation in the electoral process.

I SHALL CONDEMN the use of personal vilification, character defamation, whispering campaigns, libel, slander, or scurrilous attacks on any candidate or his personal or family life.

I SHALL CONDEMN the use of campaign material of any sort which misrepresents, distorts, or otherwise falsifies the facts regarding any candidate, as well as the use of malicious or unfounded accusations against any candidate which aim at creating or exploiting doubts without justification, as to his loyalty and patriotism.

I SHALL CONDEMN any appeal to prejudice based on race, creed, or national origin.

I SHALL CONDEMN any dishonest or unethical practice which tends to corrupt or undermine our American system of free elections or which hampers or prevents the full and free expression of the will of the voters.

I SHALL IMMEDIATELY AND PUBLICLY REPUDIATE support deriving from any individual or group which resorts, on behalf of my candidacy or in opposition to that of my opponent, to the methods and tactics which I condemn.[3]

(Reproduced by permission of the American Association of Advertising Agencies).

Political advertising enjoys such broad First Amendment protections that these ads are not reviewable by the Federal Trade Commission or, for that matter, by anyone else. Nevertheless, there are lawful limitations that can be placed on political advertising. In 1984, for example, the United States Supreme Court ruled that a city's total ban on the posting of signs, including political signs, on public property did not violate the First Amendment.[4] In that case, Roland Vincent had been a candidate for election to the Los Angeles City Council. Some of his backers entered into a contract with a political sign service company to make and post signs with Vincent's name on them. The company produced 15 " × 44 " cardboard signs and attached them to utility poles by draping the signs over the cross-arms supporting the poles and stapling the cardboard together at the bottom. The signs' message: "Roland Vincent—City Council."

Acting under a town ordinance, city employees routinely removed all posters (including the political signs for Roland Vincent) attached to utility poles and similar objects.

On March 12, 1979, Taxpayers and COGS, the political sign service company, filed suit in U.S. district court, seeking an injunction against enforcement of the ordinance as well as compensatory and punitive damages. The district court entered finding of fact, concluded that the ordinance was constitutional, and granted the city's motion for summary judgment.

One of the district court's findings was the finding that the large number of illegally posted signs "constitute a clutter and visual blight." On appeal, the appeals court did not question this or any other of the district court's findings of fact. The appeals court did reject some of the lower court's conclusions of law, however. The court of appeals concluded that the ordinance was presumptively unconstitutional since significant First Amendment interests were involved. And the appeals court ruled that:

[T]he City had failed to make a sufficient showing that its asserted interests in esthetics and preventing visual clutter were substantial because it had not offered to demonstrate that the City was engaged in a comprehensive effort to remove other contributions to an unattractive environment in commercial and industrial areas.

The U.S. Supreme Court reversed the court of appeals decision. The High Court noted that,

The problem addressed by this ordinance—the visual assault on the citizens of Los Angeles presented by an accumulation of signs posted on public property— constitutes a significant substantive evil within the City's power to prohibit.

Citing its decision in *Metromedia, Inc. v. San Diego*,[5] the Court concluded:

As recognized in *Metromedia*, if the city has a sufficient basis for believing that billboards are traffic hazards and are unattractive, 'then obviously the most direct and perhaps the only effective approach to solving the problems they create is to prohibit them' . . . As is true of billboards, the esthetic interests that are implicated by temporary signs are presumptively at work in all parts of the city, including those where appellees posted their signs, and there is no basis in the record in this case upon which to rebut that presumption. These interests are both psychological and economic. The character of the environment affects the quality of life and the value of property in both residential and commercial areas. We hold that on this record these interests are sufficiently substantial to justify this content neutral, impartially administered prohibition against the posting of appellees' temporary signs on public property and that such an application of the ordinance does not create an unacceptable threat to the profound national commitment to the principle that debate on public issues should be uninhibited, robust, and wide-open.[6]

NOTES

1. See: *Political Campaign Advertising and Advertising Agencies*, by the American Association of Advertising Agencies, 666 Third Avenue, New York, N.Y. 10017. (212) 682-2500. See also: *Advertising Compliance Service*, Tab #20, Political Ads, Article #2.

2. *Code of Ethics for Political Campaign Advertising*, adopted by 4As' Board of Directors on February 22, 1968 and approved 4As' Board July 20, 1982; also endorsed by Fair Campaign Practices Committee and League of Women Voters and Reapproved on August 12, 1982. See also: *Advertising Compliance Service*, Tab #20, Political Ads, Article #2.

3. *Code of Fair Campaign Practices*, by the American Association of Advertising Agencies. See also: *Advertising Compliance Service*, Tab #20, Political Ads, Article #3.

4. *City Council v. Taxpayers for Vincent*, U.S. Supreme Court, Dkt. #82-975, 5-15-84. See, generally, *Advertising Compliance Service*, Tab #20, Political Ads, Article #4.

5. 453 U.S. 490 (1981).

6. *New York Times Co. v. Sullivan*, 376 U.S. 254, 270 (1963).

BIBLIOGRAPHY

BOOKS

Advertising and Consumers: New Perspectives. New York: Bartos & Dunn, American Association of Advertising Agencies, 1975.

Law and the Writer. Cincinnati, Ohio: Writers Digest Books, 1985.

Legal and Business Aspects of the Advertising Industry 1984. New York: Practising Law Institute, 1984.

Legal and Business Aspects of the Advertising Industry 1982. New York: Practising Law Institute, 1982.

The FTC—1982, New York: Practising Law Institute, 1982.

Mass Media, Freedom of Speech, and Advertising: A Study in Communication Law. Dubuque, Iowa: Kendall/Hunt Publishing Co., 1979.

FEDERAL DOCUMENTS

Deceptive and Unsubstantiated Claims Policy Protocol. Washington, D.C.: Federal Trade Commission, 1975.

FCC Information Bulletin, Cable Television. Washington, D.C.: Federal Communications Commission, 1984.

FCC Publication 8310-100. Washington, D.C.: Federal Communications Commission, 1985.

Federal Trade Commission Policy Statement Regarding Comparative Advertising. Washington, D.C.: 1979.

Improving Consumer Access to Legal Services: The Case for Removing Restrictions on Truthful Advertising, FTC Staff Report. Washington, D.C.: Federal Trade Commission, 1984.

List of Cases and Staff Analyses as Submitted by FTC Chairman James C. Miller III to House Subcommittee on Commerce, Transportation on April 1, 1982. Washington, D.C.: Federal Trade Commission, 1982.

Requirements of Laws and Regulations Enforced by the U.S. Food and Drug Administration. Rockville, Md.: U.S. Department of Health and Human Services, Food and Drug Administration, 1984.

INDUSTRY GUIDELINES

Advertising Principles of American Business. Washington, D.C.: American Advertising Federation, 1984.
B/PAA Code of Ethics. New York: Business-Professonal Advertising Association, n.d.
Brewing Industry Advertising Guidlines. Washington, D.C. United States Brewer's Association, Inc., 1984.
Code of Advertising Standards: Wine Institute. San Francisco: Wine Institute—The Trade Association of California Winegrowers, 1978.
Code of Good Practice of the Distilled Spirits Council of the United States, Inc.. Washington, D.C.: Distilled Spirits Council of the United States, 1983.
National Association of Broadcasters's Code of Good Practices. Washington, D.C. National Association of Broadcasters, code suspended March 10, 1982.
Policy Statement and Guidelines for Comparative Advertising. New York: American Association of Advertising Agencies, 1974.
Political Campaign Advertising and Advertising Agencies, 4th ed., New York: American Association of Advertising Agencies, Inc., 1982.

LOOSELEAF SERVICES

Advertising Compliance Service. Greenwood Press, 88 Post Road West, P.O. Box 5007, Westport, Conn. 06881.
Do's and Dont's in Advertising Copy. Council of Better Business Bureaus, Arlington, Va.
Federal Trade Commission. Kanwit, Shepard's/McGraw-Hill, Colorado Springs, Colo.
Law of Advertising, The. Rosden, Matthew Bender & Company, Albany, N.Y.
Trade Regulation Reporter. Commerce Clearing House, Chicago, Ill.

NETWORK GUIDELINES

ABC Advertising Standards and Guidelines, American Boradcasting Company, New York, N.Y.
CBS Television Network Advertising Guidelines, Columbia Broadcasting System, New York, N.Y.
NBC Broadcast Standards for Television, National Broadcasting Company, New York, N.Y.

PAMPHLETS/SELF-REGULATION

The following informative pamphlets are available from the National Advertising Division of the Council of Better Business Bureaus, Inc.,

Advertising Self-Regulation and Its Interaction with Consumers. National Advertising Review Board, New York, N.Y. (1978).
Better Business Bureau: Code of Advertising. Council of Better Business Bureaus, Inc., Arlington, Va. (1985).

Children and Advertising, An Annotated Bibliography. Children's Advertising Review Unit, National Advertising Division, Council of Better Business Bureaus, Inc., New York, N.Y. (1980).

Dear _____, Your advertising has recently come to the attention of the National Advertising Division. . . . (an NAD Guide for Advertisers and Ad Agencies), National Advertising Division, Council of Better Business Bureaus, Inc., New York, N.Y. (1983).

Identifying Competitors in Advertising. National Advertising Review Board, New York, N.Y. (1977).

Self-Regulatory Guidelines for Children's Advertising. 3d ed., Chldren's Advertising Review Unit, National Advertising Division, Council of Better Business Bureaus, Inc., New York, N.Y. (1983).

Standards for Automobile Rental Advertising. Council of Better Business Bureaus, Inc., Arlington, Va. (1983).

Standards for Carpet and Rugs—advertising & selling. Council of Better Business Bureaus, Inc., Arlington, Va. (1978).

Standards for Home Insulation Materials—advertising & selling. Council of Better Business Bureaus, Inc., Arlington, Va. (1980).

Standards for Residential Swimming Pools—advertising & selling. Council of Better Business Bureaus, Inc., Arlington, Va. (1978).

Standards of Practice for the Home Improvement Industry. Council of Better Business, Inc., Arlington, Va. (1981).

SERIAL PUBLICATIONS

Advertising Age, Chicago, Ill.: Crain Communications Inc.
Code of Federal Regulations, Washington, D.C.: U.S. Government Printing Office.
Federal Register, Washington, D.C.: U.S. Government Printing Office.

INDEX

About the Author

JOHN LICHTENBERGER is Managing Editor of the highly respected *Advertising Compliance Service* (Quorum Reports) and the author of hundreds of published articles on a wide variety of advertising law topics. He received his law degree from Rutgers School of Law and is a member of the American Bar Association, the New Jersey Bar Association, and the Association of American Trial Lawyers. In addition to his work as an editor and writer, he maintains a part-time law practice in New Jersey.